D1570009

ON BEHALF OF
THE PRESIDENT

Don –
Thank you
for the support.
I hope you
will enjoy!

Lauren

ON BEHALF OF THE PRESIDENT

Presidential Spouses and White House Communications Strategy Today

LAUREN A. WRIGHT

 PRAEGER™

An Imprint of ABC-CLIO, LLC

Santa Barbara, California • Denver, Colorado

Library of Congress Cataloging-in-Publication Data

Names: Wright, Lauren A., author.
Title: On behalf of the president : presidential spouses and White House
    communications strategy today / Lauren A. Wright.
Description: Santa Barbara, California : Praeger, an imprint of ABC-CLIO,
    LLC, 2016. | Includes bibliographical references and index.
Identifiers: LCCN 2015050363 | ISBN 9781440848599 (hardback : alk. paper) |
    ISBN 9781440848605 (ebook)
Subjects: LCSH: Communication in politics—United States. | Presidents'
    spouses—Political activity—United States. | Clinton, Hillary Rodham. |
    Bush, Laura Welch, 1946– | Obama, Michelle, 1964–
Classification: LCC JA85.2.U6 W75 2016 | DDC 973.93092/52—dc23
LC record available at http://lccn.loc.gov/2015050363

ISBN: 978-1-4408-4859-9
EISBN: 978-1-4408-4860-5

20 19 18 17 16   1 2 3 4 5

This book is also available on the World Wide Web as an eBook.
Visit www.abc-clio.com for details.

Praeger
An Imprint of ABC-CLIO, LLC

ABC-CLIO, LLC
130 Cremona Drive, P.O. Box 1911
Santa Barbara, California 93116-1911

This book is printed on acid-free paper (∞)

Manufactured in the United States of America

Contents

Tables and Figures   vii

Preface   xi

Acknowledgments   xvii

1 The Puzzle Spouses Pose   1

2 What Martha Washington and Michelle Obama
Have in Common   9

3 Messengers-in-Chief   23

4 First, Do No Harm: Next, Do What Comes Natural   47

5 The Rhetorical Toolkit Spouses Use to Convince Us   77

6 Does It Work?   99

7 Modernizing Our Perspectives on Presidential Spouses   121

8 Epilogue: An Operative's Guide to Spouse Mobilization
in 2016   133

Appendix: Supplemental Figures and Tables   151

Notes   169

Bibliography   179

Index   189

Tables and Figures

CHAPTERS
Table
3.1   Number of Public Speeches Listed on the
       White House Briefing Room Websites   24

Figures
3.1   Hillary Clinton's Speeches by Type and Topic   30
3.2   Laura Bush's Speeches by Type and Topic   30
3.3   Michelle Obama's Speeches by Type and Topic   31
3.4   Implicit vs. Explicit Mentions of Policy over Time   35
3.5   Favorability   36
3.6   Name Recognition   37
3.7   Effect of Partisanship on Favorability Toward
       President and First Lady   41
6.1   Effect of Hillary Clinton Speech (Relative to
       No Speech)   106
6.2   Effect of Laura Bush Speech (Relative to No Speech)   106
6.3   Effect of Michelle Obama Speech (Relative to
       No Speech)   107
6.4   Effect of Hillary Clinton Speech (Relative to
       Bill Clinton Speech)   110
6.5   Effect of Laura Bush Speech (Relative to George
       Bush Speech)   111
6.6   Effect of Michelle Obama Speech (Relative to
       Barack Obama Speech)   111
8.1A   Example of Campaign Experiment Control Condition   138
8.1B   Example of Campaign Experiment Treatment Condition   139

8.2	Effect of 2016 Presidential Candidate Spouses on Candidate Favorability	140
8.3	Effect of Columba Bush on Perceptions of Jeb Bush	142
8.4	Effect of Bill Clinton on Perceptions of Hillary Clinton	143

APPENDIX
Tables

A.1	Effect of Respondent Partisanship on Favorability Toward the President and First Lady (1992–1995)	159
A.2	Effect of Respondent Partisanship on Favorability Toward the President and First Lady (1996–2000)	160
A.3	Effect of Respondent Partisanship on Favorability Toward the President and First Lady (2002–2012)	161
A.4	Speech Topics Attributed to First Ladies vs. Presidents by Survey Respondents	162
A.5	Relationship Between Treatment Group Assignment and Covariates in Speech Experiment (Means)	164
A.6	Relationship Between Treatment Group Assignment and Covariates in Video Experiment (Means)	165
A.7	Relationship Between Treatment Group Assignment and Covariates in Vice President Speech Experiment (Means)	166
A.8	Relationship Between Treatment Group Assignment and Covariates in Candidate Picture Experiment (Means)	167

Figures

A.1	Effect of Hillary Clinton Video (Compared to No Video)	151
A.2	Effect of Laura Bush Video (Compared to No Video)	152
A.3	Effect of Michelle Obama Video (Compared to No Video)	152
A.4	Effect of Hillary Clinton Video (Compared to Bill Clinton Video)	153
A.5	Effect of Laura Bush Video (Compared to George Bush Video)	153
A.6	Effect of Michelle Obama Video (Compared to Barack Obama Video)	154
A.7	Effect of Hillary Clinton Speech Among Women (Compared to Bill Clinton Speech Among Women)	154
A.8	Effect of Laura Bush Speech Among Women (Compared to George Bush Speech Among Women)	155
A.9	Effect of Michelle Obama Speech Among Women (Compared to Barack Obama Speech Among Women)	155

A.10   Effect of Hillary Clinton Video Among Women
       (Compared to Bill Clinton Video Among Women)   156
A.11   Effect of Laura Bush Video Among Women
       (Compared to George Bush Video Among Women)   156
A.12   Effect of Michelle Obama Video Among Women
       (Compared to Barack Obama Video Among Women)   157
A.13   Effect of Hillary Clinton Speech Compared to
       Al Gore Speech   157
A.14   Effect of Laura Bush Speech Compared to
       Dick Cheney Speech   158
A.15   Effect of Michelle Obama Speech Compared to
       Joe Biden Speech   158

Preface

The day following the 2012 Democratic National Convention, polling firms noted that Michelle Obama's speech received over one million more online views than President Clinton's speech, more than eight times the number of online views received by President Obama's speech, and more views than all of the speeches made at the Republican National Convention (RNC) combined.[1] Mrs. Obama's speech also drove unprecedented levels of social media activity, generating an average of 28,003 tweets per minute, nearly double the tweets for which Mitt Romney's RNC acceptance speech was responsible (some 14,289 tweets per minute, according to *USA Today*). And no less notably, the picture of Mrs. Obama hugging her husband on the 2012 campaign trail in Iowa, wearing a quintessentially American red and white gingham sundress, was the most retweeted and received more likes on Facebook than any photo in history. Michelle Obama has also been documented as the most televised American first lady, with 44 television appearances from 2008 to 2011 alone, dwarfing Laura Bush's 12 appearances from 2001 to 2004 and Hillary Clinton's 19 appearances from 1993 to 1996.[2] When she appears on primetime television, networks witness hikes in their ratings, as the producers of *The Biggest Loser*, *iCarly*, *Top Chef*, and *Parks and Recreation* recently learned.

There is no doubt that presidential spouses are media superstars. What is more surprising is that their ability to attract the attention of Americans, and their propensity to actively seek that attention, surpasses that of other well-known surrogates and sometimes presidents themselves. By promulgating stereotypes of first ladies as personal confidantes to the president and behind-the-scenes power brokers for decades, social scientists, historians, and journalists have failed to recognize one of the most important roles of presidential spouses: to enhance the president's public image and expand public support for the administration's policy agenda.

Like most labyrinthine intellectual journeys, the idea for the research that informed much of this book is rooted in a simple puzzle. Presidential spouses are some of the most recognizable figures in U.S. politics and among the least studied figures in political science. To understand why presidential communications scholars have not paid attention to first ladies, it is essential to understand that political operatives and political scientists do not agree on the importance of many aspects of U.S. politics. The lack of empirical work on presidential spouses is indeed characteristic of the enduring, although shrinking, disconnect between those who practice politics and those who study them. Political operatives and campaign professionals devote tremendous amounts of time and resources to the task of improving the public image of presidents and presidential candidates despite widespread consensus among scholars that their efforts rarely change public opinion in the aggregate. Perhaps because of my own background as a former gubernatorial campaign staffer, I thought it was critical to consult both of these groups in my investigation of the role presidential spouses play in White House communications strategy and their ability to shape public opinion of presidents and their policies. If Americans are keenly interested in the president's spouse and political operatives try to capitalize on this interest, shouldn't the people responsible for studying the presidency care?

There are a few reasons political practitioners and political scientists disagree on the importance of presidential spouses. The first is data availability. There have only been 45 first ladies in U.S. history, and because they are not elected officials, information about them was not systematically collected and organized until recently. Gallup conducted the first public opinion poll about the president's spouse in 1939, and job approval ratings for first ladies were not measured until the Clinton administration. Furthermore, public appropriations for staff to the first lady were not routinely designated by congress until 1979. For these reasons, records produced by the Office of the First Lady that facilitate empirical research on the formal role of presidential spouses are scarce, and much of the existing scholarly work on first ladies is weak. Without descriptive statistics in which to anchor their claims, American politics scholars, journalists, and historians have relied on typologies of first ladies to assess their roles. For example, scholars have largely deemed Laura Bush a traditional first lady rather than a modern or activist first lady, citing her lack of interest in politics and comparatively low educational attainment to her predecessor. The evidence I present later in this book suggests that these typologies are severely flawed. Fortunately, there has been very consistent documentation of the activities of the first lady since 1992, when the advent of the Internet enabled the National Archives to organize and preserve speeches made by first ladies as well as transcripts of their public remarks online. I make use of these materials by analyzing nearly 2,000 public speeches made by Hillary Clinton, Laura Bush, and Michelle Obama in the last three presidential administrations.

The second reason political scientists may have neglected the Office of the First Lady as a legitimate research topic is measurement. American politics scholars have increasingly moved away from questions that cannot be answered through the analysis of quantified data. Although quantifying speeches delivered by first ladies provides valuable evidence for my suggestion that the strategic mobilization of presidential spouses by the White House has become a more common practice, there are critical aspects of this pursuit that cannot be informed through the numerical analysis of public records. For example, why does the first lady appear in public so often? What purpose do these appearances serve? What makes presidential spouses appealing to the American public? As I mention later in the book, there is hardly a way to answer these questions reliably without consulting the political professionals responsible for deploying first ladies on behalf of the White House and on the campaign trail. Interviews with elites are important tools for evaluating existing hypotheses and generating new ones.

Encouragingly, in recent years there have been more examples of political practitioners collaborating successfully with political scientists. Campaign strategists have adopted some of the tools political methodology offers for gauging the impact of messaging tactics such as television advertising, and have even allowed scholars to conduct experiments that test different strategies for ad placement and content. This kind of experimentation was common in the 2012 elections, when the Obama campaign began buying air space in Montana early in the summer in order to test the effectiveness of ads in a low-risk setting. Hillary Clinton's campaign, in addition to recruiting many of the methodologically minded staff who played a part in Obama's 2012 victory, is actively looking for more data scientists to join Hillary for America, according to her campaign web site. Scholars like Ansolabehere and Iyengar (1995), Holbrook (1996), and Shaw (1999) have discovered that campaign events have a marginal, although not long lasting, effect on voting behavior. For instance, in their 2003 study, Hillygus and Jackman found that support for Bush in 2000 increased after the debates, but not during the conventions, and support for Gore increased following the conventions, but not during the debates.[3]

Although first ladies are merely one instrument in the presidential communications toolkit, studies that argue communications strategies used by White House and campaign staff do often influence the perceptions and behavior of voters are promising, especially because presidential spouses have become such a big part of these strategies. In this book, I assess the impact of public appearances made by the first lady on individual evaluations of the president and his policy agenda using controlled experiments not unlike those used in the aforementioned campaign advertising studies. Even if the first lady's influence on mass public opinion is difficult to ascertain, experiments allow opinion to be measured at an individual, personal level, where nonnumeric mechanisms like the supposed humanizing quality of presidential spouses do their work.

The final reason why some political scientists have been dismissive of the study of first ladies pertains to gender. During my search for advisors to guide me through the research process, I encountered scholars who thought the study of political spouses would demean academic discussions about women and politics. One congressional scholar declined to be part of my committee as long as my topic involved first ladies, but offered to help me identify a more appropriate topic on women in elected office. Another professor I consulted expressed concern that focusing my research agenda on first ladies could tarnish my reputation in academia, and warned that I might not be taken seriously among other political scientists. To boot, a certain strain of academic insult that would pass as a compliment in most professional settings was bestowed on me: that my topic had "mass appeal." The way political scientists see it, compared to the gender and politics literature that exists in the mainstream of the discipline—which largely focuses on the obstacles women face while running for office, their underrepresentation in appointed and elected government positions, and the difference they make when they are elected— at first glance, research centered on the president's wife appears inconsequential. It is not. The powers of the president's spouse are informal, but they are formidable.

First, first ladies have more access to the president than any single White House staff member or government official. Although the efforts of historians to assess the private influence of first ladies do not meet the standards required by social science to make definitive claims, the potential for spouses to affect presidential decision making behind closed doors should not be ignored. Second, presidential spouses receive more public attention than most elected officials. Spouses are also routinely covered by a wide range of popular media outlets patronized by Americans who may not consume a lot of political news. Finally, first ladies are more popular than presidents. In almost every year since the American National Election Studies began measuring public opinion of first ladies in addition to the president, first ladies have enjoyed higher job approval ratings than their husbands. Even as Hillary Clinton faced substantial public backlash in 1993 surrounding her involvement in the Clinton administration's health care initiative, her job approval rating averaged 64 percent while Bill Clinton's averaged 55 percent.[4] Likewise, Michelle Obama's approval ratings remained higher than President Obama's ratings during the first year of the administration when he enjoyed notable popularity. This book tests the assertions that first, the White House harnesses the first lady's popularity strategically in order to garner public support for the president and his policy agenda, and second, these appeals have a positive effect on individual evaluations of the president and certain administration-sponsored policies. I hope you will enjoy the book and keep its findings close in mind as we embark on another historic U.S. presidential election.

Acknowledgments

I am overcome with gratitude for the help and support I have received from the family, friends, and mentors who helped me realize this dream. I am principally indebted to the experts listed hereunder who participated in the interview process and lent me a much deeper understanding of the East Wing than I would have acquired without their help, and to the insiders also listed hereunder who introduced me to those experts and opened the door to more insight.

To my mom, a veritable first lady in her own right, thank you for believing in me and debriefing me after every exciting academic and career development I can recall, especially when nobody else was excited, and for offering the outlook of someone who is constantly reading and learning about politics. To my dad, the most supportive father for which a person could ask, thank you for letting me witness firsthand how our nation's greatest businesses are built around the same qualities of charisma and authenticity that beget political power in the United States, and for allowing me play a small part in your own rise to greatness. To my sister, the Gautama Buddha of our family, you are a personal and professional inspiration. Thank you for picking up the phone in the middle of the night and beating back my irrational fears and delusions. And to my husband to be, it is truly the highest honor of my life to share life with you. So many parts of this book were strengthened by your heeded guidance, adopted perspectives, and imparted knowledge. You know it. I love you. Thank you.

Mayesha Alam
Leslie Appleton
Andi Ball
Maurine Beasley
Jean Becker
Paul Begala
Russell Berman
Sidney Blumenthal
Christopher Bognanno
Betsy Boich
Amy Bonitatibus
MaryAnne Borrelli
Ann Brock
Cynthia Burleson
Barbara Burrell
Andy Chan
Deanna Congileo
Julie Cooke
Paul Costello
Anthony Eksterowicz
Emily Fasano
Jeanie Figg
Katherine Flynn
Amy Gardner
Michele Gillespie
Lou Gould
David Greenberg
Jessica Gribble
Avery Gordon
David Gordon
Myra Gutin
Sondra Haley
Anne Heiligenstein
Hugh Hewitt
Chris Hull
Camille Johnston
Mike Kazin
Rogan Kersh
Anne Kornblut
Stephen Krupin
Martha Kumar

Jonathan Ladd
Kyle Layman
Kevin Lipson
Sam Lipson
Catherine Lutge Sullivan
Anita McBride
Mike McCurry
Sally McDonough
Minta McNally
Tom Mitchell
Jonathan Mummolo
Stephen Mummolo
Chelsea Murphy
MaryJo O'Brien
Caroline O'Connell
Jessica Patterson
Dana Perino
Lindsay Pettingill
Megan Prior
Jennifer Richwine
Michael Riley
Betsy K. Robertson
Mark Rom
Lynn Ross
Fred Ryan
Greg Schneiders
Scott Stanzel
Valerie Sulfaro
Krissah Thompson
Karen Tumulty
Max Ukropina
Melanne Verveer
Charity Wallace
Robert Watson
Stephen Wayne
Wendy Weber
Susan Whitson
Ike Williams
Dickerson Wright
Katherine Wright
Stephanie Wright

CHAPTER 1

The Puzzle Spouses Pose

White House and presidential campaign strategists regularly use communications tactics designed to enhance the public image of presidents and presidential candidates despite arguments of scholars that these strategies rarely change public opinion. Public appearances of the first lady represent one strategy that has been used increasingly during the last three presidential administrations, yet is seldom studied. Michelle Obama gave more major public remarks in her husband's first six years in office than Hillary Clinton and Laura Bush during the first six years of their husbands' administrations. In fact, in most years of the last three presidential administrations, the first lady has also made more public speeches than the *vice president*, as I demonstrate in Chapter 3. Descriptive statistics like this suggest that the communications role of the first lady has expanded over time and may have even exceeded the roles of other key presidential surrogates. In what follows, I outline a plan to answer two primary questions that will guide readers through the book. How and why have public appearances of the first lady become an increasingly prominent communications strategy over the last three presidential administrations? Do public appearances of the first lady have an impact on public opinion of the president and his policies?

In 1956, Mamie Eisenhower became the first presidential spouse to be featured in a televised campaign advertisement. The ad, an overt appeal to female voters, emphasized Mrs. Eisenhower's popularity among women, who would become the majority of the U.S. voting public by 1964 and have accounted for the largest proportion of eligible voters in every

U.S. presidential election since 1980.[1] By the Kennedy administration, the public activities of the first lady were ardently followed by television journalists, and in 1961, Jacqueline Kennedy hired the first Press Secretary to the First Lady, marking the beginning of what scholars regard as a fully professionalized Office of the First Lady. Over the course of this book, we examine the increasingly common utilization of the first lady as a presidential messaging device. Through an in-depth examination of the Clinton, Bush, and Obama administrations, I document and explain the expanding role of the first lady in the White House and presidential campaign communications strategy and assess whether public appearances of presidential spouses have an impact on public opinion of presidents and the policies advanced by their administrations.

A Brief Note About What This Book Is and What It Is Not

There are three key attributes that make this book different than other books on first ladies. The first is focus. The book is unique in its focus on the communications and public relations role of presidential spouses; a role that it argues is generalizable to all first ladies and is the most critical role to understanding their influence in U.S. politics. Most books on first ladies discuss the many different roles and duties of presidential spouses and how they have changed over time (e.g., traditional and/or ceremonial duties), and the authors of these books then categorize first ladies using types (e.g., "active" versus "traditional" spouses). For example, Laura Bush is often deemed a "traditional" first lady in the literature and Hillary Clinton is deemed an "activist." However, as the publicly available data featured in this book show, Laura Bush gave almost twice as many public speeches as Hillary Clinton did in every year of the Clinton administration and many of these were speeches advocating the Bush administration's policy agenda.

The second unique trait of the book is methods. The few presidential scholars who have given attention to first ladies rely on personality-based typologies and historical anecdotes because of the perceived lack of data available on presidential spouses. I count and content analyze every documented public speech made by a first lady since 1992 when the White House began transcribing and posting speeches made by presidential spouses on the Briefing Room web sites, which have been preserved by the National Archives. I also conduct four survey experiments among more than 8,000 Americans that test whether reading or watching a speech delivered by a first lady (as opposed to a president or a vice president) affects the way survey participants evaluate presidents and policy issues.

Few people have the methodological training to conduct experiments like these, and as I discussed in the preface, the political scientists among them have dismissed the prospect of applying rigorous empirical methods to a seemingly trivial topic like first ladies. It is a shame, because experiments are really the only sound vehicles for determining whether the strategies used by the White House and presidential campaign staffers resonate with Americans and affect the way they vote. The experiments are introduced and explained in a way that is accessible to all readers and I hope will endear readers to the idea that the bold claims of political pundits and commentators to which we have grown accustomed ought to be tested.

The third qualifier is perspective. Making use of the contacts I acquired while working in California politics and the private sector, I was able to interview many prominent former White House staff members, journalists, and presidential campaign strategists, although I also interviewed numerous scholars. My professional campaign experience and formal academic training allow me to bridge the ideological gap between political operatives, to whom the idea of strategically deploying a spouse on the campaign trail or to promote legislation is an ingrained political instinct—an obvious way to garner public support for the president and his agenda—and many political scientists, who largely believe the efforts of campaign operatives who use these kinds of tactics—including or excluding the president's spouse—are inconsequential to our understanding of how or whether government works.

I wrote this book with the very broad intention, among others, of making empirically based political science research accessible to general audiences who are interested in topics that do not typically see the light of day in methods-driven political science departments, but are nonetheless critical to our understanding of how government really works. Americans really are *fascinated* by presidential spouses. In many cases in which a former first lady and a former president have both published their memoirs after leaving office, the memoirs of first ladies have outsold those of their presidential counterparts, a pattern that began with Lady Bird Johnson's book *A White House Diary*.[2] With a presidential election approaching that features a former first lady as one of the front-runners, it is the right time for a book like this to disrupt the way in which we perceive the roles of the presidential and presidential candidate spouses. In 2016, we will inevitably see many of the same traditions involving spouses of candidates carried out—joint interviews and ads featuring the candidates' families, emotional convention speeches, and even cookie-baking contests—but readers of this book will have the opportunity to view these public appearances in an entirely new light. Public appearances of the president's spouse are highly strategic, deftly planned, and targeted events designed primarily for one purpose: to make presidents, presidential candidates, and their ideas more appealing.

Readers can expect to encounter some academic language in the text, in the sections where we measure the effect of public speeches made by spouses on public opinion using survey experiments, for example, but they will not be expected to fend for themselves in a sea of mathematical notation. So, while researchers who believe that social science books must be written in the technical language of social science will perhaps be disappointed by efforts made to access a much broader population, readers looking for salacious lore about the private lives of presidents and their spouses will be even more dissatisfied. The interviews featured in this book with former White House staff are anonymous, save for indications of job title and rank, in order to ensure conversations with insiders still entrenched in political professions resulted in the most accurate, least polished accounts. The aim of the interviews was to engage West Wing and East Wing staff, the very people responsible for White House communications strategies, in the task of clarifying how and why the president's spouse appears in public, and the reasons why these appearances have become so frequent in recent years. Time spent excavating the personal lives of our government officials, although it often results in informative heuristics that U.S. voters use to make inferences about candidate quality, is time wasted for most political scientists, whose goal is to create the theories and frameworks that help journalists, activists, politicians, and the U.S. public make sense of political issues and events, rather than reporting or recounting the events themselves. *On Behalf of the President* is not as much a book *about* the president's spouse as it is a book about how presidential spouses fit into the U.S. political system and how we should think about spouses in the future.

A Roadmap for and Preview of the Book

Chapter 2 begins by surveying several areas of literature that guide my research on presidential spouses, including presidential communications and administrative organization, public opinion, and gender and politics. This chapter helps readers understand what research has been conducted on presidential spouses so far, what research is still lacking, some of the obstacles to conducting high-quality research on the president's spouse, and the theories and methods we can draw from disciplines outside political science to help us better understand the roles of spouses. Generally speaking, this literature underlies one of two explanations of the surge in public appearances of first ladies: what I conceptualize as supply-side (i.e. institutional) explanations and demand-side (i.e. social–behavioral) explanations. Supply-side explanations for public activity of first ladies in the last three administrations assume that public appearances are shaped by developments in the political, technological, or administrative environment surrounding the White House. One prospective explanation, for example, is that the proliferation of television and the Internet has created a public stage so large and conspicuous that the president cannot possibly occupy it alone. In other words, public appearances of the first lady may simply represent attempts to meet the requirements of a 24-hour news cycle.[3] Demand-side explanations of the expanding public role of presidential spouses, in contrast, suggest there is something special about first ladies that makes them popular and effective representatives of the administration's agenda. Increased appearances may be evidence that the White House has learned to tap into the public appeal of the first lady and become more reliant on communications strategies that include her, both on the campaign trail and in the White House.

Although the supply-side and demand-side explanations for increased spouse activity diverge considerably, they are inextricably linked. Extensive press coverage of the first lady generates greater demand for her public presence, and the public's fascination with the first lady makes the press more inclined to cover her. While one part of the book focuses on the task of explaining the increased public activity of spouses across and within the last three presidential administrations, another part aspires to measure the effect of these appearances on public opinion of the president and his policies. Chapter 2 also provides historical context for the bold idea that first ladies throughout history have *always* been expected to communicate with the public to a certain degree, even if they had no political aspirations. I explain why existing scholarship based on "active" and "traditional" typologies of first ladies that are rooted in personal factors like educational attainment and interest in politics is problematic, and I suggest a new way forward.

Chapter 3 provides a more thorough presentation of the theory advanced in this book as well as the hypotheses it tests. What are the driving forces and goals that underlie the phenomenon of increased spouse appearances? What purposes do these appearances serve? In this chapter, the central argument of the book is assembled, that public appearances of the president's spouse are strategic efforts to advance the administration's agenda. While it is feasible that public activity of the first lady is determined *both* by administrative demands and individual-specific factors, if the influx in spouse activity was due to changes in the technological or political environment alone (e.g., the emergence of 24-hour news), we would observe a parallel influx in the public activity of other surrogates, such as the vice president. We do not. The communications burden appears to be falling disproportionately on the shoulders of first ladies. Preliminary evidence for this argument is provided through the quantitative and qualitative analyses of 1,669 public speeches made by first ladies since 1992 and 22 years of public opinion data. The opinion data illuminate the ways in which Americans have a much more positive view of the first lady than they do of presidents and vice presidents, regardless of party, leaving the public susceptible to East Wing efforts to convince them. The speeches show that these efforts have taken a fascinating form since the end of the Clinton administration: political advocacy in an apolitical context. First ladies have adopted a tactic that allows them to promote presidential policy items under the guise of nonpolicy-oriented discussion. Domestic examples include plugs for the Affordable Care Act in Michelle Obama's speeches about childhood obesity and similar mentions of No Child Left Behind in Laura Bush's literacy initiative speeches.

Chapters 4 and 5 describe the additional data sources I enlist to answer questions about the reasons presidential spouses go public, whether these efforts are strategic on the part of the White House, and whether they are effective means to enhancing public opinion of the president. A multimethod approach allows me to discuss the usefulness of White House communications strategies that include the president's spouse, even if the relationship between presidential approval and public appearances of the first lady is difficult to discern through the analysis of large-n data sets. In addition to relying on content analysis of public remarks made by Hillary Clinton, Laura Bush, and Michelle Obama, elite interviews with former White House and presidential campaign staff were conducted, and a series of survey experiments were launched to test several hypotheses. Namely, I expect to find that public appearances of first ladies are strategically linked to presidential agenda items, and that these appearances have a positive effect on individual evaluations of the president and his policies in certain issue areas or among particular groups, even relative to public appearances made by the president himself and by key surrogates such as the vice president.

In Chapter 4, former White House and presidential campaign staff members, prominent journalists, and highly regarded scholars in the field open their diaries to us and explain the motivations behind and potential pitfalls associated with mobilizing the president's spouse. Through colorful stories and first-hand accounts, these experts demonstrate that first, in the last three decades, the White House has learned how (and how *not*) to harness public interest in the president's spouse to advance its agenda. A key finding is that strategies including the first lady shifted during the course of the Clinton administration in response to the negative public reaction to Hillary Clinton's intimate involvement in the crafting and campaign for the Health Security Act in 1993, and that Laura Bush and Michelle Obama's staffs have developed better strategies that allow first ladies to promote presidential policy while maintaining public favor. Second, increased public appearances are part of an "all hands on deck" approach to campaigns and White House communications.

The emphasis by some strategists discussed in Chapter 4 on the necessity of mobilizing as many surrogates as possible in modern campaigns and administrations to widely disseminate the president's message left one question unanswered: Why are first ladies doing most of the work? What can they accomplish that other surrogates cannot? The answer becomes evident in the three unique routes spouses and their staffs take to promote the president and his agenda that are discussed in Chapter 5. First, spouses go personal. They convey the president's priorities at home and abroad more sincerely than vice presidents and cabinet secretaries. Second, spouses go purple. They use their outsider status and lack of official responsibility to reach out to partisan audiences who may mistrust other members of the president's administration. Finally, they go positive. First ladies choose pet project initiatives that appear to be valence issues but double as favorable frames for the president's policy agenda. Specific examples of this practice are provided in the Clinton, Bush, and Obama administrations, and famous remarks delivered by first ladies are woven throughout more first-hand accounts from experts.

Although White House and presidential campaign strategists often have more than one goal in mind when they mobilize spouses, such as controlling the media narrative, attention getting, and fundraising, the most interesting and reliable test of the strategic communications theory is whether the president's spouse can change the way Americans view the president and his policy agenda. In certain issue areas and among women, they can and they do. In Chapter 6, I conduct experiments testing the effect of public appearances made by first ladies on public opinion. Reading a speech or watching a clip of a speech delivered by Hillary Clinton, Laura Bush, or Michelle Obama often produced more positive responses among survey participants in the treatment group than among participants in the control group who read the same exact speech or viewed a similar speech clip attributed to President Clinton, President Bush, or President Obama. Some strong effects are also realized when results among participants who read a speech clip attributed to Hillary Clinton, Laura Bush, or Michelle Obama are compared to results among participants who read a speech clip attributed to Al Gore, Dick Cheney, or Joe Biden.

Chapters 7 and 8 discuss the implications of the experimental results gathered and discussed in Chapter 6 against the backdrop of information we cultivated from earlier chapters. I contemplate the ways in which this book changes our conception of the ideal political spouse, what we should look for on the 2016 campaign trail, and map the future of the study of political spouses at all levels of elected office. I also introduce a brand new experiment that predicts how the spouses of candidates for president in 2016 affect the public image of those candidates. Discrepancies are measured in favorability ratings between the control group, which views a picture of Hillary Clinton or Jeb Bush alone, and a treatment group, which views a picture of Hillary Clinton with her spouse, former president Bill Clinton, or Jeb Bush with his spouse, former first lady of Florida, Columba Bush. As the insiders I interviewed appropriately conjectured, Bill Clinton may very well be able to do for Hillary Clinton's public image what first ladies have done for decades: reveal the human face of the candidate through charming anecdotes and personal information and engage the press in an informal and familiar manner.

CHAPTER 2

What Martha Washington and Michelle Obama Have in Common

Challenging "Active" and "Traditional" Paradigms of First Ladies

The role of the First Lady of the United States has evolved substantially over time, from that of hostess and supportive wife to political spokesperson, advisor to the president, and media celebrity. As this book later demonstrates, Michelle Obama has made more speeches and major public appearances in her first six years in office than any first lady in recent history. Despite this significant increase in responsibility and visibility, the majority of articles and books that have been published on first ladies primarily focus on their personal backgrounds or propose theoretical frameworks that simplify efforts to compare first ladies who occupied the White House over time.[1] Scholars who create typologies of first ladies, such as public versus private first ladies, or active versus traditional first ladies, often rely heavily on partisan affiliation and education level to categorize them. For example, Robert Watson and Valerie Sulfaro have classified Hillary Clinton as a public, activist first lady because of her high degree of educational attainment and her Democratic, progressive political ideals. This chapter surveys the existing research on presidential spouses in an effort to provide context for empirical findings that suggest scholars such as Watson and Sulfaro may not be entirely right: first ladies have become more publicly active over time regardless of party affiliation or degree of educational attainment.

In Chapters 3 and 4 of his book, *The Presidents' Wives*, Watson, one of the most prolific scholars of presidential spouses, categorizes first ladies according to a chronological framework that illustrates the evolution of first ladies' roles. These categories include *First Ladies that Shaped the Image and the Role of the Office of the First Lady* (1789–1817), when first ladies almost exclusively served as hostesses of social functions and formal affairs of state; *Absent Spouses* (1817–1869); *Transitional Spouses* (1869–1901); *Aspiring Spouses* (1901–1945); *Model Wives* (1945–1974); and finally *Modern Spouses* (1974–present), the category to which Hillary Clinton, Laura Bush, and Michelle Obama belong. The most intriguing change in first lady roles may have been the shift from the Aspiring Spouses period, best represented by active roles of Helen Taft, Florence Harding, and Eleanor Roosevelt as campaigners, speechwriters, and advisors to the president, to the Model Wives period, where first ladies such as Jacqueline Kennedy and Bess Truman resumed the role of supportive wives shared by first ladies in the late 19th century despite the major influx in media attention to and exposure of first ladies in the 1950s and 1960s.[2] Watson claims the role of the first lady fully developed into that of associate president by the Modern Spouses period.

Although these kinds of fluctuations are substantively interesting, the limited availability of data on public statements and appearances of first ladies before the Modern Spouses period makes quantitative analysis of trends in first lady roles nearly impossible. For this reason, it makes sense to focus on identifying variation in the public activity of first ladies within categories rather than between categories, as Watson does. Watson's definition of first lady activism has four components, which he calls the "4 P's of Political Activism."[3] These include *pet projects*, *public policy participant*, *political player*, and *pomp and pageantry*. Watson appears to differentiate primarily between first lady activism in areas of personal interest (i.e., pet project work) and first lady activism on the president's behalf (i.e., public policy participation and political player). Watson describes pet projects as socially oriented valence issues that are considered politically safe. Public policy participation and the political player role are slightly more controversial, where participation may entail chairing policy task forces, traveling independently of the president or speaking on behalf of him, designing policy or legislation, or acting as a politically savvy confidante to the president.

Watson has also written extensively about the Modern Spouses period. His edited volume, *The Presidential Companion*, is a compilation of essays by several scholars that provide insight into the role of first ladies in policy making, policy advocacy, and the process by which the Office of the First Lady was integrated into the White House. Two indications of the expanding role of first ladies noted by these scholars are congressional testimony and presence in legislative workshops, activities in which Hillary Clinton, Eleanor Roosevelt, and Rosalynn Carter participated. Colton Campbell and Sean McCluskie note that first lady involvement in committee hearings should be considered a form of policy influence, given the consensus among legislative scholars that the congressional committee system is the heart of lawmaking in the U.S. government.[4] Scholars also remark that Hillary Clinton's direct involvement in the health care policy formation process and her frequent meetings with lawmakers in 1993 prompted a clearer delineation of the status of the Office of the First Lady. Despite considerable controversy, the U.S. Court of Appeals decision, *Association of American Physicians and Surgeons v. Hillary Rodham Clinton*, stated that presidential spouses are the functional equivalents of government officers and employees, a role formally recognized by Congress when it established the Office of the First Lady by statute to include a full-time staff funded by the public.[5]

Another indication of first lady activism noted by scholars is the involvement of presidential spouses in international relations. Scholars such as Glenn Hastedt have combined basic frameworks for studying first ladies (he draws on the "ceremonial first lady," the "political first lady," and the "policy first lady" model) with paradigms in international politics and political psychology in order to determine the conditions under which and at what stages of the foreign policy-making process first ladies become active.[6] Hastedt draws from Fred Greenstein's work on presidential personalities and policy making to develop a stages model of involvement; he suggests that first ladies become participants in foreign relations and foreign policy making at different points in the policy stream, including agenda setting, policy formation, policy adoption, policy implementation, or policy analysis and evaluation.[7] For example, he shows that both Rosalynn Carter's and Hillary Clinton's efforts to promote human rights abroad were exercised at the agenda-setting stage of the policy process, where policies are recognized and defined. Hastedt writes that the foreign policy activities of Rosalynn Carter and Hillary Clinton "were not lone ranger actions." "They were coordinated efforts undertaken with the approval and involvement of key foreign policy bureaucracies and the White House . . . to advance the interests of the respective administrations."[8]

Unlike Hastedt, Cambell et al., and Watson, who draw a clear line between pet project activities and influence in "substantive policy issues," such as foreign relations, scholars such as Sulfaro use the terms "pet projects" and "first lady policy agenda" interchangeably.[9] According to Sulfaro's framework for activism, the first lady's policy agenda can either be public (controversial policy agendas motivated by the first lady's own interest) or private (noncontroversial or safe policy agendas focused on valence issues). In her 2007 study, Sulfaro asserts that Eleanor Roosevelt and Hillary Clinton had controversial and "public" policy agendas, while Laura Bush had a noncontroversial and "private" policy agenda. Accordingly, Hillary Clinton is classified as an activist, or untraditional first lady, an argument that Sulfaro supports by pointing to Hillary Clinton's educational accolades, her attempt to pursue a policy agenda independently of her husband (health care), and her former status as the primary wage earner in her family. In contrast, Sulfaro characterizes Laura Bush as a traditional first lady, in part, because of what Sulfaro considers a "relative absence of political activity."[10] Sulfaro concludes that voters' mean evaluations of Hillary Clinton were lower than those of Laura Bush overall, citing Hillary Clinton's image as a polarizing, activist figure who frequently expressed her opinion in public. She found that voters were relatively indifferent toward Laura Bush; very few respondents indicated either extreme affinity for or dislike of her. Sulfaro attributes this to Laura Bush's infrequent public appearances and statements. That is, voters were hard pressed to assign her negative attributes because of her low level of exposure.[11]

This book critically engages two aspects of Sulfaro's study. First, Sulfaro's study is restricted to partisan voters' evaluations of one Republican first lady, Laura Bush, and one Democratic first Lady, Hillary Clinton. Such a heavy reliance on two cases may bring readers to the unfounded conclusion that Republican first ladies are more likely to fulfill traditional roles and Democratic first ladies are more likely to be activists. I add Michelle Obama to my analysis in order to combat this notion. Second, Sulfaro's conclusions about partisan evaluations of first ladies rest heavily on the assumption that Hillary Clinton was more publicly engaged or "active" than Laura Bush, an assumption invalidated by a simple comparison of frequencies of public remarks included in Chapter 3.

First Ladies in the Public Spotlight: Passive Bystanders or Torchbearers of the President's Message?

If there were some way to accurately control for the status of women in society over time, we might find that political spouses have been more active players in presidential communications strategy than the literature suggests. There is an argument to be made that the primary role of the spouses of presidents and presidential candidates has always been to communicate with the public. The first documented speech by a first lady in history was made by Martha Washington in April 1789. On a solo trip from Mount Vernon to the U.S. capital at that time, New York, for her husband's inauguration, Mrs. Washington stopped in Philadelphia and was greeted by a cheering crowd and journalists from at least two newspapers, reportedly shouting "Long live Lady Washington!" Upon realizing that the crowd desired her attention, she stood up in her carriage and made brief remarks thanking the troops that escorted her and Philadelphians for the warm welcome.[12] Although scholars who study first ladies typically focus on Eleanor Roosevelt and Hillary Clinton as examples of publicly active first ladies, it is a well-cited fact that even first ladies who avoided the public spotlight while occupying the White House were avid spokespersons for their husbands on the campaign trail.

The United States has a long history of presidential campaigns in which candidates sought to capitalize on the appeal of their wives. Long before Eleanor Roosevelt began to hold routine press conferences and write weekly newspaper columns, the spouses of presidential candidates were expected to interact with journalists and voters. First ladies who entered the White House in the late 19th century were subjected to "front-porch campaigns," a style of campaigning that required candidates to host fundraising events, rallies, and press conferences in their homes. Some scholars suggest that the orchestrated role of the first lady on the campaign trail was born here.[13] Grover Cleveland, Benjamin Harrison, and William McKinley were elected in the era of front-porch campaigning. In 1888, Frances Cleveland and Caroline Harrison had become so popular that they were both featured in campaign propaganda. For example, images of Carrie Harrison were printed on schoolchildren's writing tablets, plates, buttons, and posters.[14] In 1896, the McKinley campaign published a biography of the prospective first lady in an effort to draw further support from a voting public that was already fascinated with Ida McKinley.[15]

Florence Harding is perhaps one of the best examples of an exuberant front-porch campaigner. Before Warren Harding received the Republican nomination in 1920, Mrs. Harding advocated tirelessly for her husband at the convention in Chicago, where historians note that she made an impression with delegates as the only woman out of 500 lobbyists and by emphasizing her personal relationship with the presidential candidate.[16] Back at home, in addition to opening her house to inquisitive strangers and reporters, Florence Harding arranged photo opportunities and press availability from the Harding front porch. Even today, pundits often recite a famous quote attributed to Mrs. Harding, "Well Warren Harding, I got you the Presidency. Now what are you going to do?"[17] Although Florence Harding seemed to accept these public relations responsibilities wholeheartedly, other first ladies were less enthusiastic about occupying the media spotlight. They campaigned for their husbands nonetheless. Mamie Eisenhower, despite holding only one press conference during her entire tenure as first lady and focusing almost solely on the social responsibilities of presidential spouses, averaged more than 10 daily press interviews on the 1952 campaign trail, and broke precedent by riding with her husband from the inauguration ceremony to the White House, taking a seat historically reserved for the vice president.[18] Eisenhower campaign pins famously stated "I like Ike"; however, pins that read "I like Ike. But I LOVE Mamie" were also widely circulated. Before Mrs. Eisenhower, Bess Truman, remembered as one of the most intensely private first ladies in history, made a few big speeches in battleground states during her husband's campaign.

The first lady's part as presidential spokesperson has undoubtedly stretched beyond the campaign trail into the White House. Public appearances of first ladies range from endorsements of presidential policies to damage control efforts. Again, the phenomenon of the first lady as a presidential defender and image softener has deeper roots than we might expect. As early as 1888 when Frances Cleveland published a statement refuting claims that her husband drunkenly abused her, first ladies have attempted to mitigate damage to the president's public image in addition to maximizing his popularity.[19] A good example of this is Lady Bird Johnson's campaign throughout the U.S. South in 1964, intended to rectify the president's standing among Democrats who had become hostile to the president's decision to support civil rights legislation. Watson echoes the statements of other scholars who often make claims about the positive impact of these kinds of appearances in his supposition that Lady Bird's trip minimized Republican gains in the region.[20]

There seems to be plenty of anecdotal evidence to support the notion that first ladies appear in public in order to improve public opinion of the president, and that Americans are responsive to these attempts. However, some scholars argue that spouses did not become surrogates in presidential campaigns and in the White House until the late 1970s. For example, Maurine Beasley, Ann Grimes, and Lisa Burns mark the Bush and Reagan administrations as the beginning of the use of presidential spouses as "image making" tools.[21] While Beasley acknowledges that several earlier first ladies such as Eleanor Roosevelt and Jacqueline Kennedy were public fixtures, she explains that they involved themselves in the media to the extent they wished and spoke only about topics of personal interest. This is to say that even if first ladies such as Roosevelt and Kennedy generated substantial media attention, their relationship with the press was not managed in an official capacity by the White House or the presidential campaigns. Eleanor Roosevelt, for instance, frequently held press conferences and spoke about women's rights issues, but keenly avoided speaking about her husband or topics germane to the White House policy agenda. As journalist Bess Furman noted, ". . . she [Eleanor Roosevelt] rules out controversial subjects, and won't be queried on anything in the province of the president."[22] Concurrently, Jacqueline Kennedy's media appearances projected style, rather than substance. If the Kennedy presidential campaign or the White House attempted to manage her appearances, they did so in an effort to downplay her extravagant lifestyle and the Kennedy family's wealth—issues that the campaign feared would alienate middle class U.S. voters. Perhaps in order to minimize public scrutiny regarding her expensive clothes and the number of employees assisting her, Jacqueline Kennedy agreed to be pictured in a *Life* spread in 1960 putting Caroline Kennedy to bed and doing household work without the help of a secretary or nurse.[23]

In contrast to these types of appearances, Grimes argues that in 1988, the "Year-of-the-Spouse," Barbara Bush and Kitty Dukakis acted as invaluable campaign commodities, speaking about issues such as "workplace democracy" and "good jobs at good wages" at the very first public forum for the spouses of presidential candidates. Grimes argues that the wives of presidential candidates served a number of purposes in these campaigns, including winnowing the primary field, aiding campaign operatives in their support functions, and narrowing the gender gap by appealing to women voters.[24] Some scholars have suggested that another function spouses serve is one of public counterweight to the president or presidential candidate. James Mueller illustrates this in his study "How Bill and Hillary Work Together to Handle the Media." Mueller argues that both on the 1992 campaign trail and in the White House, Hillary Clinton tightly controlled press access to her husband, who "wasn't very good at message discipline" and "sometimes [went] too far in his conversation with reporters."[25] Interestingly, Mueller notes a similar balancing act between the spouses when Hillary Clinton ran for Senate and the presidency; Bill Clinton generated press attention for the characteristically media-averse former first lady, and used it to promote his wife and punish her opponents.[26]

This book diverges from historical and typological approaches in its empirical analysis of public appearances of first ladies and its measurement of the effect of these appearances on public opinion. It takes particular issue with theoretical frameworks such as the active versus traditional typologies described before, which assume presidential spouses enter the White House with an idea of how publicly engaged they would like to be, the projects to which they would like to devote the most attention, and execute the job of first lady according to these personal desires and priorities. Such frameworks are unhelpful in efforts to further understand contemporary presidential administrations, which are under the relentless scrutiny of the mass media, faced with higher demands for transparency and public responsiveness than ever before. Next I summarize the four areas of literature that are most helpful in an investigation of the phenomenon of increased public activity of first ladies.

The First Lady as an Image Shaper

While a tremendous amount of scholarly attention has been given to presidential communications, first ladies are rarely mentioned in these discussions (despite their frequent presence in the news media and popular press). Robert Watson's 2003 article "Source Material" highlights this disconnect, observing that while approximately 58 major biographies of first ladies have been published since 1980, only about 18 reliable scholarly studies of first ladies were published in the same time period. Most of the biographies are classified as historical narratives or profiles rather than empirical research.[27] Some of the stronger scholarly work is part of communications literature that assumes the first lady is an extension of "the machinery of the White House [which] functions to make the president look good."[28] That is, every action of the first lady is planned and executed with the president's benefit in mind.[29] Discussion of the communications role played by presidential spouses on the campaign trail and in the White House marks a broad shift in the literature on first ladies, from scholarship focused on private power exercised by first ladies to scholarship that recognizes the potential political benefits of placing first ladies in the public spotlight. This shifting emphasis is even evident in titles of books about first ladies, differentiating authors such as Kati Marton (*Hidden Power*) and James McCallops (*Edith Bolling Galt Wilson: The Unintended President*) who emphasize the first lady's personal relationship with and access to the president as her main source of "behind-the-scenes" authority (i.e., "pillow influence"), and authors such as Gains (*Running Mates*) and Mueller (*Tag Teaming the Press*), who note that first ladies are most effective when they use their popularity and appear frequently in public on behalf of the White House. Gains acknowledges this shift and anticipates the increased activism that has been evident in the last three presidential administrations quite perceptively: "But for a political wife to be taken seriously means the public has to recognize her as a player and hold her accountable for whatever influence she wields. It means recognizing overt, not covert, power. Barbara Bush may not be willing to accept that new definition of first lady. Kitty Dukakis wasn't quite ready. But with more Liddy Doles and Jim Schroeders on the campaign trail, the phenomenon of 'first partner' is unavoidably on the horizon."[30]

Some scholars, such as Molly Wertheimer, who claim that first ladies "cannot not communicate," have argued that the essence of the first lady's political role is the use of specific, strategic, rhetorical communications devices to achieve goals.[31] Therefore, first ladies have interacted with the press in a passive manner as the subjects of news stories, through forms of nonverbal communication such as accompanying the president to public events, or even as gatekeepers of press access to the president. Instead, according to Wertheimer, in order to understand the roles of first ladies and the ways in which they are fulfilled, scholars must pay attention to what first ladies say in public, the way in which they say it, and the groups with which they interact. For example, many scholars have described Jimmy and Rosalynn Carter's marriage as a symbiotic relationship characterized by shared power and equality. However, Molly Wertheimer, Diane Blair, and Shawn Perry-Giles argue that the way Rosalynn Carter exercised influence in her roles as political advisor, independent advocate, and campaign surrogate was to use a strategy of "rhetorical coordination," in which she blended her agenda with her husband's political objectives and accomplishments so she could protect her interests from relegation to the secondary status of "pet projects."[32] Such a strong emphasis on the rhetoric of first ladies among communications scholars surely inspires the expanded use of public speech frequencies and content in studies that attempt to measure public activity of first ladies.

Two notable works, *The President's Partner: The First Lady in the 20th Century* (1989: Myra Gutin) and *Inventing a Voice: The Rhetoric of American First Ladies in the Twentieth Century* (2004: Molly Wertheimer), have made use of speeches, radio and television broadcasts, interviews, press conferences, and magazine and newspaper articles to illustrate the unique position occupied by first ladies of the United States and to provide a framework for understanding why the Office of the First Lady is an important part of the presidency. However, these studies provide descriptive, rather than deterministic, evidence for the changing role of first ladies over time; they do not quantify first lady communications in a way that might enable the identification of a measurable or even causal effect of first lady activism on the White House policy-making process or, inversely, that might explain what shifts in the institution and culture of the White House prompt increased first lady activism. While the extent and depth of the news coverage public appearances of first ladies receive are in and of itself an indication that communications strategies involving presidential spouses draw attention to the administration's agenda, the survey experiments detailed later in this book aim to measure whether appearances of spouses actually influence public opinion of presidential agenda items, among individuals who tuned into coverage of the first lady's appearance, or more specifically, read her speech.

White House Centralization and Demands for Presidential Visibility

Although White House staff size has decreased since President Nixon hired nearly 200 aides between 1969 and 1972—reaching a total exceeding 600 full-time employees—the role of the White House in domestic and foreign policy making has expanded and public demand for political responsiveness has grown. This change is partially attributed to what Matthew Dickinson calls "the paradox of politicization," a process in which presidents of both parties have increasingly politicized Executive Branch agencies by staffing them with politically responsive, trustworthy aides and centralizing control over policy making in the White House.[33] Politicization scholars argue that the White House makes these administrative changes in an effort to balance demands for public responsiveness with limited resources, given the growth of the Executive Branch.[34] It is not unreasonable to surmise that the increase in public appearances of the first lady in recent years occurred in response to the same pressures, except rather than politicizing bureaucratic agencies, the White House has politicized the Office of the First Lady, a historically uncontroversial office chiefly concerned with nonpartisan causes, social gatherings, ceremonies, and the restoration and preservation of the White House.[35]

The expanding communications role of presidential spouses is arguably the strongest evidence of a politicized Office of the First Lady, considering the arguments of scholars like Samuel Kernell who claim that the growth of the White House communications operation is itself a form of increased politicization. This notion is also supported by scholars such as Eksterowicz and Paynter who trace the beginning of the professionalized Office of the First Lady to the hiring of the first official Press Secretary to the First Lady under Jacqueline Kennedy.[36] Indeed, as media interest in Mrs. Kennedy grew and she became more publicly visible, the first lady's office became integrated with the office of the president and she required a full-time communications staff. Tracing the expanding public relations role of the Office of the First Lady alongside the maturation of television and Internet news from the Kennedy through the Obama administrations provides a strong foundation for the argument that the Office of the First Lady has become a fully professionalized organization, tasked with delivering the president's message, and completely integrated with the White House communications operation.

Public Opinion of the President

The literature that assesses the way in which political strategists measure public opinion may explain why White House officials increasingly place the first lady in the public spotlight despite evidence in quantitative studies that these kinds of appearances have a negligible impact on presidential approval and popularity.[37] Susan MacManus and Andrew Quecan affirm that the enormity of mass media attention placed on spouses in recent elections and the amount of space in both the Bush and Kerry 2004 campaign playbooks devoted to the strategic use of spouses do not match the lack of empirical study of the frequency, timing, and structure of presidential spouse appearances on the campaign trail.[38] A small group of scholars has argued that the employment of spouses in presidential elections is perceived by Republican strategists as a way to close the gender gap, but hardly any have identified a causal relationship between vote choice and candidate wives.[39] It is possible that first ladies only affect public opinion under certain circumstances, or in a way that has not and perhaps cannot be identified by survey research. For example, first ladies may impact public opinion on an implicit, cognitive level. Some of the perceived benefits that have been noted by scholars and journalists include the ability of spouses to "humanize" candidates and the effectiveness of psychological messages sent by spouses to the public that reassure voters and legitimize the candidates. For example, regarding the 2012 presidential campaigns, Catherine Allgor wrote, ". . . Americans believe that a wife can tell us about her husband in ways that we can't discern from ads, stump speeches, or even debates: about his personal morality, his character, how he reacts to crisis—in short, who he really is."[40]

Gender and Credibility

A final area of literature about gender and political credibility points to several reasons why the first lady may be an effective communicator.

Gender scholars have argued that the presidency is the most intensely masculine post in the U.S. government, and political scientists such as Borrelli claim that any valuable study of first ladies must be as deeply rooted in gender as it is in presidency studies because public expectations of the first lady's role are fundamentally based on perceptions of gender and gender role modeling.[41] The small number of studies that focus on first lady approval ratings find that public evaluations of first ladies vary significantly according to respondent partisanship, respondent gender, and respondent attitudes about women's rights and gender. More specifically, Sulfaro finds that among other variables, young, female voters evaluated Hillary Clinton more positively and that older voters evaluated Laura Bush more positively.[42] Progressive views about women's rights are significantly and positively associated with high evaluations of Hillary Clinton. The powerful impact of partisanship that Sulfaro identifies, in addition to her postulation that "there is something associated with first ladies that women find appealing," may have implications for further study of increased involvement of first ladies and their longer-term impact on political views.[43] The possibility that first ladies are viewed as partisan figures rather than impartial figureheads by the public provides support for the argument that the Office of the First Lady plays an increasingly political rather than ceremonial role.

While the work of Sulfaro and others suggests that the first lady is evaluated according to the same partisan frameworks used to evaluate the president and other politicians, it is also possible that the first lady's lack of formal responsibility or connection to controversial policy issues actually makes her a more likeable public figure. Even if the first lady is viewed through a partisan lens, she may be considered a less controversial figure than other surrogates such as the vice president. This possibility is supported by a 2013 poll that found Michelle Obama to be the most trusted political figure in the United States, outranked only by a handful of movie stars, television hosts, and media personalities who have little or no association with politics.[44] Some scholars suggest that first ladies who have been particularly successful in their efforts to promote the president's agenda frame their public sphere work as an extension of their private sphere priorities, a strategy that distances them from partisan politics and makes them relatable to everyday Americans. Borrelli cites Laura Bush's rhetoric as an example of this strategy, in which she campaigned as a wife and mother, stressing her familial role and downplaying her partisan affiliation.[45] Sulfaro's findings track most closely with the "belief" approach to gender stereotypes, which posits that female politicians are more competent to deal with "compassion issues" such as education, health care, welfare and poverty, and child-related issues because they are perceived to be more caring by nature than their male counterparts.[46]

In contrast, the "trait" approach to gender stereotypes claims that female politicians are perceived to be more qualified to deal with compassion issues because gender-based personality traits make women better on some issues and men better on others (i.e., not because they have different political views, but because they have different experiences, interests, and perhaps values). Whether the first lady's communications efficacy is determined by her gender or her greater ability to maintain a nonpartisan or more trustworthy image, the literature on compassion issues prompts an investigation of the types of issues the first lady addresses in public, why the first lady and the president may speak about the same policy in different manners, and the impact of these actions. Do White House strategists place the first lady in the public eye because they believe women can speak about compassion issues more effectively?

CHAPTER 3

Messengers-in-Chief

Public appearances of presidential spouses have become more common over time as public expectations of first ladies have grown and the Office of the First Lady has become more professionalized. In fact, presidential spouses have made more major public speeches and remarks than vice presidents in most years of the last three presidential administrations (Table 3.1). Vice presidents are comparable to presidential spouses because they lack institutional power, except in the senate, yet play a highly visible role as presidential running mates. Although it is not the topic of this book, the notion that presidential spouses make more public remarks than vice presidents challenges the arguments of scholars such as Goldstein who claim vice presidents are becoming more powerful.[1] The findings in Table 3.1 may mean, for example, that the president's spouse is shouldering some of the communications responsibility traditionally delegated to other surrogates, allowing vice presidents to engage in other policy making or administrative activity, or instead that spouses are more effective in public relations than vice presidents in some cases. The frequency distribution displayed in Table 3.1 also shows that Hillary Clinton made fewer major public remarks than Laura Bush in almost every year of her husband's presidency, and that in merely six years in the White House, Michelle Obama's public activity has outpaced that of both her predecessors.

The tabulated remarks are part of an original data set of 1,669 public speeches made by presidential spouses from 1993 through 2014, manually collected from the White House Briefing Room web sites preserved

Table 3.1 Number of Public Speeches Listed on the White House Briefing Room Websites

	Hillary Clinton	Al Gore
1993	10	20
1994	21	45
1995	21	51
1996	7	27
1997	31	83
1998	71	100
1999	86	108
2000	7	57
	Laura Bush	**Dick Cheney**
2001	42	19
2002	67	27
2003	51	45
2004	92	149
2005	68	33
2006	152	74
2007	120	38
2008	116	41
	Michelle Obama	**Joe Biden**
2009	74	60
2010	85	35
2011	97	30
2012	178	19
2013	77	22
2014	108	28

by the National Archives and coded for a multitude of attributes to be discussed later in this chapter. Speeches that may be considered private, such as remarks made in intimate settings as family gatherings, are not publicly available and are not considered in this research. In the interest of maximizing reliability and validity of results gleaned from this data set, remarks shown in Table 3.1 do not include television or radio interviews, public appearances during which no remarks were made, or written statements such as op-eds or press releases from the Office of the First Lady. These forms of communication were not archived consistently until the Bush administration and including them in the analysis would make for an unrepresentative measure of Hillary Clinton's public activity. Frankly, the best data sources for assessing public activity of presidential spouses are the first lady's daily schedules, which were recently released by the Clinton Library but remain unavailable for the Bush and Obama administrations. These schedules list all events and meetings attended by the president's spouse, whether the event was open or closed to press, and even meeting participants in some cases.[2]

However, speeches listed on the White House Briefing Room web sites for each administration are useful for a different reason: they provide a great window into how the administration packages and presents the first lady's remarks to the public. They also link to full-text speech transcripts, which are stored separately from the daily schedules and are not linked in any way. An analysis of daily schedules would require the researcher to rely on the way in which the event was labeled to categorize the speech and trust the schedule's author to accurately describe it. As I discuss later in this chapter, titles of speeches can be very informative or very misleading, depending on the content of the speech. For example, a speech titled "First Lady's Remarks at a Mother's Day Reception" may contain an in-depth discussion of health care policy although the event is described in a different manner. It would indeed be rare for a first lady speech title to read "First Lady's Remarks on Healthcare Reform at a Mother's Day Reception" even though this would be a much more accurate label in many cases. As I also discuss in greater detail later, the palpably low number of remarks delivered by Hillary Clinton may also reflect the public relations concerns of Clinton communications strategists. Just as staff responsible for the content of White House Briefing Room web sites were mindful of the titles they attached to first lady speeches, they may also have restricted the total number of speeches that appeared on the White House web site during the Clinton administration. Because this book is chiefly concerned with the role of presidential spouses in White House communications strategy, these intricacies are exceedingly interesting.

Three primary theories are proposed and tested in this book.

1. *First, public appearances of the president's spouse are strategic efforts to advance the administration's agenda.* Even when the appearances are not overtly related to policy or the president's popularity, they are intended to influence the public's opinion of the president and presidential policy items. In other words, what seems apolitical has political ends. While it is feasible that public activity of the first lady is determined both by administrative demands and individual-specific factors, I maintain that it is highly unlikely that first ladies act independently in the public arena. Presidential spouses have become fixtures of the 24-hour news cycle, and they are the functional equivalents of government officers and employees, a role formally recognized by congress when it established the Office of the First Lady by statute to include a full-time staff funded by the public.

2. *Second, public appearances serve several key purposes.* These include fulfilling ceremonial duties traditionally ascribed to the East Wing, such as hosting state dinners and Christmas at the White House, garnering public support for the president's domestic and foreign policy agenda, garnering public support for the president on the campaign trail, and relaying the president's message to women and families.

3. *Finally, I theorize that for presidential spouses, going public is an effective strategy for improving public opinion of the president and his policy agenda.* According to the gender literature discussed earlier, for example, the first lady may have more credibility on certain issues than the president, including education and health care. It is also possible that certain groups such as young people, women, or mothers may find her more convincing than the president on these issues.

The next section of this chapter details the theoretical and empirical motivations for each of these expectations. In Chapters 4 and 5, the methods used to test the first two hypotheses and the results of these tests are discussed, and in Chapter 6, the methods used to test the third hypothesis and the results of these tests are discussed.

Preliminary Support for the Strategic Communications Theory

Policy Speeches Are Decreasing, Political Speeches Are Increasing

After content analyzing the data set of speeches made by Hillary Clinton, Laura Bush, and Michelle Obama from 1993 through 2014, it is clear that public appearances of presidential spouses have changed substantially over the last three administrations, which may suggest that communications strategy involving the first lady shifted. The first noticeable change, besides the fact that the number of speeches increased across and within administrations, is that the topics, audiences, and types of speeches changed. Designing a typology of speeches was the first phase of my analysis. Five major types of speeches were identified in my investigation: *Ceremonial* speeches, *Policy* speeches, *Women and Family* speeches, *Pet Project* speeches, and *Campaign* speeches. Spouses seem to go public for three strategic reasons: to appeal to women and families, to garner support for the president's agenda through campaign or policy speeches, and to garner support for pet projects that often frame the president's agenda. The phrase "going public" was coined by Samuel Kernell who argues that presidents have increasingly made direct appeals to voters in order to persuade congress to pass a legislation of what the president wants and to improve presidential approval in general.[3] Like presidents, first ladies appear to go public in an effort to mobilize support for a particular policy agenda and their appearances are highly organized and often targeted at a specific group or constituency.

The types of speeches presidential spouses make can be identified as follows. Ceremonial speeches include remarks delivered at annual White House events, such as the White House Easter Egg Roll, or Christmas at the White House, as well as award ceremony and dedication speeches. Ceremonial speeches also include remarks that pertain to traditional duties of first ladies. For example, it has become customary for the first lady to visit each cabinet department at the beginning of each presidential term. What distinguishes ceremonial speeches from other types of speeches is the conventional or classic nature of the venue. In other words, there is nothing about the event that is specific to that particular spouse's interests or initiatives, or to the administration's agenda. The most common types of ceremonial remarks are made at award ceremonies, dedications (e.g., groundbreakings and naming ceremonies of naval ships or fleets, for example), state dinners or official White House events, trips overseas (remarks are usually made with the equivalent of the first spouse in the host country), and high school and college commencements. Ceremonial events are largely generalizable across first ladies. Groundbreakings and award ceremonies tied to one of the first lady's signature initiatives were coded as pet project speeches.

Pet project speeches are among the easiest to identify. Each first lady has had between two and four principal causes, which presidential scholars often call pet projects.[4] For example, Hillary Clinton's pet projects included health care reform, foster care, and child abuse legislation. Laura Bush's pet projects included literacy, elementary education, and Afghan women's rights. Michelle Obama's pet projects include military families and childhood obesity, and in 2014 and 2015, she launched domestic and global education initiatives, Reach Higher and Let Girls Learn. Over time, pet project initiatives have become more formal, highly organized efforts and thus easier to identify through content analysis. In the Clinton and Bush administrations, pet project initiatives encapsulated broad themes and were not staffed in a way that distinguished one project from another. However, the Office of the First Lady under Michelle Obama assigns specific personnel to Let's Move! and Joining Forces, and each of her initiatives is a professionally branded and marketed campaign. Each White House web site in the last three administrations has featured a page of the first lady's initiatives, supplying specific criteria with which to determine whether an appearance should be coded a pet project.[5]

Speeches pertaining to women and family include remarks delivered to parental, youth, or women's organizations that fall outside the umbrella of the first lady's pet project causes. Examples may include Michelle Obama's speech at a women's health care center about breast cancer prevention, or one about the importance of mentoring at a local elementary school. Similar to ceremonial speeches, all first ladies are expected to make women and family speeches. What ties them together is the first lady's unparalleled ability to reach out and relate to women and mothers on particular issues. At times it becomes difficult to separate ceremonial remarks made at women's organizations or award ceremonies from remarks categorized as women and family. Again, titles are very helpful here. If a spouse delivered remarks titled "Remarks at an Award Ceremony for Women Leaders," this would be coded a ceremonial speech. Alternatively, if a spouse gives a speech titled "First Lady Speaks to Moms about Education," this would be coded a women and family speech.

Policy appearances are explicit remarks given to boost the president's agenda or a specific administration policy. Like pet project speeches, policy speeches were coded according to lists provided on the White House web sites of the president's signed legislation.[6] In order for remarks to be coded a policy speech, a particular policy, let us say No Child Left Behind or the Affordable Care Act must have been named at some point during the speech or specific elements of the legislation must have been discussed. The title of the speech must have also included the name of a presidential agenda item or policy. This rule is especially important during the Clinton administration, because one of Hillary Clinton's primary pet projects was health care reform and she retained a formal role as the chair of the president's task force that helped shape the Clinton health care over-haul. For this reason, speeches that specifically mentioned the Health Security Act of 1993 or detailed its objectives and content were coded policy speeches rather than pet project speeches. The difference between a speech coded as a policy speech and a politicized pet project speech is discussed further in the next section of this chapter.

Finally, campaign speeches, while also intended to amass support for the president's agenda, follow a particular format and are usually deliv-ered in swing states. During midterm elections, first ladies are often sent to a competitive district to speak on behalf of the president's party for congressional and gubernatorial candidates. Titles of campaign speeches will almost always contain the word "campaign," just as policy speeches will almost certainly have the policy's name in the title of the speech.

It should be noted that the five speech "types" identified in this research are not entirely novel. Presidential scholars have made fairly comprehen-sive lists of the various roles and responsibilities of first ladies that the typology of speeches discussed here closely mirrors. Watson provides a useful summary of the typologies of various authors in the second ver-sion of *The Presidents' Wives*.[7] I should again clarify that in the process of placing speeches into categories, I largely take the White House's word regarding the type of speech being made. This is to say that as a general rule, if the White House web site titled a speech "Campaign Remarks," it was also coded a campaign speech in my analysis; if a speech was titled "Mrs. Obama's Remarks at a Lets Move! Event," that speech was coded a pet project speech; and if a speech was titled "Mrs. Clinton's Remarks on Health Insurance Reform," it was most often considered a policy speech. However, speech *type* and speech *topic* are decidedly different variables. What is more original is the second phase of coding, in which I determined whether a speech was politicized. Unlike the process of assigning speeches to one of five types, which heavily factored speech title into categorization, coding for politicization accounts for the possibility that the first ladies do not discuss what the White House purports they discuss in these speeches. In other words, the possibility exists that even remarks not overtly geared toward the administration's policy agenda are actually intended to garner public support for the administration and its policy positions.

Figures 3.1, 3.2, and 3.3 summarize the percentage of speeches in each administration that were categorized as ceremonial, policy, women and family, and pet project, as well as the percentage of speeches within each of these categories that mentioned a particular presidential policy item. The first major finding to note is that ceremonial speeches and policy

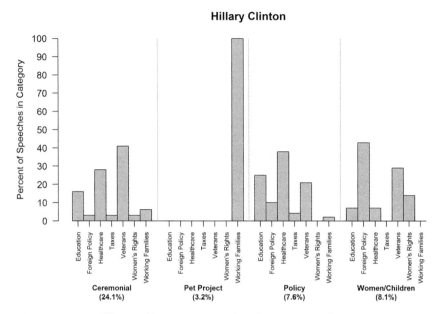

Figure 3.1   Hillary Clinton's Speeches by Type and Topic

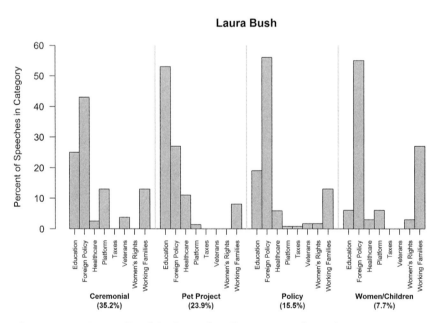

Figure 3.2   Laura Bush's Speeches by Type and Topic

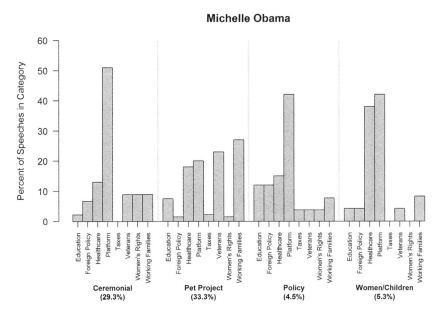

Figure 3.3   Michelle Obama's Speeches by Type and Topic

speeches have decreased dramatically over time, while the percentage of speeches dedicated to pet projects and campaigning has conspicuously increased across the administrations. Speeches dedicated to women and family have decreased. While more than half of the speeches given by Hillary Clinton from 1993 to 2000 were ceremonial speeches and almost 20 percent of speeches were policy speeches, only 35 percent of speeches given by Laura Bush and 29 percent of speeches given by Michelle Obama fall into the ceremonial category. Laura Bush gave a surprising number of policy speeches (about 16 percent of her total speeches were geared toward policy), although fewer than Hillary Clinton. But the share of policy speeches dropped severely in the Obama administration. Less than 5 percent of Michelle Obama's speeches were explicitly about policy. Pet project speeches and campaign speeches account for the biggest surge overall; while less than 1 percent of the speeches made by Hillary Clinton were delivered on the campaign trail, 18 percent of Laura Bush's speeches were campaign speeches, and almost 30 percent of Michelle Obama's speeches were campaign speeches. The low number of campaign speeches during Hillary Clinton's tenure should be considered a very conservative figure. It is well known that Hillary Clinton was active on the campaign trail in 1996; the speech she delivered at the Democratic National Convention (DNC) in Chicago was merely the third time in U.S. history that an incumbent first lady gave a convention speech (Eleanor Roosevelt was the first in 1940, followed by Pat Nixon in 1972). Elizabeth Dole's 1996 speech also marked the first year nonincumbent spouses began to give convention speeches. Although it is unclear why the White House archived and published some of Hillary Clinton's campaign speeches and not others, it is fair to say that this number is probably an incomplete picture of her *public* campaign appearances. Campaign appearances are often *private* events, such as fundraisers or small gatherings with interest groups and donors, but these are not included in the data. What is more central to the exercise of illustrating how public speeches of first ladies have changed in number and in nature over time is the fact that even if we removed campaign remarks from the tabulations in Table 3.1, we would see the same increase in number of speeches across the Clinton, Bush, and Obama administrations. Bluntly put, the absence of campaign remarks in the Hillary Clinton data is not the reason why Laura Bush appeared to give more speeches than Hillary Clinton. Finally, 24 percent of Laura Bush's speeches and 30 percent of Michelle Obama's speeches were attributed to their pet project initiatives.

The second major finding to highlight from the content analysis is that speech types historically considered to be unrelated to presidential policy have actually become more politicized over time. Although we observe a drop in policy speeches overall after the Clinton administration, the number of ceremonial, women and family, and pet project speeches given by Laura Bush and Michelle Obama that contain policy cues or discussion of policy increased substantially. In fact, only 43 percent of the speeches made by Hillary Clinton were politically charged according to my framework, compared to 57 percent of all speeches made by Laura Bush and 65 percent of all speeches made by Michelle Obama that contained discussions of policy. These statistics are disruptive to the established body of political science literature that labels Hillary Clinton an activist first lady and Laura Bush a traditional first lady. If we take a look at these numbers annually (Figure 3.4), a clearer narrative emerges. In 1993, 1994, and even 1995, the majority of speeches made by Hillary Clinton were politically charged policy speeches. In each year after 1996, however, most of her speeches contained no overt reference to policy at all.

This within-administration shift in volume of policy speeches tracks closely with another in the topics of Hillary Clinton's policy speeches. In the first two years of the administration, nearly all of the politically charged speeches Hillary Clinton delivered pertained to health care reform. After 1994, most of Hillary Clinton's speeches that mentioned policy either belonged to the women and family or pet project category, and the most frequent policy mentions were about women's rights and human rights abroad, as well as social programs aimed at helping children and families. From her speeches alone, it could be suggested that Mrs. Clinton retained her interest in health care, but discussed it in terms of women's health and families, for example, throwing her support behind the Newborns' and Mothers' Health Protection Act of 1996 and the Women's Health and Cancer Rights Act of 1998. Most of her policy mentions after 1994 related to the Adoption and Safe Families Act of 1997 and the Foster Care Independence Act of 1999, two issues that tracked seamlessly with the first lady's pet projects.

These patterns buttress what some scholars have labeled a failed communications strategy in the Clinton administration: placing the first lady at the forefront of the health insurance reform effort. Matthew Corrigan, for example, attempted to measure the impact of Hillary Clinton's 1993 and 1994 campaigns for health care reform on public attitudes toward the bill through opinion surveys.[8] While he finds a negligible effect (due in no small part to the inherent difficulty of tracing a shift in mass attitudes to a single speech or appearance through the analysis of observational data), he offers several reasons why the administration's efforts were unsuccessful. Corrigan claims that media coverage and public evaluations of Mrs. Clinton were positive when she testified in front of congress emphasizing her role as "a mother, wife, sister, daughter, woman" and declined sharply when she adopted a negative tone and attacked the health insurance industry. The administration may have noticed this downturn in favorability; in the spring of 1994, Mrs. Clinton changed the audience of her health care speeches to university students and small town hall meetings with women and health care providers. But these efforts may have been made too late, as the Health Security Act was already in serious trouble in congress by June, and was declared dead in August.

Corrigan concludes that the president's spouse can be a tremendous asset in courting and persuading supporters of the president, but should not engage in attacking his opponents. He also suggests that the public may have found the first lady's involvement in drafting health care legislation more acceptable if the President and Mrs. Clinton made more joint appearances when speaking about health care reform. This is an interesting suggestion, and actually, there is some evidence that the first lady made more of an effort to appear alongside the president when speaking explicitly about policy. In 1999 alone, 15 percent of the first lady's appearances were about policy remarks made at joint appearances with the president, and a growing number of policy speeches in both the Bush and Obama administrations were made at events at which the president also made remarks. This style of tandem policy speeches has actually become very common in the Obama administration, and about a third of Michelle Obama's overt remarks about health care reform were made at town-hall style events with President Obama. Finally, Corrigan suggests that Hillary Clinton's campaign for health care reform was not nearly robust enough, that she gave too few speeches on the topic overall, and, more specifically, that she spent too much time in Washington, precluding her from engaging friendly audiences in a nationwide campaign.

Just as we can see evidence of a possible shift in White House communications strategy involving the first lady from 1994 to the end of the Clinton administration, we can see evidence of a change between administrations. It is possible that the Bush and Obama administrations learned from mistakes made in the Clinton administration and adopted new strategies to mobilize the first lady. The most obvious way in which this appears to have occurred is through politicized pet project speeches, particularly in the Bush administration. Although it is possible that the apparent link between Laura Bush's pet projects and the administration's policy agenda was one of happenstance, the sheer volume of speeches Laura Bush made to audiences of women and families about human rights in the Middle East and the importance of a military presence there and the frequency with which she discussed standards-based education reform in the context of her literacy initiatives and book festivals are difficult to overlook. More than 50 percent of speeches made to women and families and 30 percent of her pet project speeches about Afghan women contained discussion of the War on Terror and about 49 percent of her pet project speeches on literacy and early childhood development mentioned No Child Left Behind. Although slightly more opaque, a similar connection can be deciphered between Michelle Obama's Lets Move! initiative and the Affordable Care Act, as well as her veterans' initiative and the president's removal of troops from Iraq and Afghanistan. Figure 3.4 summarizes the point that although the frequency with which presidential spouses make policy speeches has decreased over time—perhaps a reaction to the unsuccessful attempts of the Clinton administration to place the first lady at the center of the public policy-making process—the number of speeches that have been politicized through covert rather than overt mentions of policy has greatly increased. The White House communications operation may have discovered a new way to exercise the public appeal of presidential spouses: political advocacy in an apolitical context.

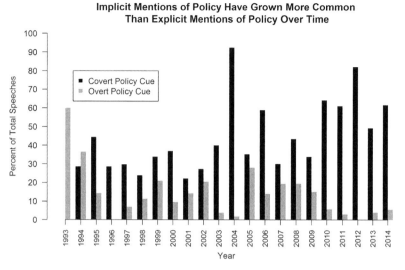

Figure 3.4   Implicit vs. Explicit Mentions of Policy over Time

Presidential Spouses Are Unmatched Surrogates

Popular and Recognizable

Now that I have established some of the ways in which public appearances of presidential spouses have changed over the last three administrations, suggesting, first, that first ladies promote the president's policy agenda in their speeches more often than not and, second, that a shift in strategy may have occurred between the Clinton and Bush administrations concerning the first lady as a communications asset, it is important to outline some of the motivations that may underlay the White House's efforts to mobilize the first lady in addition to, or even in place of, other presidential surrogates. The first reason is the popularity of the president's spouse and her high visibility. Figure 3.5 demonstrates that in most years of the last three presidential administrations, presidential spouses have enjoyed higher favorability ratings than the president and the vice president, with the exception of the public opinion backlash Hillary Clinton suffered at the beginning of the Clinton administration surrounding her prominent roles in the health care policy overhaul, Whitewater, and Travelgate.[9] These numbers are largely derived from feeling thermometers indicating favorability toward the first lady, president, and vice president in the American National Election Studies (ANES). Survey respondents were asked to rate a political figure on a scale of 0–100,

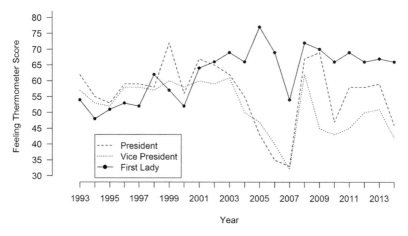

First Ladies Tend to Be More Favorable Than Presidents and Vice Presidents

Figure 3.5   Favorability

where ratings from 51 to 100 degrees mean they feel warm or favorable toward the person, ratings between 0 and 49 degrees mean they do not feel favorable toward the person and do not care very much for them, and a rating of 50 degrees indicates they do not feel particularly warm or cold toward the person. I focus on feeling thermometers instead of job approval mainly because job approval ratings for the first lady have not been measured in many years of the ANES and other major public opinion polls.[10]

We can also see from Figure 3.5 that the first lady's favorability tracks less closely with the president's favorability than the vice president's favorability. In other words, the president's spouse appears to be somewhat invulnerable to swings in presidential popularity compared to her vice presidential counterpart. This difference almost implies that Americans evaluate the president's spouse according to different criteria than they use to evaluate the president and the vice president. For example, the president's spouse may not be strongly associated with political scandal or legislative successes and failures. That sort of imperviousness may make public opinion of the first lady more difficult for the White House to control, but it may also prove a valuable tool on the campaign trail and when approval ratings of the president and his administration are low. Figure 3.5 shows us that it is even possible for the first lady's favorability to rise in years in which presidential and vice presidential favorability is sinking. Remarkably, Laura Bush's favorability increased from 2004 to 2006 at the

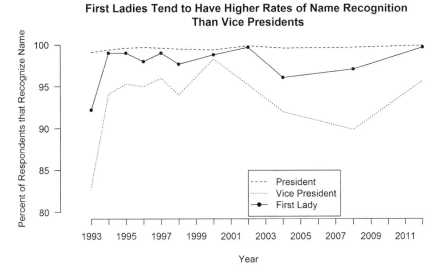

Figure 3.6   Name Recognition

height of controversy surrounding the Iraq War and Hurricane Katrina, and remained more than 10 points higher than that of President Bush and Vice President Cheney in 2007.

One might propose that we see these outstanding differences in popularity patterns because the first lady is a peripheral figure in the administration, compared to presidents and vice presidents. Perhaps most Americans do not know or care enough about the first lady to have a negative opinion of her. Figure 3.6 demonstrates that this explanation is wrong. Not only does the U.S. public feel warmly toward the president's spouse in most of the years they are asked but they also recognize her name at much higher rates than they recognize the vice president's name. Not surprisingly, the president's name is the most recognizable of the three names. Figure 3.6 depicts percentages of ANES respondents who recognize the first lady's name compared to the percentage of ANES respondents who recognize the president's and vice president's name. This measure is constructed from the same ANES feeling thermometer variable exploited in Figure 3.5. In other words, when respondents were asked how they feel toward the president, first lady, and vice president, a small percentage in each case would respond that they did not recognize the name of the person in the question. While a better measure of recognizability may have been responses to a name recollection question, in which survey participants are simply asked to name the president, first lady, and vice president, like approval, the first lady question is not consistently asked across all ANES years and would provide a limited picture of recognition at best. In conjunction, Figures 3.5 and 3.6 validate the president's spouse as both a highly likable and visible public figure—often outrunning the president's official running mate—who has the potential to be a valuable part of White House communications strategy.

Less Susceptible to Partisan Evaluations

In her 2007 study "Affective Evaluations of First Ladies," Valerie Sulfaro hypothesizes that first ladies, rather than remaining above or immune to partisan politics, are actually evaluated according to the same partisan and ideological criteria used to evaluate political candidates.[11] She finds that indeed, more than religious values or other demographic variables typically associated with political attitudes, partisanship and ideology are the strongest predictors of evaluations of Laura Bush and Hillary Clinton. Sulfaro's treatment of the president's spouse as a serious political player about whom the mass public has strong opinions (instead of the president's private confidante) and her application of quantitative methods to the study of presidential spouses are an admirable departure from political science literature that still seeks to understand first ladies through historical anecdotes, secondary opinion data, and media coverage. The study of presidential spouses would do well to evolve in the direction of Sulfaro's work.

The analysis of speeches conducted in the first part of this chapter avers Sulfaro's placement of Laura Bush in the "controversial policy, supportive of husband's agenda category," rather than the "nonpolicy oriented, nonindependent agenda category"; however, Sulfaro still robs Laura Bush of some credit she is due by labeling her White House activities traditional and implying that Hillary Clinton held a graduate degree, whereas Laura Bush did not. Laura Bush does in fact have a Master's degree in Library Science from the University of Texas at Austin.[12] My speech analysis again showed that traditional, ceremonial speeches accounted for a much larger percentage of Hillary Clinton's total remarks than those of Laura Bush, and that after 1994, the topics of Mrs. Clinton's speeches became much less controversial and much more loosely linked with policy. Finally, Sulfaro's assertion that Hillary Clinton pursued a policy agenda independently of her husband has little support among experts on the Clinton administration, who instead claim that Hillary Clinton's involvement in health care reform was a central part of the administration's communications strategy on that issue and that the president appointed his wife to head the task force on health care reform to signal his legislative priorities and commitment to making the changes he campaigned on in 1992.

I replicated and expanded Sulfaro's 2007 study of the impact of partisanship on public opinion of Hillary Clinton and Laura Bush to include more years of the ANES as well as evaluations of Michelle Obama. The original research design uses data from the National Election Studies in years 1996, 1998, 2000, 2002, and 2004 and Sulfaro regresses a variety of independent variables, including the key explanatory variable, partisanship, on the dependent variable, what she calls "affect," measured using the same ANES feeling thermometers discussed before in my comparison of presidential, first lady, and vice presidential favorability. When we speak of regression analysis in political science, we are referring to statistical tools used to describe the relationship between an independent variable, like a person's partisanship, and a dependent variable, such as how a person feels about the president or the first lady. Bivariate regression is not all that different from a correlation between two variables, but multivariate regression, of the kind Sulfaro uses, allows us to understand how the dependent variable of interest changes in relation to an independent variable of interest, while the other independent variables we believe that are relevant to our understanding of the dependent variable are held constant. The independent variables in Sulfaro's study include partisanship, ideology, women's place, gender, religiosity, marital status, age, ethnicity, and education. I followed Sulfaro's coding scheme as precisely as possible and realized similar results for Laura Bush and Hillary Clinton. The results for Michelle Obama in 2012 follow a similar trajectory, where partisanship and ideology are strong and significant predictors of affect toward the first lady. Statistical significance, as it appears in this book, refers to the probability that a result was not reached by chance alone (i.e., sampling error). I have several concerns with the coding scheme and variables included in Sulfaro's study, mostly those that affect toward Hillary Clinton should not have been measured in 2000 or afterward, when Clinton's campaign for U.S. Senate was already underway and strong partisan evaluations of her were undoubtedly influenced by the fact that she was a widely known political candidate herself at the time the ANES were conducted.

However, improvement upon these details was not the chief motivation for my replication of this study. Sulfaro may be missing the big theoretical picture when it comes to public opinion of first ladies. Of course, her discovery that partisan identification plays a major role in the way we think about the president's spouse is a useful one, but the president's spouse, like any other political actor, does not exist in a vacuum. She is an integral part of a White House machine that functions to advance the interests of one principal, the president of the United States. The first lady's reign over the East Wing and all of its capabilities is a consequence of her relationship with the president of the United States. For this reason, public opinion of the first lady, just like her communications role, should be examined in relation to the president and other members of the administration, not as an independent statistic. A more appropriate question becomes, then, how powerful is partisanship as a predictor of public favorability toward the first lady, *compared* to the power of partisanship in predictions of attitudes toward the president? Even if the first lady is evaluated according to partisan criteria, if these criteria play a less outstanding role in evaluations of spouses compared to evaluations of the president or other surrogates, interesting implications for the first lady as a communications asset abound alongside her favorability and recognizability.

A first stab at this question taken through the examination of correlation and bivariate regression coefficients would lead us to believe that the relationship between partisanship and favorability toward the first lady is not as strong as the relationship between partisanship and favorability toward the president or vice president. This is the case in every year that these variables were measured in the ANES.[13] For example, even in 1994 when Hillary Clinton's favorability was very low, only 21 percent of the variation in feeling toward Hillary Clinton could be explained by respondent's partisanship alone, compared to 27 percent of the variation in feelings toward Bill Clinton. However, these results may change once we control for other important covariates. Replicate estimations of first lady affect conducted by Sulfaro for the same years of the ANES (and additional years) are presented beside estimations of presidential affect in the Appendix. As a reminder, the coefficients in the first row of Tables A.1 through A.3 in the Appendix, estimated using ordinary least squares, should be interpreted as the increase or decrease in feeling toward the president or first lady on a scale ranging from 0 to 100 associated with a one-unit increase in partisanship. Partisanship is coded on a seven-point scale where higher values indicate Republican preferences and lower values indicate Democratic preferences, so for example, as respondent partisanship increases by one point, favorability of Hillary and Bill Clinton decreases by the number shown. This makes sense because Republicans typically evaluate Democratic politicians more negatively and Democrats usually evaluate Republican politicians more negatively.

Again, at first glance, in Figure 3.7 as well as Tables A.1 through A.3 in the Appendix, we can see that the magnitude of the effects of partisanship and ideology is almost always smaller for first ladies than they are for presidents, even in the case of Hillary Clinton. Party identification seems to play a much larger role in the way ANES respondents feel about the president than it does in the way respondents feel toward the first lady. Another way to say this is that Democrats did not evaluate Laura Bush as negatively as they evaluated George W. Bush, and Republicans did not evaluate Hillary Clinton and Michelle Obama as negatively as they evaluated Bill Clinton and Barack Obama, holding critical factors like views about women's rights, religion, and educational attainment constant. A prudent question for many researchers and savvy readers will inevitably be exactly *how different* are these differences? Figure 3.7 helps illustrate the answer to this question while also allowing us to discern effect sizes. In some years, the difference in the relationship between partisan identification and feeling thermometer ratings for the president and first lady appears to be very small. We can see that in these cases the 95 percent confidence intervals on the estimates actually overlap. However, in other cases (1992, 2002, 2004, and 2012), the difference in size of the estimates appears to be sufficiently large to draw our attention to a discrepancy in the way the partisan affiliation of respondents shapes attitudes of presidents

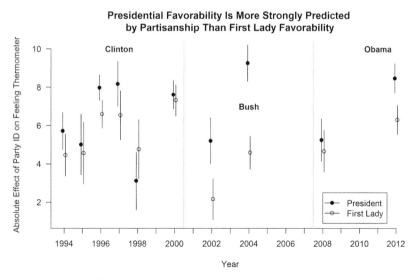

Figure 3.7   Effect of Partisanship on Favorability Toward President and First Lady

and their spouses. This discrepancy is particularly impressive in presidential election years when partisan attitudes are so salient.[14]

Taken as a whole, these estimates stress that there are substantial differences in the ways Americans evaluate first ladies and presidents, even if partisanship has a robust effect on both sets of evaluations. The first lady is still a unique player in the public eye and may have more potential than the president and other surrogates to transcend partisan politics and party identification. The first lady's apparent disconnection from strong partisan evaluations, combined with her high favorability ratings and widespread name recognition, solidifies her potential to be a tremendous communications asset on the campaign trail and in the White House. The first lady may be able to connect with and extract support from groups the president and other proxies cannot.

Different Expectations (Press and Public)

The president's spouse is one-of-a-kind because she is not an elected or appointed official and does not share the formal responsibilities ascribed to other members of the administration, yet she is undoubtedly the closest person to the president. Of course, U.S. presidential spouses have also been women thus far, which makes them unique players in the predominately male world of the executive branch. In many of my interviews with former White House staff, the president's spouse is described as a "sovereign," the closest thing the United States has to royalty. For this reason, many experts have claimed, the public and the press have different rules of engagement concerning the first lady. In other words, the media does not interact with spouses the same way it interacts with White House staff, campaign operatives, or politicians. Television and print journalists often refrain from asking first ladies tough policy questions, instead sticking with lukewarm inquiries related to the president's personal attributes or the first lady's pet project interests. A conservative talk show host I interviewed with ties to the Nixon and Reagan administrations underlined this point. He told me: "You don't attack the sovereign. Those people [who criticize the first lady] are fringe. They're crazy." Put differently, the president's spouse commands a certain amount of respect and a gentle touch, a sort of treatment rarely granted to other members of the president's administration. A communications staffer for George W. Bush made a similar claim:

> The way I think of it . . . I almost liken it to the separation of State and Government. The first lady represents that State portion and the

president represents Government. So it makes sense that the press doesn't ask the State representative complicated questions about government and they don't ask the head of government questions about state affairs. You wouldn't ask the British Prime Minister about china for a state dinner and you wouldn't ask the Queen of England about a piece of legislation. So we don't.

Mostly all of these comments were supplemented with the point that our modern first ladies have been so highly educated, talented at public speaking, and qualified to govern in their own right that they would likely have no trouble answering a tough question from a journalist about policy. But journalists seem to perpetuate the status quo in interviews of first ladies nonetheless. This sort of special treatment, whether warranted or not, presents a huge opportunity for political strategists to capitalize on guaranteed media coverage of the first lady without risking the negative press attention that often results from a clumsily answered question. What strategists have in a spouse is essentially a surrogate who is more popular, more well known, and less polarizing than others such as the vice president, yet does not share the same obligations of politicians to the press and the U.S. public. Why *not* mobilize that kind of person on behalf of the administration?

In a pretesting phase for several randomized survey experiments I completed as part of my research (detailed in Chapter 6), I sought to assess whether the public has different expectations of the first lady and the president when it comes to public speeches. I found strong evidence that Americans do in fact have very different conceptions of the topics first ladies discuss in public and the topics presidents discuss in public, although these conceptions are often inaccurate. As we saw from the speech analysis earlier in this chapter, first ladies make speeches on a variety of subjects, including those on which the literature on gender and politics tells us that women are perceived to be less credible, such as the economy and foreign policy. Laura Bush, for example, actually made a sizable amount of speeches about the War on Terror and the importance of maintaining a military presence in Iraq and Afghanistan, accounting for most of her policy speeches. She also made several speeches on Burma toward the end of her husband's administration. Mrs. Bush participated in a United Nations policy roundtable on Burma in 2006 and numerous press conferences on the topic, even addressing members of congress on the formation of the Senate Women's Caucus on Burma in 2007. Mrs. Clinton was no stranger to making speeches on the economy, federal budget, or foreign affairs, although it may surprise some that Michelle Obama has delivered remarks on foreign policy. For example, in 2011, she made a speech alongside the president on the administration's strategy for removing troops from Iraq. Although the majority of campaign speeches made by presidential spouses are all-purpose remarks that recount the president's record over a number of issue areas, Mrs. Bush's and Mrs. Obama's campaign speeches were sometimes focused on only one topic, such as health care or the economy. A small percentage of Laura Bush's campaign remarks were exclusively focused on taxes, small business, and the economy—a repudiation of political science and gender literature that claims female politicians and presidential spouses most often undertake valence issues such as educating children and improving women's health when making public appearances—policy areas in which they are often perceived to be the most qualified communicators.

To probe for these public perceptions, I designed a survey that showed a group of 628 Americans excerpts from real speeches made by the president and the first lady in each of the last three administrations on the economy, foreign affairs, health care, and education, and asked survey respondents to guess whether the speech was made by the president or the first lady.[15] The speech category with the strongest gender-based expectations appears to be the economy. On average, 58 percent of survey respondents thought that economic speeches made during the Clinton administration were attributed to Bill Clinton, 64 percent thought that economic speeches were attributed to George W. Bush, and 64 percent thought that economic speeches were attributed to Barack Obama. The results were similarly strong for foreign affairs in the Bush and Obama administrations, with 56 percent and 58 percent of respondents, respectively, answering that foreign affairs speeches were made by the president, although interestingly, the majority of respondents thought Hillary Clinton (53 percent vs. 47 percent) made the foreign affairs speeches. This divergence can reasonably be attributed to the fact that Mrs. Clinton was secretary of state when the survey was launched and respondents probably had trouble separating her from this role. The results on health care and education were more varied, and overall, respondents seemed to expect that education and health care speeches were made by Laura Bush and that Barack Obama made most of the education and health care speeches. Respondents only attributed one category of speeches most often to Michelle Obama: fair pay for women. A table summarizing all of these results can be found in the Appendix (Table A.4) and the survey methods are considered in more detail in Chapter 6.

It is important to remember that these survey results are descriptive in nature and the survey design contained no experimental manipulation.

It is highly possible that some other variable, rather than speech topic alone, caused respondents to believe that the first lady or president made a speech. However, this survey still lends meaningful support to the idea that Americans hold presidents and first ladies to different standards and have strong preconceived notions of their public activities, furthering my argument that first ladies are special surrogates. If Americans already expect first ladies to go public on certain issues such as health care, education, and women's rights, perhaps first ladies can more effectively garner support for the president in those policy areas.

Proximity to the President

Finally and briefly, we cannot forget that the first lady is special because of her personal relationship with the president of the United States. Because this book is concerned with the public role of spouses as vehicles through which the White House can effectively promote the president's agenda, I have largely avoided the first lady's marriage in contemplations of her influence. First ladies are media superstars whose activities are most appropriately analyzed through the lens of White House communications strategy. Yet, the first lady's *private* relationship with the president is part of what may make her an effective *public* messenger. Americans view the first lady as the closest person to the president, and when she speaks on his behalf, we are inclined to believe what she says. When she says something is important to the president, something angers the president, or something saddens the president, our instinct is to trust her. And since she is not directly driven by the professional concerns of elected officials, we are largely convinced that her interpretation is a genuine one. If White House strategists are at all aware of positive public perceptions of the first lady, it seems almost implausible that they would refrain from mobilizing her with the administration's interests in mind.

The first lady's unmatched access to the president is another reason we should view her public appearances as strategic, political activities. An interview participant who worked in the Reagan East Wing helped me understand this point. "The first lady has the ear of the President of the United States," she said. "If she wanted to influence policy, she is in the best possible position to do that, behind the scenes, away from the cameras, in private. So that should tell you that the bus tours, the speeches, the photo opportunities—those are not for her. They are hard work and they're not always fun. Those are for the administration. They're to help the president." Indeed it is imaginable, especially after the repercussions suffered by Hillary Clinton in the early years of her husband's administration surrounding her involvement in health care reform, that influencing policy behind the scenes is a much safer road for spouses to travel if they are in fact interested in a particular issue or cause. Would White House staff likely place the president's spouse in the public spotlight and expend the federal resources required to do so if they did not think these actions would help advance the administration's goals? In Chapters 4 and 5, I discuss the elite interviews conducted as part of my research and the information gleaned from them about spouses and their communications roles.

CHAPTER 4

First, Do No Harm:
Next, Do What Comes Natural

It is a cornerstone of good scholarship to consider potential weaknesses of the theories that underpin our hypotheses and the foreseen challenges associated with the methods used to test them. The first possible weakness of the proposed strategic communications theory pertains to direction. I hypothesize that the administration's needs and goals are driving public activity of spouses, although as I noted in Chapter 2, some scholars have suggested that the first lady uses the White House platform to further her own agenda. Another possible weakness of the notion of strategic appearances is that public activity of the first lady varies substantially within and across presidencies. Many factors specific to each first lady besides the administration's decision to mobilize her determine what appearances she will make, including her personality, career experience, and the demands of parenting, if applicable. This variation limits the extent to which a theory of presidential spouses as instruments of the White House communications operation can be generalized.

For example, one possible explanation for the low number of first lady speeches in the Clinton administration is that Hillary Clinton was simply more active behind the scenes in the policy-making process than Laura Bush and Michelle Obama, and thus made fewer public appearances. This assertion complements scholarship that claims that the public involvement of first ladies is determined by individual factors such as education and interest in politics. In other words, some first ladies choose to occupy the public spotlight, and some do not. This perspective yields descriptive categories of first ladies such as "public," "private," "active," and "traditional" that have little or no basis in empirical evidence. The fact that Laura Bush (deemed a "traditional" first lady in the literature) gave more than twice the number of speeches Hillary Clinton (the archetypal "activist" in the literature) did in each year of each administration, and that many of these were policy speeches, contradicts these theories. By focusing on personal attributes, theories centered on "types" of spouses also completely exclude the president from assessments of first lady activity.[1]

Fortunately, elite interviews with former White House staff, communications consultants, and public relations professionals who have worked on presidential campaigns provide an ideal avenue to assess my expectation that White House communications specialists mobilize the first lady strategically. By asking seasoned communications staff why the first lady appears in public so often, I was able to paint a more complete picture of the first lady's role in White House communications strategy than that achieved from speech analysis alone. Many of my interview participants were the architects of these appearances.

I conducted formal and informal interviews with experts on White House and campaign communications strategy and/or presidential spouses as part of my research for this book. Of the interviews, eight were White house staff during the Clinton administration, three of whom had the title of Special Assistant to the President or higher, nine were White House staff during the George W. Bush administration, four of whom held the same title or higher, and five were White House staff during the Obama administration, one of whom held the title of Special Assistant to the President or higher. Interviews were conducted with presidential staff from earlier administrations: Nixon, Ford, Carter, Reagan, and H.W. Bush. In all, 20 interviews were conducted with Republican presidential staff and/ or elected officials and 14 interviews were conducted with Democratic presidential staff and/or elected officials. Although an even number of Republican and Democratic interviews would have been preferred, this discrepancy can be attributed to the difficulty of conducting interviews with staff to sitting presidents and presidential spouses, as well as former presidential staff still working in politics. Because many of the Clinton senior West Wing staff and Hillary Clinton's East Wing staff from 1992 to 2000 followed her to the U.S. Senate, worked with her at the State Department, and are currently wrapped up in the 2016 presidential run, getting Clinton insiders to interview proved almost as difficult as interviewing Obama staff. Seven interviews were conducted with Chiefs of Staff to either the President or First Lady, two White House Press Secretaries, and eight people who served as Press Secretary, Deputy Press Secretary,

Communications Director, or Deputy Communications Director to the First Lady. Directors of advance, policy directors, social secretaries, speech writers, and schedulers were also interviewed. Several interview participants worked for more than one presidential administration, and roughly one half of the interview participants were staff to the president's spouse. The remaining number of interviews was conducted with professors of political science, history, and communications whose areas of expertise included White House communications or the First Lady of the United States, or with journalists and political consultants who have written about or worked closely with presidential spouses. Roughly half of the interview participants were male and roughly half were female.[2]

While interviews are first and foremost an interpersonal exchange and the structure and content of each discussion are highly improvised, each interview participant was asked a minimum of three broad questions that frame the book: (1) Why have public appearances of presidential spouses increased in recent administrations? (2) What purposes do these appearances serve and/or what goals drive them? (3) Do the appearances effectively fulfill those purposes or meet those goals? Of course, I was most interested in responses to the first and second questions, because unlike the third question, they cannot be answered through any of the other research methods used in this book, such as survey experiments.

Regarding the first question, recall my hypothesis in Chapter 3 that appearances of first ladies are strategic in nature. And recall in the literature review that the increase in appearances over time can be explained by supply-side forces (changes in the technological and media environment that have created more platforms and mediums through which the president's spouse can communicate with the public) or demand-side forces (factors specific to presidential spouses, rather than the environment, that have increased public interest in the first lady and have made her a more central player in White House communications strategy). While it is likely that these explanations have worked together to create an influx in public activity of the president's spouse, the strategic appearances hypothesis coincides most closely with demand-side explanations. That is, I expected to hear in elite interviews that there is something special about presidential spouses that makes them useful surrogates, relative to others, and that the White House has tapped into this potential in recent administrations.

Regarding the second question, although the goals underlying a spouse's public appearance can be determined somewhat by reading transcripts of her public remarks and following clues provided in the title, the venue, the audience, and the content, we cannot be nearly as confident about the purpose of these speeches and appearances by analyzing them as we become by asking the producers and organizers of the appearances themselves. A variety of architects of these public appearances exist, and in fact, as the next section of this chapter reveals, many hands go into every major and minor appearance the first lady makes. And many times, as I surmised previously, the purposes and goals of an event are not what they appear to be. Finally, recall in Chapter 3 my hypothesis that the objectives for mobilizing a president's spouse included fulfilling traditional responsibilities ascribed to the East Wing such as hosting state dinners (e.g., attending events coded "ceremonial" in Chapter 3), garnering public support for the president's domestic and international policy agenda, garnering support for the president during elections, and relaying the president's message to women and families. Keep in mind that the last three objectives mentioned are strategic objectives and the first objective mentioned is not innately strategic. Ceremonial or traditional appearances serve particular purposes but these purposes are not relevant to the legislative or electoral success of a sitting president. For this reason, I expected to find a greater emphasis in interviews on the strategic mobilization of the president's spouse (i.e., demand-side mobilization) rather than non-strategic mobilization (i.e., supply-side explanations for increased mobilization, such as that the number of traditional events the first lady is expected to attend has increased).

Why Have Public Appearances of the President's Spouse Increased over Time?

In the Last Three Decades the White House Has Learned How (and How Not) to Harness Public Interest in the President's Spouse to Advance Its Agenda

Social scientists schooled in the many possible threats to the validity of their findings hesitate to make bold claims about their research results. Quantitative research methodology offers more tools to deal with these threats systematically. In statistical analysis, for example, confidence levels allow us to gauge the probability that a finding that satisfies our hypothesis may have occurred due to chance alone or if it is in fact the "real" finding. Yet neither quantitative nor qualitative researchers can ever be 100 percent certain of their findings. Researchers conducting interviews to test their hypotheses must be particularly careful that their interactions with interview participants do not affect the outcome of the study and that their interpretations of the interview data do not favor their hypotheses. They must also consider that the data collected exclude responses from participants who could not or opted not to participate in the study, and that there is a chance these responses may have been different from those the researcher had an opportunity to include. In my interviews with a variety of political professionals as well as scholars, I found results that both confirmed and weakened my initial expectations about the manner in which presidential spouses go public. However, the evidence provided by former White House staff for one of my hypotheses was overwhelming: public appearances of presidential spouses are carefully planned, highly strategic efforts to further the administration's political goals.

The first reason why public appearances of the president's spouse have surged over the last three presidential administrations is because the East Wing has mastered them. This appears to be the same reason why the content and distribution of speeches changed, as I demonstrated in Chapter 3. Policy and ceremonial speeches decreased in frequency overall and pet project speeches that indirectly endorse certain presidential policies, along with campaign and women and family speeches, increased in frequency. Over the last 30 years, the White House has sharpened and perfected its strategy for mobilizing the president's spouse strategically in order to bring attention to the president's political agenda, to control the media coverage of that agenda, and to boost public support for those policies and their authors when possible. Moreover, the overarching narrative of the East Wing from the Clinton through Obama years seems to have been a trial-and-error approach to leveraging the Office of the First Lady to its fullest potential, and there is evidence that this approach reached maturity by the end of the Bush administration. It is arguable that the Obama administration is even more sophisticated in its design of Mrs. Obama's public appearances. According to one scholar I spoke with, the potential for the first lady to become an image-shaping asset to the administration has grown in the last 30 years, in part, because the Office of the First Lady has become more professionalized and more integrated with the West Wing. He pointed to the following three pieces of evidence of integration:

> First of all, first ladies have been giving their staff more influence. And generally, the way they do that is have more of their staff hold presidential commissions or become presidential advisors. We have seen an increase in that occurrence since Watergate. It is important because it means they [East Wing staff] can attend West Wing briefings if they have the title Advisor to the President. So they are on an

even keel with a lot of advisors in the West Wing. The second important thing that has happened in the last 35–40 years is Public Law
95–750 and what that has done is basically integrated the budget of
the West Wing and East Wing.[3] So that the first lady now, when she
carries out tasks of the president's office, she is budgeted. And the
third thing that has done that [increased integration] is an important decision that happened in the Clinton administration. And that
is the *Association of American Physicians vs. Hillary Rodham Clinton*
which indicated that the first lady is a government employee when
she is performing tasks . . . when she is tasked to perform jobs by
the president.

Indeed, in each of the last three presidential administrations, the first
lady's chief of staff has participated in the president's morning briefing,
the so-called 7 AM meeting during the Bush administration, open only
to the president's senior staff. The first lady's staff typically convenes in
a daily meeting that begins an hour later. In the Clinton and Bush administrations, this practice originated in the Arkansas and Texas Governor's
office, where the first lady's chief of staff and/or communications director
was included in the governor's daily meeting. Yet unlike some scholars,
who suggested the first lady's close relationship with the president has
always created "turf wars" and tension between top-tier staff in the West
Wing and East Wing, and that the East Wing staff is discredited by the
West Wing "until they realize her [the first lady's] approval ratings are
higher," the senior East Wing and West Wing staff I interviewed told me
the purpose of involving the first lady's chief of staff in the president's
morning meeting and communicating with the West Wing throughout the
day is to ensure that both the first lady and the president are "on the same
message" and to orchestrate synchronous goals and activities for the
president and his spouse on a daily basis.

The speech data presented in Chapter 3 revealed that the proportion
of total public speeches and remarks delivered by the president's spouse
that mention policy has grown substantially over the last three decades,
even when the main topic of these speeches is extraneous to policy. I
became interested in the possibility that White House staff responsible for
the first lady's public appearances limited the number of policy speeches
the first lady delivered, or at least tried to downplay the image of the first
lady as a policy maker because of Hillary Clinton's unpopular involvement
in health care reform.

There is evidence that the White House "learned" this lesson in the
second term of the Clinton administration and the Bush administration

was careful not to make the same mistake. First, the content and packaging of Hillary Clinton's appearances changed. When we look at speech transcripts from the second half of the Clinton administration, we can see that Hillary Clinton remained interested in health care and continued to engage with Americans on the issue, but she did so in a different context. Mrs. Clinton made more appearances outside Washington, went to women's groups, and talked about the importance of health care reform for U.S. families from the perspective of a mother and a wife. The other policy areas in which she was interested, such as child care and foster care, resulted in legislation, but when Clinton remarked on these issues in the second term, she usually appeared alongside the president, especially if the event was a bill signing or overtly related to policy. Again, she tackled the issues from the perspective of a woman and mother. Examining Hillary Clinton's speeches before and after the Health Security Act was declared dead in congress in 1994 yields convincing evidence that a shift in strategy involving the first lady occurred. In Mrs. Clinton's 1993 speeches about health care, she frequently uses "we" in her discussions of reform, or mentions "the president" in her remarks, and the speeches are fairly technically laden with specific bill content. In 1995 and 1996, she mentioned the president less, more often opting for "my husband" or "Bill" and describing her relationship with the administration's policy agenda in more personal and less professional terms. A paradigmatic example of this shift is her 1996 Democratic National Convention (DNC) speech, in which she says "I decided to do tonight what I have been doing for over 25 years. I want to talk about what matters most in our lives and in our nation: children and families."[4] Clinton continues:

Bill was with me when Chelsea was born in the delivery room, in my hospital room and when we brought our baby daughter home. Not only did I have lots of help, I was able to stay in the hospital as long as my doctor thought I needed to be there. But today, too many new mothers are asked to get up and get out after 24 hours, and that is just not enough time for many new mothers and babies. That's why the President is right to support a bill that would prohibit the practice of forcing mothers and babies to leave the hospital in less than 48 hours.

She uses the same rhetorical strategy later in the DNC speech in her discussion of family medical leave and health care reform, emphasizing the president's and her personal experience with workplace flexibility and hospital bills rather than legislative details.

You know, Bill and I are fortunate that our jobs have allowed us to take breaks from work, not only when Chelsea was born, but to attend her school events and take her to the doctor. But millions of other parents can't get time off. That's why my husband wants to expand the Family and Medical Leave Law so that parents can take time off for children's doctors appointments and parent-teacher conferences at school . . . Our family has been lucky to have been blessed with a child with good health. Chelsea has spent only one night in the hospital after she had her tonsils out. But Bill and I couldn't sleep at all that night.

But our experience was nothing like the emotional strain on parents when their children are seriously ill. They often worry about where they will get the money to pay the medical bills. That is why my husband has always felt that all American families should have affordable health insurance.

A prominent journalist who covered both Clintons for many years pointed to a change in the tone and audience of Hillary Clinton's speeches after 1994, claiming that major resources went into the reconstruction of Hillary Clinton's image to soften it, and that after health care reform failed, she was most often photographed "tousling the curls of elementary school children" rather than holding policy roundtables. Indeed, Clinton's focus on health care reform was redirected from the well-being of all Americans to children's well-being. She began to pursue a practice perfected in the Bush administration: highlighting organizations and traveling to locations where excellent health care was being provided to children and adults rather than attacking those responsible for the decline of the health care system, as she did, for example, in a November 1993 statement to the American Academy of Pediatrics when she stated the insurance industry had "brought us to the brink of bankruptcy because of the way they financed health care"[5] or in 1994 at a health care reform rally. She warned ". . . the forces of negativism, the forces of cynicism, the forces of the kind of pessimistic view about what we are capable of as a nation will flood the airwaves . . . . They will preach hatred and divisiveness and bigotry and intolerance. They will appeal to the worst emotions in people."[6] The contrast between these aggressively toned appearances and her heartfelt speech about children's health care at a Little Rock, Arkansas hospital in 1998, for instance, is striking:

If we were to take a report card on the health of America's children today, we would show that we are improving our record in almost every subject. And I am proud that much of the impetus of the work that my husband and his administration have done came directly from our experience here in Arkansas, very particularly from our experience at this hospital . . . Hearing about the needs for new technology or learning about incredible gains that could be made by simple preventive measures and outreach—all of that was really an ongoing lesson as we saw here in Arkansas that we tried to incorporate into everything that we have done in the last years in Washington.[7]

In addition to changing the way she discussed policy, Hillary Clinton discussed policy less often. This serves as the second piece of evidence that there was a shift in communications strategy involving the first lady beginning in the second term of the Clinton administration. As a Clinton administration insider shared with me, "For Hillary it was always about policy. She really cared about it. She personally cared about education, health care reform, and equality. She cared deeply about child care, she lobbied Congress directly . . . she became recessive after 1994 and rarely brought up health reform after that." Hillary Clinton also began to make more speeches about women's rights internationally after 1994 and received less press scrutiny for those efforts despite the controversial content of some of the speeches, perhaps, because as another Clinton aide told me, "Women's equality wasn't a sexy issue. The press didn't care," or possibly, because as I discussed in Chapters 2 and 3, first ladies are considered credible speakers on women's issues and there is a baseline expectation that they will reach out to women on behalf of the administration.

It seems clear that although Hillary Clinton's public involvement in health care reform was partially driven by her personal interest in policy, noticeable adjustments to the style, substance, and frequency of her public appearances after 1994 tell us that her public activity was fundamentally driven by the needs and goals of the president. If this were not the case, and if scholars who claim that the public activity of first ladies is determined by personal factors like their interest in politics were right, then perhaps Hillary Clinton would have continued her crusade for the Health Security Act even after she weathered a public opinion backlash and the bill was defeated in congress. But, clearly, when push came to shove, she proceeded in a different direction with the administration's image in mind. As a senior White House press officer recapped, "There used to be a Wednesday night strategy meeting with all of us [the president's top aides, the president, the first lady's top aides and the first lady].

We used to map out communications strategy for all four principals on a white board [the president, the first lady, the vice president, and the second lady]. After 1994, there was no communications strategy involving Hillary. She was off the board. The East Wing took over at that point and I think they did a really good job."

It should also be noted that considering Hillary Clinton's involvement in health care reform solely through the frame of personal ambition is a misdirected endeavor. Tapping Hillary Clinton to chair the taskforce on the health care system overhaul was as much an indication of President Clinton's personal commitment to and interest in the policy area as anything else. And surely, by doing so, as my interview subjects confirmed, the administration intended to send a positive message to the public about how closely the president was paying attention to the issue. If the administration had predicted the negative outcome of Hillary Clinton's health care campaign, it seems they would not have placed her in such a prominent position, or would have at least executed communications strategies that implicated her more carefully. Indeed, some of the best evidence that presidential spouses are deployed strategically is that the first lady often acts in ways she would not have otherwise. In Mrs. Clinton's case, this happened in the form of withdrawing from events or activities that were important to her, but as I learned from many former staff, it also happens when first ladies attend events and make appearances they would rather not.

Even stronger evidence that the public activity of first ladies serves the needs of the president's administration above the first lady's personal interests can be found in the Carter, Reagan, George H.W. Bush, and finally George W. Bush administrations, which was perhaps the first modern administration to begin using the first lady's pet project agenda to frame the president's policy agenda, and to mobilize the first lady on issues where the president was weak or unpopular. While much of Laura Bush's East Wing staff in the first term consisted of campaign staff from 2000 and staff from the first lady's office in Texas, staff who joined the White House in the second half of the Bush administration shared a more strategic, politicized, conception of the Office of the First Lady. I will return to this point shortly.

Rosalynn Carter, commonly cited by scholars as an active first lady with an independent agenda from her husband's, famously sat in on her husband's cabinet meetings so she could stay informed on current affairs questions she figured she might be asked while traveling or giving interviews. What is not as often mentioned by scholars is that Mrs. Carter's presence was requested by President Carter, and that the source of the first lady's involvement was her concern for her impact on her husband's image and presidency.[8] "She wasn't raising her hand or dictating policy or telling people what to do. She was in the back of the room taking notes," a former staff member of Mrs. Carter's explained to me. Nancy Reagan, like Rosalynn Carter, is often portrayed by historians as a rainmaker behind the scenes, providing her husband advice about staff management and rumored to have been responsible for several major personnel changes. As a former Reagan staffer told me, "Nancy Reagan was involved in the substantive side of the presidency. She was the only person who could interrupt every meeting—any person in the meeting—the president. Some say he wasn't engaged in the substantive side of the presidency. But Nancy Reagan was a strategist. She protected his image." Part of the way Mrs. Reagan protected the president's image was watching his back in the West Wing, but she also made public appearances she did not want to in order to enhance the president's reputation. A Reagan press office veteran shared some of those experiences with me:

> You know, this is a political job. They don't get there without politics and they don't stay there without politics. She didn't like to give speeches. In fact, when her husband said, "I'm going to run for president," she goes, "That's fine so long as I don't have to give any speeches." Well, that didn't last long. She traveled 200,000 miles for the anti-drug abuse campaign alone.

She continued:

> I mean, I can't believe what she did. The places that she went and all the people that she met. And, you know, things she'd rather not do and she did. She was a soldier. In the five-and-a-half years I worked for her, we canceled two events, I think, and there were thousands. One of them because she was snowed in going down to Nashville, Tennessee. Even when she was sick. She had laryngitis and there were Christmas parties at the White House. She even showed up one year and just wore a sign that said "I have laryngitis. Merry Christmas." They don't get to do what they want when they want to do it. It's just the opposite.
>   But she knew the value. When they reopened the Statue of Liberty in 1986, she not only cut the ribbon for it. But the photo-op that we all dreamed about was of her waving out of the crown of the Statue of Liberty. And to get up to the crown, she had to take her shoes off and walk this tiny spiral staircase. And the Secret Service said "I don't

think you should do that." But she knew the value of this photo. I was in the helicopter with the press pool getting the photograph. And she was there with a French boy and a little American girl because, you know, it was a gift from the French children to the American children. And that photograph made the front page of every newspaper in the country.

By the first Bush administration, East Wing and West Wing staff began to realize the inherent value of the first lady's bully pulpit—not simply to make headway on a few issues of the first lady's choosing but to enhance the president's public image and mask his deficiencies. I spoke with Barbara Bush's former staff about the public appeal of the former first lady and the potential to mobilize her strategically as a surrogate. A former deputy press secretary to Mrs. Bush recounted three events that generated a surprising amount of positive press coverage for the White House:

Probably one of the first ones, well all three of these got huge press; this was pretty much right in the middle of the AIDS crisis in this country. People were afraid that if you were in the same room with someone who had AIDS, that you were going to get AIDS. So she made a very public trip to a place in Washington, DC called Grandma's House. They took care of babies who had AIDS. And then also . . . she met with this group of men, all who had AIDS. Then there were pictures of her hugging and kissing everybody there. That was something that was her idea. That was something that she wanted to do, because she just wanted to make a statement, that there was just so much ignorance about this disease.

A second example was right around Christmas time. There was a big article in *The Washington Post*, that a number of the major malls in Washington, DC were going to kick the Salvation Army bell ringers out of the mall . . . because they felt it was inconvenient to their customers . . . to be harassed by the Salvation Army bell ringers. She [Barbara Bush] was so appalled by this story. And she said, "I want to go the mall and make a donation to the bell ringer, and I want to take the national media with me. And I'll be ready to go. Just call me when you all are ready." Again, it made a huge difference.

The third story was during Desert Storm. There was a feeling in the country that it was not safe to fly commercially; that Saddam Hussein and the Iraqis were going to target American airlines. I do remember at the time, when all of us were thinking, how ridiculous, what a stupid rumor. Again, this was 10 years before 9/11, and we just found all that rather inconceivable. But she made the decision—the First Lady of the United States has a private plane that she uses, a military plane—and for the duration of Desert Storm, she kept flying commercial, which the secret service were not happy about, and it made our job a lot harder. But I still remember the first morning she did it, and we took U.S. Air somewhere, like Kentucky or North Carolina. I remember it was looked at as a huge deal, and the media covered her getting on the plane, they covered her getting off the plane. But she just wanted to send the message that yes, it is safe to fly, and you all are being ridiculous.

Barbara Bush's staff was very in tune with her potential to humanize the president, to make him seem less distant from the middle class and more relatable. Mrs. Bush also avoided the type of negative press coverage Mrs. Reagan generated with her expensive wardrobe and entertaining expenses. As an aide to Mrs. Bush shared with me, first ladies were the "feel-good coverage for the White House," she caveated, ". . . pretty much up until Mrs. Clinton. Mrs. Clinton created a rat's nest with her sound bite of not being a cookie baking, stand by your man type wife. And then her involvement with health care. The public didn't like her getting personally involved with something she had not been elected to do." She added: "Mrs. Bush became very popular right away as first lady. Coming in behind Mrs. Reagan, she was very cognizant of Mrs. Reagan's image and at an early luncheon, she, with humor, made it clear that she was not a designer driven dresser. What you see is what you get. The audience loved it and the press coverage was massive." Considering this popularity, some of Mrs. Bush's staff wished that she had been mobilized even more often on behalf of the president. She could have communicated certain issues to Americans on which President Bush had difficulty gaining traction, such as the economy, they explained:

We should have used her to better explain where President Bush was coming from on the economy. He was sort of painted as the "out of touch" president . . . didn't understand the economic woes of the middle class. I think it maybe would have been smart to have used her to combat that. We didn't, and now that I think about it, that would have been quite brilliant, but we didn't do it. Certainly during Desert Storm, she was very helpful in helping garner public support for that. Oh my God, we traveled to so many military bases. She started travelling to military bases all over the country, targeting military bases where their contingence of troops had been shipped from that base overseas. And we would do these big events with the families back home. Those were very popular, so that was a case where we were really smart.

When George W. Bush entered office, the East Wing had become a completely professionalized body, with a large staff more capable of and knowledgeable about deploying the president's spouse in a beneficial manner than perhaps any modern administration before it. Perhaps most germanely, the Bush administration learned an important lesson from the Clinton years about the apparent U.S. aversion to presidential spouses as policy makers. Laura Bush had another unprecedented advantage: she was already familiar with the White House from her father-in-law's time in office. She understood how the Office of the First Lady worked and she had a better handle on public expectations of her. However, Laura Bush's comparable comfort in her new role did not prevent communications strategy reliant on her from evolving over the course of the administration. In contrast to the strategy shift concerning Hillary Clinton during the Clinton administration, the strategy shift involving Laura Bush was much more of a ramp-up, rather than a tamp-down, of the first lady's messaging role after 2004.

When the Bushes arrived in the White House, they brought many friends with them from Texas and much of the staff from the Governor's office. The East Wing was no exception. Andi Ball, Mrs. Bush's chief of staff until 2005, was her chief of staff in Austin and on the presidential campaign trail. Karen Hughes and Margaret Spellings also came from the Governor's administration. Furthermore, much of Mrs. Bush's public activity in the first half of the administration was a continuation of her work in Texas: the National Book Festival, for example, and her other literacy projects. The first term in the Office of the First Lady was characterized by offensive (as opposed to defensive) communications strategy. The president was popular before and after September 11 due to a rally 'round the flag effect among Americans in the early years of his first term, and Laura Bush was nicknamed "Comforter in Chief." There was not yet much of a need for the first lady to step in and save the day. Mrs. Bush did nonetheless delve deeply into the No Child Left Behind Act of 2001. "She was *very* involved," a communications director told me. On 9/11 in fact, as many of her staff reminded me, Mrs. Bush was on her way to the Capitol with Margaret Spellings, then Secretary of Education, to testify before the Senate Education Committee on No Child Left Behind. In fascinating response to my question about why Laura Bush may have retained such high popularity throughout the administration, a former White House press secretary shared "Maybe it's because she wasn't really playing a policymaking role. Actually, no, you know what, that's not fair. First ladies make policy all the time. Mrs. Bush was very involved in policymaking."

A pivotal question naturally becomes: Why was the public reaction to Hillary Clinton's promotion of the Health Security Act so harsh while Americans hardly noticed Mrs. Bush's push for No Child Left Behind? The answer is *not* that Laura Bush was secretly engaged in crafting the education initiative while Hillary Clinton was openly active in the health care reform debate. Although Mrs. Clinton was officially designated chair of the president's task force on health care reform and Mrs. Bush held no such title, both first ladies occupied the front lines of public relations campaigns designed to accumulate public support for these bills as well as congressional lobbying efforts. A brief look at Figures 3.1 and 3.2 reminds us that the bulk of Mrs. Clinton's and Mrs. Bush's public activity was attributed to health care and education, respectively, in the first terms of their husbands' administrations. An investigation into each spouse's tenure as the first ladies of Arkansas and Texas would also show that Clinton and Bush had abundant experience with the issues at the state level and created initiatives geared toward their amelioration long before entering the White House. In 1979 when her husband was elected governor, Hillary Clinton became chairperson of the Arkansas Rural Health Advisory Committee, where she helped develop programs that expanded health care coverage in the state's most isolated areas,[9] and by 1999, Laura Bush had established Reach Out and Read and Ready to Read, two elementary educational programs she elaborated at the White House.[10] In other words, both spouses were qualified to grapple with these subjects.

What *was* markedly different was the style and context of their speeches about health care and education. Laura Bush's literacy initiatives and her work in early childhood development (i.e., her pet projects) allowed her to make public appearances that highlighted the importance of the president's education bill while keeping her at an arm's length from the language of lawmaking. She spoke *covertly*, not *overtly*, about the No Child Left Behind Act. Enlisting the president's spouse to promulgate policy without alarming the press is an impressive tightrope walk perfected in the Bush administration that deserves the attention of scholars. Whether the strategy of priming Americans on a particular policy issue through the first lady had a measurable impact on public opinion is a question tackled in Chapter 6. But to Mrs. Bush's staff, it made common sense to link the first lady's literacy projects and the president's education agenda. Take this speech from 2001 at a Ready to Read, Ready to Learn event:

> I also want to thank every teacher here because you do so much more than teach. You inspire, you challenge and you mentor children who need your guidance. I know you don't hear often enough how much we appreciate you. I know, because I've been there. I worked in public schools as a teacher and a librarian. It's often a difficult job, but it's a rewarding one. What you do in the classroom determines the future for your students . . . and for our country.
>
> President Bush knows that, so he's made education his number one priority: He wants to give America's teachers and schools greater flexibility, freedom and support to do your job . . . so that every child is educated and no child is left behind.[11]

As I argue later, the incorporation of policy rhetoric into a pet project speech should be conceptualized as the gold standard for remarks delivered by a president's spouse. While the earlier speech is not overtly related to No Child Left Behind, Mrs. Bush makes the case that teachers and students are personally important to her, personally important to the president, and that No Child Left Behind is an outgrowth of these priorities. She also stays positive. Positivity is another stark difference between Hillary Clinton's speeches on health care reform in the first half of the Clinton administration and Laura Bush's speeches on education. Criticism sounds partisan; accolades for a job well done do not. Rather than place blame on the public school system, congress, or teachers for underperforming, Mrs. Bush praised the schools and teachers that were succeeding. She talked about providing more resources to exemplary schools instead of extracting funds from failing ones. And finally, what cannot be ignored is the policy itself. No Child Left Behind had bipartisan support in Congress. As a policy director for Laura Bush and former communications staff member explained:

> I think with Mrs. Clinton, what happened was . . . education is something where I think there was more consensus that American education has to get fixed. You can stop any person on the street, and they'll tell you, "We're so far behind other countries, etc." Or, "Our kids are not doing well." Health care, that was a lot bigger. That also had big economic ramifications. The message of holding adults in schools accountable—because you can't hold schools accountable unless you hold the adults who are running and teaching in the

schools accountable—that's not a tough message to sell, I mean it really isn't. But when you start talking about reforming the health care system in America, that's a pretty tough challenge; that brings in all kinds of economic concerns, not just for Mom and Pop, but for the medical industry, for the medical device manufacturers.

To say that there's not politics to it, of course there's politics to it. Laura Bush never [said], "Tell your congressmen to vote for the No Child Left Behind bill." That was Margaret Spellings's job with Ted Kennedy, that was not Laura Bush's job. Her job was to go out to significant locations of regional press, and rather than criticize what was going on locally, her strategy was, I'll compliment who does it well.

The East Wing became even more strategic in its mobilization of the first lady in the second term, reflected in staff changes. Many of the first lady's new hires were savvy Washington veterans or strategic recruits from the private sector, hired to hone Mrs. Bush's communications role in a way that would best reinforce the overarching goals of the administration. From interviews with these staff members, I realized that clearly, Mrs. Bush intended to help her husband above all else, who would soon face sinking approval ratings associated with the invasion of Iraq and the disaster of Hurricane Katrina. A senior member of Laura Bush's staff told me that in her first substantive meeting with the first lady a week after the 2004 election, Mrs. Bush made it clear that she wanted to use her skills and time to support the president's foreign and domestic policy initiatives:

And her guidance to me . . . was "I'm not here for me. I'm here for George. I want to support him where I can and where it makes the most sense. How I can use my experience, my background to support him?" And there were extraordinarily important global initiatives that were launched by President Bush. The President's Emergency Plan For AIDS Relief, the president's malaria initiative. She became the lead advocate for those and was a very effective and astute foreign policy advocate for President Bush. We were able to do it because we were totally in sync and in tandem with what the overarching goal was of the administration. We weren't running a shadow government. We were there very seriously to support what the President was trying to do. On the freedom agenda, on the human rights agenda and on the renaissance of foreign assistance, which is what it was.

Perhaps one of the most successful applications of Mrs. Bush's voice was on Afghan women's issues, an effort that commenced shortly after September 11. Mrs. Bush became the first spouse to deliver the president's weekly radio address and she used the platform to inform Americans of the plight of Afghan women and children.[12] Again from the standpoint of a wife and mother, she intertwined the president's foreign policy objectives with the fate of women and families. A portion of one of her 2001 radio addresses exemplifies the sophisticated rhetorical strategy:

> Afghan women know, through hard experience, what the rest of the world is discovering: The brutal oppression of women is a central goal of the terrorists. Long before the current war began, the Taliban and its terrorist allies were making the lives of children and women in Afghanistan miserable. Seventy percent of the Afghan people are malnourished. One in every four children won't live past the age of five because health care is not available. Because of our recent military gains in much of Afghanistan, women are no longer imprisoned in their homes. They can listen to music and teach their daughters without fear of punishment. Yet the terrorists who helped rule that country now plot and plan in many countries. And they must be stopped. The fight against terrorism is also a fight for the rights and dignity of women.[13]

Similarly to her education initiatives, Laura Bush's post at the Afghan Women's Council (which she has continued to chair since 2002) and other women's groups provided her with an apolitical route to make hefty political strides. She could highlight the president's freedom agenda on the ground in Afghanistan and Iraq in a noncontroversial manner. Mrs. Bush made two solo trips to Afghanistan beginning in 2005 and one accompanying the president. She actually made more solo trips abroad than any other first lady in history, except Pat Nixon, who traveled to 81 countries compared to Laura Bush's 77. According to senior White House staff, Mrs. Bush stepped into a sweeping communications role in the second term on issues the administration feared would be overshadowed by reporters' preoccupation with the Iraq war, such as PEPFAR. A member of her communications team expressed frustration with the president's inability to control the narrative, citing an interview with President Bush and journalist Ann Curry in Africa in 2008 in which she [Ann Curry] ". . . didn't even talk about Africa . . . she asked about the war."

Despite their awareness that Laura Bush did not have quite the same media penetration as the president, Mrs. Bush's staff began to deploy her on behalf of the president abroad because of the "likability issues" challenging President Bush in his second term. According to another senior staff member, "History will show her [Laura Bush's] passion [for humanitarian issues and Afghan women] but will also show that she saw the need to be the ambassador in a space where her husband just couldn't be given what he was focused on and needed to do, which was leading the war. And so I think she's probably not yet given credit for that role that she moved into and spending time in the Middle East and spending time in Africa and spending time globally."

A domestic version of the same kind of strategic deployment became prevalent in the wake of Hurricane Katrina. As former staff noted, most people probably do not remember that Laura Bush made 25 trips to the gulf coast in the aftermath of Katrina, most of them alone or with administration officials other than the president. Although it is not clear whether the short-term memory of the U.S. public or the messaging strategy that drove these trips is to blame for the lack of credit Laura Bush was allegedly awarded for her efforts, it became clear through interviews that Mrs. Bush's trips to the Gulf Coast were indeed a political play. A senior staff member recounted:

> On the domestic front probably the place where it was so important for her to go was to the Gulf Coast after Katrina. We went every month for the first year and then it was a little less than that but we kept going. When restaurants would reopen, when hotels would reopen, when schools would reopen, when libraries would reopen, when job training programs were established, she was there. And we went with cabinet officers and we went with the secretary of labor. We went with secretary of education. We went with HHS. Playgrounds were being rebuilt, volunteer organizations were coming in. That dominated a lot of our schedule . . . to go to each. She would equally hit Mississippi, Louisiana . . . we went to Alabama too. So that was a play and the president as you know got intense criticism. It's not that all of her visits there were going to totally change that perception and there was a lot of misinformation about the coordination between state and local and federal authorities. But the Gulf Coast wasn't forgotten by President Bush and [that] certainly manifested in the frequency of visits made by Laura Bush.

Exactly what prompts strategists to mobilize first ladies in a damage control capacity is discussed later in this chapter. As interviews with many experts confirmed, Mrs. Clinton was deployed in such a way on the 1992 campaign trail to combat allegations that Bill Clinton had an affair with Gennifer Flowers, and again in 1998 during the Monica Lewinsky scandal. While some of these targeted efforts may have been less effective than others—the famous sound bite Mrs. Clinton gave in an interview with Matt Lauer regarding the "vast right-wing conspiracy" comes to mind—communications strategists I consulted from various administrations concurred that Mrs. Clinton's willingness to loyally "stand by her man" did a great deal to uphold the president's public image in the threatening face of controversy. Without her, they suggested, public resentments would have been much stronger.

While it is difficult to pinpoint an instance in which Michelle Obama immersed herself in the national spotlight in order to restore the president's public image, like Laura Bush, she has advocated for her husband tirelessly on the campaign trail, complimented his policy agenda through her pet project initiatives, and communicated the goals and interests of the administration to women and families. Evidence uncovered through the analysis of speech transcripts underpins the idea that strategic deployment of the first lady has increased markedly in the Obama administration. The majority of Mrs. Obama's public appearances fall into the category of campaign speeches or speeches on her two primary initiatives, Let's Move! and Joining Forces. Unlike the Bush administration, which merely hired directors, deputy directors, and associate directors of policy and projects for Laura Bush, Mrs. Obama's office assigns personnel to specific initiatives, for example, designating executive, deputy, and assistant directors of Let's Move! and Joining Forces. Such a highly specialized operation signifies a more organized East Wing operation than existed even in the second term of the Bush presidency.

Although it may come as a surprise to commentators like Glenn Beck and Rush Limbaugh who alleged the first lady had a staff size of 40 or more people in 2011 and 2012, Mrs. Obama's staff is not larger than that of Mrs. Bush or many of her predecessors. Since the 1970s, staff sizes in the Office of the First Lady have hovered in the range of 16–25; in 2008 and 2009, Laura Bush and Michelle Obama both had roughly 25 total staff members.[14] What is perhaps more interesting is the growing number of communications and press hires in Mrs. Obama's office who have private sector or nonprofit communications experience. There is some indication that the practice of hiring public relations experts reached new heights in the Bush administration, when Mrs. Bush's second-term communications team began reaching out to alternative media outlets to improve "surface-level-only" coverage of Mrs. Bush, unapologetically capitalizing on her popularity and what it could contribute to the image of President Bush and his administration. Mrs. Obama's team kept the new tradition alive, courting alternative media organizations and restricting coverage of the first lady to a few key issue areas. "She was going out on way too many issues" a senior communications staff member told me, when she arrived at the White House to work for Laura Bush:

> I was fairly deliberate in not going through the press briefing room to get to press. Which the West Wing was very supportive of but they took a lot of complaints about . . . although my understanding is that the Obamas aren't respecting the rules. But you go in rotation from networks to print coverage and . . . they would argue for Mrs. Bush to be in the rotation when they wanted to go but they didn't guarantee that they would actually send someone. And I'm like, "Well, I'm not going to let you only cover the cool stuff. Either you're in and we always can count on you or you're not my first choice, because you have a filter." They [the White House press corps] had a president filter. Low approval rating, high approval rating . . . So we went around the press room which gave Dana [Perino] a lot of heartache because she had to stand in front of them every single day but we got better coverage and we were able to tell the story more authentically . . . if you're going to talk about women in Afghanistan, women's magazines are a really good place to take that story . . . so we kind of went the non-White House tradition route and obviously the Obamas have taken that to the next level.

"She was a brilliant strategist," another senior staff member to Laura Bush said about the communications staff member quoted earlier.

> She was so brilliant in her strategies, pushing Mrs. Bush to do non-conventional media, to do *Vogue*, because people weren't doing those types of things. She came from the outside. She had a PR point of view, which helped a great deal. You know what? It's that classic thing in politics. If something goes wrong, it's not the policy. It's communications. Which is not true. I mean we know that sometimes but for us it was not that the policies weren't good or the things that Laura Bush was promoting. It wasn't that the communications plan wasn't great. It was the perception that the media and the public had of the president.

Like Laura Bush's communications team, communications staff to Mrs. Obama acknowledged the opportunity present in the East Wing to control press access to the first lady and coverage of her. The West Wing does not share this luxury, subject to daily inquiries from the White House press corps and the basic rules of the press room rotation, as a communications strategist for Mrs. Obama explained:

> You aren't engaging the press each week . . . I never did a Sunday Show with Mrs. Obama. So in some ways you have to be more strategic. The West Wing eventually has to . . . give everybody access. The East Wing does not. You get to pick and choose. And you can't hide your head in the sand, because when you do have something important to say, people [in the press corps] have all this pent up anger, so your interviewers don't care about your topic, they care that you've never given them an interview. And so, you do have to do things periodically to feed the beast and keep people engaged. But you don't have to do it in the same way the West Wing does. There's a network strategy for the West Wing, for example, where they try to play fair: Someone got the first crack at it last time; now you're at the end of the line.

The Obama administration has also seized opportunities to communicate with the public directly. Mrs. Obama is a regular social media presence. Technology has granted her office the ability to restrict and expand public exposure to the first lady as they see fit. As a staff member to Laura Bush explained to me:

> First it was 24/7 [news] then it was technology and you know Facebook, Twitter. We didn't have it. It was around but it wasn't a demand that we use it. They [the Obama administration] came in and they did a great job with it on the campaign and kept it up . . . I mean we did video blogging and writing . . . we did "ivillage" from the road, which back then was fairly breakthrough. We didn't have pool press giving pool rotation notes and that was a little frustrating to them that they were learning from a blog, but they have different rules of engagement. And I think they should. I mean they [first ladies] either get treated with mandatory coverage the same way a president does or they don't.

Seasoned journalists I consulted also cited the explosion of social media as a key reason the Obama administration has been able to amplify Mrs. Obama's public relations activity while also tightly controlling traditional news coverage of her: "The Obama administration hasn't been

tied to traditional ways of communicating with the public. The 'no filter' approach as they say. They have been very innovative. Some of
what Michelle Obama does—her staff wouldn't say it but I will—is reinforce the Obama brand with the public. They love to break viral video
records, dunking with the Miami Heat, etc. Those are huge wins for them.
And of course there is always an underlying policy issue."

The primary underlying policy issue in Mrs. Obama's case, according to her former staff members and journalists who have covered her,
is health care, although Joining Forces (her military families initiative
with Jill Biden) has certainly framed the president's push for the removal
of troops from Iraq and Afghanistan. In the fashion of Laura Bush's
projects to improve the lives of Afghan women and promote literacy,
Mrs. Obama's initiative to combat childhood obesity, Lets Move!, facili-
tated her participation in larger debates about the cost of health care in
the United States and the importance of preventative approaches to medi-
cine while distancing her from the policy-making process. Mrs. Obama's
efforts to frame her husband's policy agenda have accounted for a much
larger percentage of her total public speeches than Mrs. Bush's efforts
did. Although ceremonial or traditional appearances often also serve to
reinforce the administration's political program, Michelle Obama has
attended few ceremonial events overall, instead making mostly pet project and campaign-related remarks, accounting for more than 60 percent
of her public activity. As the same journalist explained to me:

> I think they knew they wanted to do health care very early on and
> she actually did talk about health care quite a bit—but from the
> perspective of a mom. The staff makes it clear that she is interested
> and passionate about this but she is the face and the spokeswoman.
> I've been trying to find out more about Michelle Obama's role in
> drafting legislation but what I've seen is that she delegates her input
> to trusted aides. She gives her staff the input and then they make the
> changes or edits. She had a tough time in the campaign and I think
> they have been very careful about making sure the public doesn't
> think she's involved in drafting policy. The goal is to help and not
> hurt.

Just as we observed in Laura Bush's speeches about literacy and Afghan
women, the administration's policy interests are artfully woven through
Mrs. Obama's Lets Move! and Joining Forces speeches. Here is an example of a reference to health care reform in a speech by Mrs. Obama in
2009:

As we look at tackling some of the biggest health problems that our nation faces, like obesity, diabetes, heart disease, and related issues like access to primary care and preventative health services, I've realized that little things like a garden can actually play a role in all of these larger discussions. They make us think about these issues in a way that maybe sometimes the policy conversations don't allow us to think. And it has truly inspired me and the White House staff to look for opportunities to put the topic of healthy eating right on the table and at the forefront of health care discussions. And this is one of the reasons why we're here today, why we're here supporting this effort today.[15]

The speech previously mentioned was titled "Remarks by the First Lady on What Health Insurance Reform Means for Women and Families" on the White House Briefing Room web site and was coded a policy speech in my data set because of her expressed focus on the Affordable Care Act and the general audience that attended her speech at the Eisenhower Executive Office Building that day. Yet, as we can see, the way in which Mrs. Obama qualifies herself to discuss the Affordable Care Act is first, by defining herself as a woman and a mother, effectively removing herself from the Washington world of policy making and partisan interests and second, by channeling her antiobesity initiatives. This acute rhetorical strategy is common in Mrs. Obama's speeches. Here is a different example of the same strategy in a 2011 speech concerning the end of the war in Iraq. The first lady and president appeared together in this case:

And that's why I've been working so hard, along with Jill Biden, on a campaign we call Joining Forces . . . businesses are hiring tens of thousands of veterans and military spouses. Schools all across the country and PTA's are reaching out to our military children. And individuals are serving their neighbors and their communities all over this country in your honor. So I want you to know that this nation's support doesn't end as this war ends. Not by a long shot . . . We're going to keep finding new ways to serve all of you as well as you have served us. And the man leading the way is standing right here. He is fighting for you and your families every single day. He's helped more than half a million veterans and military family members go to college through the Post-9/11 G.I. Bill. He's taken unprecedented steps to improve mental health care. He's cut taxes for businesses that hire a veteran or a wounded warrior. And he has kept his promise to responsibly bring you home from Iraq.[16]

The way in which pet projects such as Joining Forces and Let's Move! are used as frames for the administration's policy agenda is discussed in further detail in Chapter 5. So far, I should have also made the case that Michelle Obama's role as subtle spokeswoman for the Affordable Care Act in 2009 and Laura Bush's promotion of No Child Left Behind in 2001 were retreats from Hillary Clinton's aggressive campaign for the passage of the Health Security Act in 1993, but highly organized and focused efforts all the same. Chapter 5 also illustrates how the unique status and public appeal of spouses permit them to shape public impressions of the president in ways other surrogates cannot: by going personal, going purple, and going positive. I now turn to another reason interview participants claimed first ladies appear in public on behalf of the administration.

All Hands on Deck

In addition to the fact that White House staff have attempted to capitalize on public appearances of the president's spouse to a greater degree in recent years, public activity of the president's spouse has also grown as a result of increased demand for presidential responsiveness. Pressure has thus been placed on surrogates such as the first lady to shoulder more of the burden. One senior advisor to President Clinton traced the influx in first lady appearances back to Watergate, which mandated improvements in overall White House transparency and visibility. "Watergate was a really transformative moment in the presidency because it raised in a much more highly visible way the question of character," he said. The first lady is uniquely qualified to vouch for the character of the president, as I discuss shortly, but we also expect to see and know more about presidents than ever before. This is perhaps most obviously the case on the campaign trail. White House and campaign communications experts point to the emergence of the permanent campaign, a vetting process for presidential candidates and running mates that becomes longer and more arduous every year, and a governing period that becomes shorter and less focused on policy than public approval.[17]

A Clinton communications advisor recounted that first ladies can be "force multipliers" on the campaign trail. "It wasn't merely that she [Hillary Clinton] humanized him; so yes, she would go to a rally and people would see a loving couple, but also to send her out independently. And man, that helps, because there are so many places you've got to be, 20 or 30 states in play, and you can only be in one at a time." Another Bush campaign veteran lamented the superhuman requirements of the modern campaign trail: "If you think about the time of 24-hour news and how much they [the networks] have to fill it is unbelievable. And I think that's why presidents have to be younger to keep up the schedule. I asked the Reagan advance people . . . they said he would give a major speech once every three weeks . . . we were lucky if we had three days to plan something like that." Many other interview participants cited the explosion of 24-hour news and social media as a central part of the increased appearances phenomenon:

> I think a huge thing in the communications effort to look at now is the access to information. I always say that one of the things that really diluted news was 24-hour cable news and that's interesting because it has helped give [Americans] rights to a public personality [the first lady's and president's] that they didn't have 20, 30, 40, 50 years ago. I mean you think about Mrs. Obama and Twitter; she can tweet something and you know it's her and you get that "MO" there. And that's a different way of communicating and putting yourself into the public conversation that you didn't have any other time. So the perception I think is that something is more accessible, more relatable . . . in some ways those outlets create an increased demand on your time. But I think there is that greater interest as a result too. That would be the biggest learning curve for me, if I went back into [White House] communications . . . knowing how to use that strategically.

The proliferation of media platforms with which the first lady can communicate with the public, in addition to or even instead of network news, in turn creates a greater expectation for her to engage with the public and generates more public interest in her. Public access begets public interest.

One journalist deftly attributed the increase in public appearances of first ladies to the "celebrity-fication" of political figures. "Aren't we just fascinated with celebrities in general?" a former staffer to Barbara Bush asked. "It's what they were wearing, it's the details of people's personalities and lives. It's a window into a different world." Others pointed to Michelle Obama's satellite appearance at the Oscars in 2013. Mrs. Obama presented the award for Best Picture from the White House. "The administration was saying 'she just loves movies', but even I was like, 'come on', it's great optics, her in that dress in front of all the military personnel, and they get to see a bit of her life in the White House." When I asked a communications strategist about the same appearance and the White

House's defense of it, he said "I wouldn't buy that for a second. Every move they make is strategic and well thought out and planned weeks, if not months, ahead of time. Everything I do in my current capacity and everything I have done in the past as a campaign manager has been well thought out and executed, even at the congressional level . . . it's optics." If the first lady has in fact become a national celebrity, she can appear before the same high-yield audiences that Hollywood icons do, such as the Oscars, late night talk shows, and in Michelle Obama's case, guest roles on scripted and reality television shows such as *Biggest Loser*, *Top Chef*, and *Nashville*.

While I agreed with the assertions of interview participants that presidential campaigns are becoming more demanding, that cable news and new social media outlets have provided more tools for spouses to communicate often with the public, and that first ladies have become part of American celebrity culture, none of these reasons adequately explains why presidential spouses, in particular, *not* other presidential surrogates such as vice presidents, have become more active. As I demonstrated in Chapter 3, first ladies appear more often in public than vice presidents and they are more widely recognized than vice presidents. Vice presidential speech frequencies have not surged according to the same pattern as first ladies, which we would expect to observe if the increased communication workload was divided evenly among surrogates. The reality is that the workload is not evenly divided and that the president's spouse is unlike other surrogates. According to interview subjects, the first lady is invariably the most in-demand surrogate on the campaign trail, the most successful fundraiser, and, as the polls in Chapter 3 suggested, the most popular presidential representative in the eyes of the American voter. Volume of requests for appearances on the campaign trail and fundraising prowess, in fact, are two of the ways presidential campaign operatives measure the effectiveness of spouses in elections. When I pushed interview participants to explain the difference between the president's spouse and other surrogates, they reiterated some of the discoveries I made through observational data analysis: first ladies almost always enjoy higher likability than their presidential and vice presidential counterparts and they are not subjected to the same critical style of news coverage as most politicians.

But what drives this likability and public interest? What makes donors more likely to open their checkbooks for the spouse of a president than another surrogate? What can the first lady provide the public that another surrogate cannot? "Because they are without question the closest person to the president," a former staffer to Laura Bush explained. "It's the closest person to him," confirmed former aides to Jimmy Carter and Michelle Obama. The first credential the first lady brings to the bully pulpit is proximity to the president. And in an age when presidential character is a prime focus of campaigns, closeness is a critical asset. "I think what they [first ladies] all bring . . . is this credential about what kind of person is my husband and what kind of person are we electing president. And they can speak almost uniquely to their characteristics as a husband, as a father, as a family person. That takes on a very special role because the public detects it pretty quickly if there's any dysfunction there," said a former senior Clinton staff member. He continued: "I make this point a lot: the unique relationship the American electorate has with the president is totally unlike governors, senators, congressmen, mayors, and other elected officials because there's much more of this personal relationship. I mean, everybody in the country knows something about Barack Obama and Michelle." These personal cues and stories about the president's character were almost universally mentioned messaging tools by both Democratic and Republican campaign veterans. A Bush communications staff member who worked in the White House and on the 2004 campaign explained that these cues not only help the electorate evaluate the president but also galvanize volunteers and grassroots staff:

> There was a tremendous desire among, say Republican candidates or even grassroots activists or donors to see and hear from First Lady Laura Bush. She was immensely popular. Because she has a very warm and funny down to earth demeanor, she was able to tell stories and share things about President Bush that no one else obviously could. And was able to make the case for him as a leader and as President in a way that no one else could. And that is something that is tremendously powerful on the campaign trail and something that people really enjoy because it's a more human side of politics. She is able to talk about his motivations and why he is doing what he is doing and the kind of person he is. And people really identified with that and appreciated her sharing that on the campaign trail because it made them more interested in trying to help the campaign and trying to work on his behalf . . . It really sort of bonded them with the idea that they were part of this effort to get him elected.

Although vice presidential running mates can ostensibly make the same case spouses do regarding the candidate's character, they are squarely outmatched by a person who has observed the candidate in a variety of phases of professional and personal life. In other words, spouses are privy to a "behind-the-scenes" view of the president that is exclusive to his friends and family. As one communications expert told me, "It's odd, but the opinion of the spouse becomes more believable—more authentic—because he or she is not necessarily invested personally in the process. Of course they are invested but not exactly professionally—they're not running, but they have this kind of window [into the candidate] that you don't have unless you're that person." This account reveals a second quality presidential spouses can convey to the public that other surrogates cannot: the appearance of authenticity and relative impartiality. Perhaps because the president's spouse acquires no formal responsibilities or powers when her husband wins office, Americans are more likely to wonder "What's in it for her?" when they see the first lady on television or the Internet. The efforts of spouses to communicate with the public appear more genuine and less opportunistic.

A senior Clinton administration official suggested that the decision to campaign under the "two for the price of one" slogan in 1992 thwarted Hillary Clinton's ability to benefit from the public perception of her as Washington outsider, or at least someone with nothing to gain from her husband's success. The slogan, he claimed, automatically gave the public an excuse to evaluate her according to the same criteria as her husband. "I think that's what put Hillary Clinton in such a vulnerable spot: that whole elect-one-get-one-free . . . because people said, 'No, wait a minute, we're not electing her. We're electing her husband,' " he said. The public may be more comfortable, and first ladies can be better assets to campaigns and administrations, when they resemble independent political actors.

CHAPTER 5

The Rhetorical Toolkit Spouses Use to Convince Us

In the previous chapter, I shared answers gleaned from the elite interview process to the question: Why have public appearances of the president's spouse increased in frequency over the last three administrations? I discovered that first, appearances have surged because the first lady's staff has become more professionalized and adopted a more strategic approach to her public role. Second, the influx in appearances can be explained, in part, by the explosion of conventional and social media outlets with which the first lady can communicate with the public. However, among the many surrogates the president can choose from to share the increased communications burden, first ladies are still the first choice of the White House and campaign operatives for a variety of reasons. The following subsections of this chapter address a different question: What are the purposes and/or goals that underlie public appearances of the president's spouse? In other words, what needs and concerns drive her activity? Why does she go public?

To answer this question fairly and thoroughly, the first notion that must be made clear is that all public activity of first ladies varies slightly according to the particular person and to "the power dynamics of the couple's relationship" as one communications strategist suggested. That is, "how involved one is in the other's life and wanting him or her to succeed or not succeed." Or as a former chief of staff to a first lady shared with me, "The three you are focused on [Hillary Clinton, Laura Bush and Michelle Obama] are the first three professional first ladies; they had very thoughtful agendas. But you must remember every first lady brings her own unique experience, interests and talents to the office; they each must figure out where they can make a contribution." A president's spouse must *want* to participate in the political process. Participation is the first way a president's spouse can have a positive impact on the presidency. Recall from the literature review my appraisal of scholarly work that overemphasizes the personal interests and experiences of first ladies. It would be very difficult for a modern president's spouse to avoid the media spotlight without raising concern. The expectation that first ladies communicate, to be certain, has been set in stone at least in the last three administrations, if not earlier. What would happen (or what has happened) if a president's spouse declines to be publicly engaged was a major point raised by communications strategists I interviewed, who suggested that involvement of the president's spouse on the campaign trail is "requisite" for success in our current electoral environment. As a Bush communications staffer told me:

> Would the first lady, or the vice president for that matter, be enough to change who is elected? I think there have been a lot of polls that say no. But I actually think who actually gets there is a completely different piece of it . . . they have to go through a primary, they have to go through a lot. And I think you'll hear living first ladies say that one of the most important roles is to support their spouse and that is both private and public and cannot be underestimated. And you think of some, you know, Hillary Clinton. Man, she really stood by her man. There is a genuine partnership and the partnership is you have to be as engaged in the process and supportive of the process or it is highly unlikely that they're going to get there.
>
>   And if you think really contemporary, I mean, Chris Christie. He didn't throw his name in the hat. And around the water cooler, the family isn't supportive of it. Mrs. Heinz, actually, Kerry . . . she hurt his campaign and you know they might not be the reason they get elected but could be the reason they don't. So what is interesting . . . what I've seen from people who haven't worked on a presidential campaign . . . is they often don't support the spouse early enough or appropriately enough until there has been either a misstep or a mistake or something has happened. And it's a whole new territory for everyone.

Interview participants often pointed to the trouble Howard Dean and John Kerry's spouses caused on the 2004 presidential campaign trail due to a lack of participation. A former senior communications staffer to

Michelle Obama indicated Howard Dean's problem with his wife, Judith Steinberg Dean, in particular:

> If you don't have a spouse, it's considered a liability . . . and it's considered a detriment if you have one who won't participate. Look at Howard Dean. Howard Dean's wife refused to campaign. That was a huge detriment. If you're bad at it, it's [also] not good. I don't think Mrs. McCain was an asset to John McCain. Her daughter was probably a very good campaigner for him. You need them for a couple reasons: There's a lot ground to cover, so you need that extra voice out there. There's this notion out there that they make you human because they know you best, which is probably true. It feels little weird at this point, but that part is true. I don't think you can win a campaign these days without people feeling like they know you. This "Who do you want to watch your kids?" test. They throw one of these new things out there every single time and it's almost impossible if you haven't had the validation of the spouse to tell the person why they'd be fun to have a beer with or who you pick to watch your kids. Those are two crazy litmus tests, but the American public uses them.

If doing no harm depends first and foremost on some level of participation, then the second phase is avoiding controversial statements while participating. Most presidential spouses have sparked some kind of controversy on the campaign trail, as a member of Laura Bush's communications team explained before, often because they were not given the adequate support and attention of strategists early on. Or, as another staff member noted, spouses may not notice how closely they are being watched by press. Even Barbara Bush, whose popularity floated 40–50 points above her husband's for most of his administration, has drawn negative press attention at times. Bush even inspired a *Vanity Fair* article about how "scary" and "mean" she was compared to Nancy Reagan.[1] Many of Mrs. Bush's staff reminded me of her gaffe on the presidential campaign trail in 1984 when she was the vice president's wife. When asked what she thought of Geraldine Ferraro, then Democratic nominee for vice president, the sharp-tongued Barbara Bush replied, "I can't say it, but it rhymes with rich." "I don't think she realized she was on the record," a member of her former press team told me.

In March of the 1992 presidential campaign, as President H. W. Bush fought Bill Clinton for a second term, Hillary Clinton famously remarked to television reporters, "I suppose I could have stayed home and baked cookies and had teas, but what I decided to do was fulfill my profession which I entered before my husband was in public life."[2] And perhaps most recently, Michelle Obama stated during the 2008 presidential campaign in Milwaukee: "For the first time in my adult lifetime, I'm really proud of my country."[3] Like Hillary Clinton's March remark, Michelle Obama's comment was uttered fairly early on in the campaign (February), a point in time when she was not always prepped by strategists before going on camera. During election season, spouses learn to speak in a very careful and controlled manner, as Mrs. Obama claimed in an interview for a *Newsweek* profile, "This is what I haven't learned how to do . . . I can't think out loud, I can't sort of meander through because then somebody takes a clip of the first part."[4] What the controversial comments share, in addition to generating considerable press scrutiny, is a negative overtone or implication. Negativity of any sort often proves a problematic rhetorical strategy for presidential spouses, as we saw with Hillary Clinton and the Health Security Act of 1993. As a prominent journalist who has covered the Clintons for more than a decade iterated, Americans react unfavorably to first ladies who attack the president's political adversaries:

> The times they used her [Hillary Clinton] strategically, I mean obviously healthcare, became counterproductive. You know at the lowest moment of his presidency they sent her out to do the Matt Lauer interview, about the vast right wing conspiracy. And then it is over that year that her public approval soars, because you know that's sort of the great story of Hillary Clinton . . . people have always liked her best as a symbol or a victim. It's like, as much as she came into this job thinking she was going to have these great achievements, you know, in fact people weren't comfortable with her . . . and don't forget she was the first first lady ever forced to testify in front of a grand jury . . . I think it will be a very, very long time before anyone tries to do what Hillary Clinton did.

"Our job was only to help and not complicate," a senior communications strategist for Laura Bush added. Aside from staying positive and eschewing controversy, presidential spouses face a delicate "tightrope walk" in which they attempt to exercise message control while retaining authenticity. Thus, first ladies often choose safe topics to discuss in public—subjects about which they are knowledgeable. As a former advisor to President Bush said, ". . . they should do what they're most comfortable with. Because I think if you try to pressure them to do something outside of their comfort zone it becomes contrived and then it's not authentic and the American people can sniff out insincerity in a second." Communications advisors to Laura Bush and Michelle Obama agreed that on top of augmenting the reputation of the president and certain policies, the topics of public remarks made by Mrs. Bush and Mrs. Obama were fundamentally defined by their personal preferences. One of Laura Bush's staff members summarized the trade-off between Mrs. Bush's interests and West Wing needs that drove messaging strategy in the East Wing:

> No Child Left Behind . . . very involved; that's a good example. Tax bill . . . same time frame . . . she wasn't that involved. Now whether she tangentially worked on that, maybe, but in all that I've done with her that's not been an area.[5] Also in his first term was developing the volunteerism/faith based initiative. Involved. So you kind of look at different initiatives that could she have had the skill set also to attack. Sure, she's a smart, smart person, but did she have the luxury of being a first lady who could choose where she spent her time? Absolutely. And so that's [education] where she spent her time in the first term and obviously post-9/11 their focus shifted and . . . she got such a response from doing the president's radio address on Afghan women.

She continued, later in the interview:

> I went to a daily communication meeting in the West Wing. From a policy point of view, Mrs. Bush's Chief of Staff would be with President Bush's Chief of Staff deciding where Mrs. Bush's priorities could be from an interest and a need [perspective]. But you have to remember, so much happens without staff, between two principals, and so Mrs. Bush's interest could have been driven from President Bush, right? They have a very very close relationship so there's that factor. You can have all the staff in the world . . . but for the most part, particularly in the second term of the Bush administration we knew which issues we were helping with and we continued to go out on them. AIDS. PEPFAR. His global work. Working with women in Afghanistan. Education, pushing for reauthorization of No Child Left Behind in the second term. They [West Wing staff] didn't have to ask us to do that but we planned and reported in. They didn't necessarily drive our agenda. There would have been times where Dana [Perino] would have called me and said "If you could convince Mrs. Bush to actually do this interview it would be helpful because

she could add a side of the story that they're just really not listening to."

A former senior staffer to Michelle Obama drew on similar themes in her explanation of the multifaceted concerns that inform the issues first ladies embrace, confiding that teen pregnancy and AIDS in the African American community were a couple of projects interest groups wanted Mrs. Obama to focus on:

> Knowing how polarized the country is . . . she intentionally did not give people a target. People had all these agenda arguments where they thought, "Oh, I finally got [an African American first lady]. She's going to be doing what I think she should be doing." And there was all of this projection on her. [Teen pregnancy and AIDS] were things she was not engaged with before she was first lady. There was no reason to pick them as first lady. Are they important causes? Absolutely. But you can't take on every important cause. So, take on the ones you think you can actually have an impact on, that the country would appreciate . . . and that are somewhat aligned with your husband's agenda. So, Joining Forces, all about veterans. This is a country that won president's office while they were fighting three wars. So, it was a natural offshoot. Affordable Care Act, health, wellbeing, early intervention. All part of the healthcare conversation. So, that's out there. The engagement of young people in public life. Go back to the president's speech in Cairo, go back to how to engage Muslim youth . . . no different than her mentoring program here in D.C.
>
> Every bit of her agenda is intertwined in his and there's nothing that would give you an opportunity to take a pot-shot at her. If she had been a healthcare expert, she might have been more engaged in the Affordable Care Act. She was certainly engaged in talking about the need for preventative healthcare for mothers, for children, in ways that she has experienced herself and that she learned at the University of Chicago. So, her world was that, but advocating for a piece of legislation wasn't necessarily the same thing. Choose your battles kind of thing and do that piece well.

Going Personal: Conveying the President's Priorities at Home and Abroad

One of the three ways spouses shape the president's image is by making personal appeals to the American public on his behalf. As I mentioned before, proximity to the president is a unique asset first ladies such as Nancy Reagan and Hillary Clinton often wielded in private, but has also been used in public to vicariously communicate the president's concerns. When the president sends the first lady to an event or meeting on his behalf, he conveys a stronger message of personal interest than could be communicated through a vice president or secretary of state, despite the formal powers these other officers possess. It seems counterintuitive, but according to interview participants, first ladies often impart the priorities of the White House more effectively than the president himself. First of all, first ladies have less security than presidents and they travel with a smaller entourage. Disparities in the security details of presidents and first ladies are sometimes concerning to staff, such as a Reagan press aide who told me: "She [Nancy Reagan] had a bulletproof raincoat. I mean, the president is always in front of the Blue Goose, the podium that goes with him wherever he goes and it's bulletproof. She doesn't have that . . . and anybody who goes to see the president has to go through a magnetometer . . . the first lady doesn't have that kind of security."

But as a former chief of staff to a first lady put it, there are major public relations benefits attached to deploying the president's "number one person": "I think people really feel close to a first lady . . . maybe it's because you can actually touch them. I mean they have security but it's not quite as tight. You can shake their hand and they have enough time that they can smile at people and talk to them . . . that goes such a long way, that connect. I think it's all about how much time you can spend with people." A former director of advance for Laura Bush discussed the way in which different diplomatic responsibilities ascribed to the president and first lady during foreign trips can work to the administration's advantage:

> She was able to raise the profile of policies. So if [President and Mrs. Bush] were taking a trip together, a joint international trip, he always had to be at meetings . . . with his counterparts, the head of state or head of government. He didn't a lot of times get the opportunity to go out into the field and see the international policies [in effect]. Mrs. Bush and first ladies can do this . . . their schedule will break off from the president's schedule and they will go out and spotlight [the administration's policy on the ground]. They can highlight it in a way that shows what is actually going on. We got to see so many more people, hear their stories. The president didn't get to, but it is harder to move a president than it is a first lady, for security reasons, and the package that comes with the president is so big and

it is such a huge imprint. And so first ladies have an opportunity to be a little bit more mobile and flexible . . . they can do some of the public diplomacy work more easily I think than presidents.

I do remember on one of our trips that the president's advance team . . . said, "We want our trip to look like a first lady trip." It was harder . . . they waited, they planned the trip. They front-loaded his trip with . . . the bilateral meetings and things like that and then got him on into the field. And so it enabled him to actually get to see everything. It was in Guatemala. That is what Mrs. Bush got to experience all over the world.

Another senior staffer to Laura Bush in the second term confirmed the special appeal of first ladies overseas: "She was so well received. The president's spouse is probably the most highly regarded surrogate that you could send to a foreign country . . . it's just human nature. She couldn't sign memorandums of understanding or things like that . . . but she is there [to say] this really matters to the president. She could say that better than anybody." The Obama administration has also deployed the first lady strategically abroad, although they have closely guarded the aims of these trips, according to a journalist who covers Mrs. Obama. Following in the footsteps of the Bush administration, Mrs. Obama usually visits disenfranchised groups when she arrives in a host country and she is careful not to project the image of an official foreign envoy. The insider shared a couple of examples with me:

With her trips to South Africa and Botswana, the goal was somewhat personal; [Michelle Obama] had said she wanted to make a sort of pilgrimage there but the other reason was that the president hadn't spent as much time in Africa as the administration perhaps thought he should. Because both President Bush did with PEPFAR and so did the Clintons. So they wanted that presence and it looked good. With her trip to China, there wasn't nearly as much press access and the administration said it was because of the laws in China and the different media environment there. But really they had begun tightly controlling her appearances and press access to her at that point. And even though she did make some controversial policy speeches, with pointed terms about open access, she spent time with minority groups that were discriminated against in China. So it was painted as a goodwill tour and I think they were wary of sending a message that she was there to do diplomacy, but the trip came before president Obama's trip to China where some very serious things were discussed.

A staff member who traveled extensively with Rosalynn Carter abroad recounted how deeply Mrs. Carter was affected by a trip she made to Asia in 1978. He accentuated the personal message presidents communicate to the public when they send their spouses to distressed regions and the immense impact on foreign policy first ladies can have if they so choose:

> During the time we went to Thailand was the Pol Pot regime . . . there was a refugee crisis on the Thai border and the president didn't go but he wanted to send his wife to be his emissary and tell the world the United States cared about what was happening there. It was really a day of jarring contrasts. We saw masses of humanity. We were at one camp and . . . right after we left [Mrs. Carter] was told that the baby that she had held ten minutes before had died. And she was just completely wiped because of the experience. And then we flew from there to the Summer Palace of the King and Queen and sat in the backyard gardens for tea. You know, it was such a disconnect . . . a contrast. And she came back to the United States and she said to the president, "We have to do something about this crisis," and . . . the foreign aid package to Thailand for the refugee crisis was increased after that. She came back and really moved the needle . . . because it is so personal, it is so intimate . . . it's not the vice president and the secretary of state who are going to say, "Jimmy we have to do something about it! Jimmy we have to do something about it!" And so it is someone who carries the eyes and ears of the president in a very different way than other people do.

While it is not the focus of this book, it is fascinating to consider the possible policy implications of the intense personal interactions many first ladies share with impoverished populations. Due to security concerns and time constraints, presidents and other high-ranking officials are often protected from the calamitous situations over which they preside. There is a normative argument to be made for the increased mobilization of presidential spouses, talented political actors with celebrity status, few formal responsibilities, and the trust and attention of the president of the United States. In addition to personalizing international diplomacy, experts claim that spouses can fill gaps and balance deficiencies in the president's public image. Campaign speeches provide one stage for this improvement process to take place. In her 2012 Democratic National Convention (DNC) address, for example, Michelle Obama called attention to President Obama's nightly ritual of reading letters from struggling U.S. families, emotionally sharing, "That's the man I see in those quiet moments late at night, hunched over his desk, poring over the letters people have sent him . . . I see the concern in his eyes . . . and I hear the determination in his voice as he tells me, 'You won't believe what these folks are going through, Michelle . . . it's not right. We've got to keep working to fix this. We've got so much more to do.' "[6] A prominent journalist confirmed:

> If you looked at these last three first ladies, you would find instances where they're talking about how hard their husband is working, how committed he is to whatever it is, healthcare reform, the war on terrorism . . . so they are kind of reinforcers of the message, and also they're able to offer a little bit different perspective. They're able to not just speak on the policy, but give you the kind of personal dynamic. For example, "You don't know how late my husband stays up at night fighting the war on terrorism, trying to make healthcare affordable, trying to increase wages." Whatever the specific policy agenda is at the time.

The ability of first ladies to soften or humanize the president's image was an especially common declaration of former Obama administration staff and advisors, although a famous strategist suggested that the need for humanizing varies by president. About Laura Bush, he bluntly stated, "She was a real asset to Bush though. Because she was seen as smart and he was seen as dumb, and that helped. Because it was like 'Okay, he married a smart woman. He has smart people around.'" In her book, *Spoken From the Heart* Laura Bush admitted that the "cockiest" thing George W. Bush ever said was that he wanted to get Osama bin Laden "dead or alive."[7] The first lady reportedly quipped "You gonna get 'im Bushie?" in front of some staff after hearing the vulgar remark.[8] Regarding whether Michelle Obama fills a void in President Obama's personality, the same Democratic strategist suggested that what she brings to the table is a greater ability than the president has to convey emotion: "Well he's Mr. Smart, you know, he's just so very controlled. And she is so warm and human and impressible. She's an enormous asset."

Another celebrated Clinton strategist argued that Bill Clinton did not need the sort of emotional accompaniment that other presidents required from their wives, slyly commenting "Hillary Clinton had a competent husband so it was different than other administrations." Other communications advisors claimed that Mrs. Clinton was central to the Clinton campaign's efforts to dispel rumors about the candidate's infidelity. A senior Clinton campaign advisor referred to the couple's first joint interview in 1992 on *60 Minutes* with Steve Kroft in which Hillary Clinton famously asserted: "You know, I'm not sitting here like some little woman standing by my man like Tammy Wynette. I'm sitting here because I love him and I respect him and I honor what he's been through and what we've been through together. And you know, if that's not enough for people, then heck, don't vote for him."[9] "The fact that he had this brilliant, strong, independent woman [by his side] that said 'I'm not just anyone who'd stand by my man', that was enormous, the most important asset you can have. Because people would say, I think, sensibly, 'Well he can't be all bad, she likes him,'" the advisor argued. In fact, damage control was one of the main functions a Republican strategist suggested the spouses of candidates can serve: "If you can put a wife out there to show they're human, they're dads, they're husbands, it helps. That's more interesting to the voter. We've also seen the wife up on the podium standing by her man. If you can show that image of solidarity, show the wife supporting her husband, a lot of people will say 'Well I don't have to like the guy or what he did but if she can stand by him I can hold my nose and vote for him.'"

Finally, a former aide to Michelle Obama compared the current first lady's contributions to the president's public image to the dynamic between Hillary and Bill Clinton:

> [Michelle Obama] is popular because she tries hard to be a normal role model. She's not overtly political, she's very accomplished and very smart, but she's the converse of the president, she humanizes him and she is very arms-open to the public, where he is not. She's as non-confrontational as possible and has had to step away from her own interests while doing this. It's interesting to compare them to the Clintons because president Clinton had a very open and emotional demeanor; people didn't need Hillary to balance him out in that way because he provided it. President Obama is criticized all the time for being stoic and unemotional . . . it is off-putting to some people to always seem like the smartest person in the room, which Michelle Obama almost always is, but she can be human about it. The president doesn't do that as well and that's what she does for his public image.

Going Purple: Addressing Unfriendly or Unfamiliar Audiences

As a Clinton insider put it, first ladies also bring to the bully pulpit "a way of being able to depoliticize an issue," which no president or presidential surrogate can match. To be sure, the ability of spouses to remove partisan politics from a policy conversation is wrapped up in the public's conception of them as political outsiders or unofficial representatives of the administration. As we saw in Chapter 3, this understanding is evident in the distinct ways in which Americans evaluate first ladies and presidents. Spouses are also able to "stay above the fray" because they do not directly engage with journalists on controversial subjects, and they benefit from the freedom to pursue alternative forms of media coverage to the White House press corps. The Office of the First Lady works hard to preserve her positive reputation, which initially surprised me. I often wondered over the course of my research why such a popular surrogate was not overexposed when the president's approval ratings suffer. A political scientist I spoke with claimed he had the same thought during the botched rollout of the Healthcare.gov web site in fall 2013 as well as troubled budget negotiations with congress. "Where's Michelle? Why isn't he pushing her out there?" he exclaimed. "Because you can't stick the first lady with your crappy policy," a senior communications staffer to Michelle Obama answered during our interview. She elaborated:

> And I don't mean it's crappy policy. It may be good policy, but it's also controversial. She's not the cleanup batter. That's not the right role for them. She could do policy-related things where she's not expected to win, but she's expected to contribute. She can't be the closing argument. It's not useful to have the first lady lobby, which is what you have to do in order to get policy passed. I think Mrs. Obama has gone to the Hill once or twice for her nutrition stuff. But there's a whole army of lobbyists on both sides of that thing and to put the first lady on a lobby doesn't really suit the role. It doesn't really suit your staff either. You have one head of policy and maybe two or three people. The first lady's staff is very small, so you couldn't do that without the West Wing side of things and then it would be considered West Wing.

Naturally, since the death of the Health Security Act in 1994, first ladies and their staffs have avoided the image of policy maker and lobbyist. While they readily discuss policy in carefully crafted and practiced public remarks, in the rare instances in which first ladies are startled by controversial policy questions from journalists, they simply decline to answer:

> [The Obamas] have been trying to look for ways to effect change, but not through congress. Like they did on the campaign, they have sought funding from independent groups, through private foundations, and she's definitely lobbying but in different ways. She's not going to Capitol Hill and neither is he. It's private phone calls, conference calls and using her fame and influence that way. Press relations have also changed from more round tables to more pop culture appearances where the White House can control the narrative. She's in some situations where traditional press is there. In one instance she was in the Oval Office with some moms when the [Healthcare .gov] website wasn't working and it gave the press corps a chance to shout at her but she didn't even respond. They said "Why are you here?" and she said "I'm a mom." So you know, three words. They pick and choose their relations with the press and the first lady's press pool is very well trained. We would never shout at her.

According to a Carter communications advisor, what little tension does exist between East and West Wing staff is derived from the unwillingness of East Wing staff to compromise the first lady's public appeal in an attempt to mold the president's. "Who is most popular? Who can we count on not to mess up? You're trying to leverage that popularity to help the president . . . but you ideally want to keep first ladies above the fray. The East and West Wing are often at odds over that because her staff is personally loyal to her and any request to use her . . . in a potentially controversial way can dampen her popularity and they don't want to see her take the fall for that." A former presidential chief of staff stressed a similar point in his comparison of first ladies to other presidential surrogates: "First ladies, they target their appearances, they keep their powder dry and they do selective events. If you do that, it always keeps the appeal there, so I think that's another reason [that they're more popular]."

Event requests are exceedingly common in a campaign season, specifically during midterm elections. Laura Bush's former staff boasted her widespread appeal in 2004 and described the strategic decision of operatives to send Mrs. Bush to swing districts where the president would not have been greeted with open arms. "Mrs. Bush was definitely seen as more moderate than her husband. And really by virtue of staying silent on a lot of the issues that may have been more controversial. That may have allowed her to go into areas in the country that were more moderate . . .

that her voice may resonate a little easier than the president himself. She was very, very strong in that area," said a press aide. A senior staff member confirmed:

> During the midterm elections and during the 2004 reelect absolutely she was an incredibly important surrogate for the president. And a lot of people would tell you she helped tip the balance on what women thought of him when she gave her convention speech in New York in 2004. And really from that podium talked about how she watched him struggle, making the decision to go to war in Iraq. And so . . . she put a human face on what was then a very controversial war time presidency. During midterm elections in 2006, she was out there. She raised about $15 million, I mean she was deployed in so many of the moderate races where it was more difficult for the president to go because she was more popular. So . . . we worked with political affairs. We worked with the RNC. So yes, we worked very closely with the entities that had the full picture and the full map of what was happening politically and where she could be best deployed and she only wanted to go places where she could help.

Not only did Mrs. Bush's popularity soar in the second half of the administration at home, but also she remained very well-liked abroad when the president's decision to invade Iraq had squandered much of his approval overseas, as a press officer discussed with me.

> We really had a very strong reception wherever she went. We would go into places where she was literally clapped for on the streets all the time. I mean, I remember specifically being in Italy and thousands of people gathered outside the restaurant where she was eating . . . she walked out and the entire crowd erupted. I didn't always see that with President Bush. But he also has to take a stance on issues and policies that not everyone is going to like. I remember sitting in a meeting with Dan Bartlett, the president's communications director one day and I was telling him what we're doing. And he was like "Are you all *ever* on defense?" and most days no, we're not, we were always on offense, so it was always great stories we were able to tell him. Rarely was the first lady's office on defense in communications.

Although first ladies largely have the luxury of evading tough policy questions, when they do engage in policy discussions they tread lightly. For example, when traveling abroad, Mrs. Bush usually centered her comments on the human rights ramifications of foreign policy. Mrs. Bush's staff often brought state department personnel with them on trips to sensitive regions, such as Liz Cheney, deputy assistant secretary of state for near eastern affairs at the time, so they could "drill down" on policy issues the first lady was not comfortable discussing in detail. As a former staffer to Laura Bush reminded me, Mrs. Bush spoke about breast cancer in the Middle East "at a time when you couldn't even say the word breast there," and made very strong statements deploring Burma's ruling regime. In an unprecedented White House Briefing Room press conference by a first lady in 2008, Mrs. Bush urged Burma to accept foreign aid after Cyclone Nargis devastated the country's shores and called for the release of political prisoners. Here is an excerpt from a statement Laura Bush made about the Burmese refugee crisis in 2008:

> Burma's regime has ignored the entreaties of the international community. It has treated the United Nations Special Envoy with disregard. Through its actions, the regime has reaffirmed its disdain for the will and the well-being of the people of Burma. The military leaders carried out a sham constitutional referendum, extended Aung San Suu Kyi's house arrest, and continued to arrest political activists. The United States reiterates our long-standing call for the Burmese regime to engage in a genuine dialogue with all democratic and ethnic minority leaders, with the goal of making a credible transition to civilian, democratic government. We call on the regime to release Aung San Suu Kyi and all other political prisoners.[10]

"If you closed your eyes she did almost sound like Hillary Clinton . . . people were not recognizing again, that she was overseas becoming a very important voice. And by the way Hillary Clinton too . . . you know in many ways after she was dealt her big setback at home on healthcare, she became a much more important voice overseas," a journalist said as she described the strides modern first ladies have made abroad with human rights and women's rights. Laura Bush's staff claims that part of the reason she was able to make political statements without aggravating the U.S. public was because of the style in which she spoke. "To me, Hillary Clinton and Laura Bush had done the same amount for women. But Mrs. Bush is seen as traditional, I think partly because she is conservative. And because of her mannerism; she is reserved. And she is a quieter-type person. But she . . . has so much to say on topics that are significant. It's just she doesn't say it loudly—and I actually mean volume-wise."

One of the best explanations I received for the efficacy of women's rights campaigns led by first ladies belonged to a former senior advisor to Hillary Clinton, who noted changes in her rhetorical style after the health care reform debate in the early 1990s. People did not like Clinton's pointed remarks and "how she would come back with a sharp answer" if she were asked a question she did not like. But Mrs. Clinton took a much more nuanced rhetorical approach abroad when she advocated for microloans and women's economic freedom later in the administration. Referencing Hillary Clinton's historic trips to South Asia in March of 1995 and her speech titled "Women's Rights are Human Rights" at the September 1995 Beijing World Conference on Women, the advisor urged: "If you are in the art of persuasion, the worst way to persuade is to call them [your opponents] out or be critical. You want to be diplomatic. The *how* of this is part of one's effectiveness. She was masterful about this. She did it in a way that was very compelling and demonstrated that this has huge payoffs." "You point out what they're doing right," a policy advisor to Laura Bush said.

Barbara Bush was a master at the art of persuading or seducing a hostile crowd. Her staff reminded me of her 1990 commencement speech at Wellesley where Mrs. Gorbachev was her guest. Prior to the speech, a petition to retract Mrs. Bush's invitation was signed by thousands of students who thought her conservative ideals and lack of career experience were a poor representation of their own aspirations, sparking protests, and a campus-wide debate on feminism, according to a *New York Times* article.[11] Mrs. Bush complimented the crowd and made fun of herself, her staff recounted. Perhaps in the best lines of her speech, she joked, "Now I know your first choice today was Alice Walker, known for *The Color Purple*. Instead you got me, known for the color of my hair." And later, "Who knows? Somewhere out in this audience may even be someone who will follow in my footsteps and preside over the White House as the president's spouse. And I wish him well."[12] "The students loved it," a press aide recalled.

Going Positive: Pet Projects as Soft Frames
for Presidential Policy Items

According to former White House staff, professors, and journalists I consulted, the projects first ladies pursue must meet a variety of criteria. One of these criteria was mentioned briefly in an earlier section of this chapter: the personal interests and experiences specific to each first lady. In addition to Hillary Clinton and Laura Bush, who had successfully tackled health care and education reform, respectively, at the state level while being governors' wives, Michelle Obama accrued extensive knowledge of higher education as well as health care from years spent in a management capacity at the University of Chicago as Associate Dean of Student Services, and at University of Chicago Hospitals where she worked on community outreach.[13] Armed with a formidable professional background in the health care industry, Mrs. Obama could have surely embraced a more tangible role in the development of the Affordable Care Act. She opted for the peripheral role of spokesperson instead, wedding herself to Let's Move! an offshoot of the president's health care reform agenda partially funded through federal programs and the Affordable Care Act. Former White House staff claim this series of decisions can be attributed to certain criteria good pet project choices must meet. First, pet projects must be valence issues that enjoy relatively widespread public support and, second, pet projects must reinforce the administration's policy agenda. An academic expert on first ladies with whom I spoke summarized the centrality of these criteria:

> There are a couple of things that make these social projects effective. One, do they resonate with their husband's policy agenda? So if you look at Obama's policy agenda, he's pushing universal healthcare. Michelle is pushing healthy kids, nutrition, diet and exercise. Obama's pushing getting us out of Iraq, better benefits for Veterans. She's pushing military families. So her issues resonate and gel perfectly with her husband's issues. Secondly, they have to be sort of a velvet glove pulpit, rather than a bully pulpit. They have to have that necessary quotient of femininity to them. Michelle could not talk about better body armor [for our military], because that would be seen as a force, a masculine issue, because society is still hung up on such things. But, by talking about military families, and she wraps it all up by saying, "As a mother," so she's on safe ground with that. And perception is reality. So it has to be the necessary quotient of femininity, and it should also dovetail nicely with something the first lady did before her career.

Adhering a first lady's pet project to a presidential agenda item accomplishes a few things in the eyes of the White House. Pet projects can frame policies in a way that makes them appear less polarizing or more relevant to certain groups. Pet projects can also alter the culture surrounding a particular policy issue. As a former journalist and political strategist shared, Laura Bush's and Michelle Obama's literacy and childhood obesity initiatives have acted as soft frames for their husbands' more controversial domestic policy agenda items: No Child Left Behind and the Affordable Care Act. "Every coin has two sides, right? So . . . the notion that literacy is a way into or an echo of No Child Left Behind, for instance. Clearly, a linkage there. Health, obesity, with ACA, they're absolutely all tied together. It's like any political messaging, you know, you want your speeches, your interviews, your commercials, all of those, to reinforce one another . . . but it's a different framing of it. It's warmer, it's softer, it's less controversial."

One of the ways in which Laura Bush and Michelle Obama have been able to soften signature presidential agenda items is by focusing the attention of their projects on children who can also benefit from the administration's policies. "Who's against kids?" a Republican political strategist asked me. Laura Bush oriented her public remarks on education toward the expansion of opportunities for children in the U.S. to succeed academically, rather than the failing schools and ill-equipped teachers the No Child Left Behind Act sought to eradicate. Michelle Obama's Let's Move! speeches are similarly centered on giving parents and children access to more nutritious food and encouraging them to lead active lifestyles. She does not belabor the severe cost of health care due to our nation's obesity epidemic. "It's a great play if you take the long view and I'll tell you one thing," a Democratic strategist divulged about administration efforts to link the first lady's obesity project to the larger discussion of health care reform. "This president [Obama] takes a long view . . . frequently talks about 10, 20, 50 years down the line. We don't see the fiscal benefits of preventative care for 50 years but oh my gosh, they will one day. I'm quite sure that's part of what the administration is thinking."

First-term Clinton insiders acknowledged that when Mrs. Clinton took on the health care overhaul as chair of the task force, the issue was simply too controversial for any remote possibility of success. "Well with healthcare you are remaking a quarter of the economy," a senior advisor to Hillary Clinton told me. "It was a combination of being hit with a national policy undertaking . . . and there was a tremendous opposition effort. People showed up with guns at a rally, she was hanged in effigy in some places." Clinton herself admitted in retrospect of the Health Security Act failure in 1994 that the "process and the plan were flawed" and that through the process she "learned . . . the wisdom of taking small steps to get a big job done."[14]

However, contrary to the claims of commentators and journalists, Clinton did not abandon health care reform entirely after 1994. She simply refocused her attention on children's health care and smaller legislative packages, shifting her strategy from Capitol Hill appearances to school and hospital visits, where she communicated with audiences mainly comprising women and children. The same White House advisor confirmed that Clinton's focus on the State Children's Health Insurance Program (CHIP) was a purposeful change in communications strategy regarding Clinton's involvement in the health insurance reform debate: "There were news stories after 1993 about how she receded and moved out of the issue entirely. That's not true, but she did it differently. In 1994 Newt Gingrich became Speaker there was a Republican congress. She encouraged the president to work with the new Speaker at least to try to get something for the children . . . and that was CHIP. She made many speeches about that. They achieved pediatric labeling for drugs, among other things." The passage of CHIP in 1997 was no small accomplishment for Clinton, accounting for the largest increase in public funding for children's health care since President Johnson's creation of Medicaid in 1965.

Perhaps had Clinton dealt with a smaller chunk of health care reform or accepted an honorary chair of the president's taskforce, as other first ladies such as Rosalynn Carter have done in the past with causes like mental health advocacy, she would have been more instrumental in the administration's effort to garner public support for the Health Security Act. Historians who have studied first ladies reminded me that Hillary Clinton's takeover of the president's health care reform directive was not the first time a first lady adopted a controversial cause, but perhaps it was the first time such a cause was not carefully tailored in order to avoid public criticism: "Ladybird Johnson's advocation of beautification . . . and she hated the name beautification. She wanted to call it conservation, but in the 1960s, the country just wasn't ready for a woman to say . . . well . . . we weren't ready for conservation. But she was involved in serious things, like, while she's pushing beautification, it dovetails perfectly with LBJ, who's passing the wild and scenic rivers preservation legislation." Head Start, the original board of which Lady Bird Johnson presided over as honorary chair, was also "a heavy legislative lift," a former chief of staff told me.

Communications staff to Laura Bush and Michelle Obama learned from Clinton administration mistakes and made more educated decisions about which initiatives to bring to the first lady's desk, which to sidestep, and perhaps most importantly, how to tie those pet project initiatives to the president's policy agenda without ruffling the feathers Mrs. Clinton did in the early 1990s. "Mrs. Clinton's time in office was the precursor to everything we see about politics now," a communications strategist told me. "It cannot be ignored that the copresidency concept that they termed with President Clinton hurt those moving forward to some degree," said a senior staffer to Laura Bush. Again drawing a clear line between Laura Bush's successful lobby for No Child Left Behind and Hillary Clinton's unsuccessful attempt at health care reform, a former chief of staff emphasized the importance of careful planning and a soft touch while advocating for presidential policy at home and abroad: "One of the reporters that covered Mrs. Bush's briefing in January or February of 2002 . . . said what a contrast it was to Hillary Clinton's briefing on healthcare reform which was such a spectacle . . . she made a contrast to sort of the calm and no-nonsense approach that Laura Bush had, meaning that there was no furor . . . and part of that was again here's this librarian-teacher, she is expected to know about this. This is a safe issue, non-controversial for a first lady to be talking about education. Yet No Child Left Behind was a controversial piece of legislation." That article, published in the *New York Times*, compared Mrs. Clinton's entitled tone to Mrs. Bush's modest testimony from the perspective of a former schoolteacher.[15] The former chief of staff spoke with me at length about the way the administration was able to deploy Mrs. Bush successfully abroad.

> Her style is very non-confrontational, very inclusive . . . she's a listener. After 9/11 again . . . the lens through which foreign policy was conducted was completely changed. And where we had asked ourselves a question is "Why are we so hated around the world and what can we do to start changing the face of a new generation, of young people in the region of the world which seemed to have the greatest problem with us?" And President Bush launched a very important initiative called the Middle East Partnership Initiative that really was targeted a lot on women because he really believed, and so did Mrs. Bush, that women are the key to peace in the Middle East. And there was a whole range of programs under the Middle East Partnership Initiative that focused on education, that focused on political empowerment for women, for rising democracies, and focused on health diplomacy. Laura Bush could be a voice in all of those.
>
> We worked really closely with the state department to develop an opportunity for her to travel to some of the countries in the Middle East that had the highest incidences of breast cancer. And again why did we do that? One was a part of a health diplomacy initiative . . . AIDS was not a problem in the Middle East, cancer was. We put together a trip for her into Saudi Arabia which is a very difficult place as you can imagine to talk about this openly. But there were

opportunities there. So this was another way that she could be deployed . . . and reform policy perspective. [Departments and agencies within the U.S. government] came to Laura Bush and said "Will you help us advocate this?" So some of it comes from them, from agencies that have been charged by the president to succeed . . . So they're going to look at who are their best surrogates and assets? And hands down on these issues of global health, global education, women's rights, you couldn't have a better person and everybody in the agencies knew that. And she was wildly aggressive with her schedule. Anything that we presented her made sense if it fit with the initiative. If it felt authentic to her then she would do it, absolutely would do it.

Pet projects allow first ladies to highlight strides the administration is making in a particular domestic or foreign policy area without talking explicitly about policy. As a former aide to Michelle Obama provided:

The East Wing and the West Wing are actually very independent. But the East Wing is a solid strategic entity on its own. Of course Michelle Obama chooses valance issues and of course they're issues she's passionate about, but choosing them and planning events is an intricate process. They have to be events that are high profile, they must align well with policy issues the first lady is interested in, and finally they have to align with the president's agenda, and how much they help the president is very important. Different overseas trips are about different things. The Ireland trip we did was about his family roots so we did cultural things—Riverdance—we crafted the trip around that. But really the goal is primarily diplomacy when the first lady travels internationally. Michelle Obama has acted as the softer face to the White House. The "face" before and after that diplomacy. Domestic events, so events with high school kids for example, the event we did at Howard, people need to see what the administration is doing and she always uses subliminal messaging and the administration's talking points, so the goals are very interconnected. Let's Move! was connected with the president's agenda . . . it's possible about Joining Forces too.

Some administration officials and Democratic strategists suggest that Joining Forces redefined the culture surrounding veterans returning home from unpopular wars. A Clinton administration communications strategist with close ties to the Obama administration praised

Mrs. Obama's work with Joining Forces: "She's tried to move the culture. And look, it has an effect . . . no matter how you feel about the war, in Iraq or Afghanistan . . . soldiers can rejoin their families and the community notices and cares. If you ever go to a Washington Nationals game, every single game in a full block of seats they give priority to military families. And in every single game, the entire audience stands and cheers for those guys . . . that never happened in the '70s, when soldiers came back from Vietnam, believe me. I mean, that's how I look at Michelle Obama. It's really, really important for the anti-war Democratic President to recognize these families and the troops."

Chapter 6 tests the bold assertions of strategists who profess the powerful impact of first ladies on public attitudes. A series of randomized survey experiments is used to isolate the effect of reading or watching a speech made by a presidential spouse on evaluations of the president and certain policies.

CHAPTER 6

Does It Work?

In Chapter 4, I discussed the inherent difficulty of research designs that conceive of the public activity of first ladies as the dependent variable. Studies preoccupied with the identification of forces that influence the extent to which presidential spouses go public, such as fluctuating approval ratings of the president and his spouse, changes in the political media environment, or communications skills or assets unique to the president's spouse, are burdened with the complicated task of parsing these deeply intertwined factors, among others. There are also potential pitfalls associated with examining the first lady's public appearances as independent variables.

Scholars attempting to measure the impact of public appearances made by the president or his surrogates on approval ratings point to limitations in the abilities of political actors to lead public opinion.[1] A large part of this challenge can be attributed to the complexity of approval ratings and the ongoing debate among experts concerning the factors that affect approval. For example, presidents may be able to improve public opinion of certain policies if they are already popular or have the support of elites. However, this can only occur under specific circumstances such as a favorable economic climate or in the absence of political scandal or war.[2]

Yet, most of these opinion studies use aggregated polling data, not randomized experiments, to measure the president's effect on public evaluations of particular policies. A researcher might ask, for example: To what degree does President Obama's health care speech persuade the public to support his health care plan? In *On Deaf Ears*, Edwards compares

presidential approval before and after presidents have made major televised addresses since 1981, paying special attention to presidents who
were considered to be stellar communicators such as Ronald Reagan and
Bill Clinton. He concludes that presidents vastly overestimate their ability to sway public opinion on an issue, and that on average only 40 to
60 percent of the public can recall something about the speeches presidents make after they air.[3]

There are a few problems with this general approach to causal questions,
what Gerber and Green describe as the exercise of drawing inferences
from intuitions, anecdotes, or correlations.[4] First, studies like Edwards's
do not account for the possibility that the messenger matters. Although
Edwards compares different presidents, he does not consider the different effect a president may have on public opinion compared to that of
another surrogate, such as the president's spouse. He also neglects to assess
the effect of the message itself. Herein lies the problem of an imprecise
treatment; we do not know whether the message or the messenger is doing
the work.

Second, correlations can be a problematic guide to causality because
they may arise (or may not arise in the case of Edwards) for reasons that
have nothing to do with the causal process in question.[5] For example,
the way in which a random sample of survey respondents evaluated a
presidential policy item, even one day after the address was televised,
could be caused by extraneous factors to the president's speech. We
cannot accurately ascertain in studies like Edwards's that respondents
watched the speech (i.e., received the treatment), nor can we account for
the uncontrolled setting in which the study was conducted. Certain events
may have interacted with or counteracted the experience of watching the
president's address, for example, the commentary of television pundits
or newspaper coverage of the address (i.e., competing treatments).

While it is perhaps unlikely that a "first lady effect" will be detected
through the analysis of a large aggregated data set, randomized survey
experiments offer a vehicle for dealing with observed and unobserved
confounders, the lurking variables discussed before. In addition to the
hypothesis that public appearances of presidential spouses increase support for the president, I want to test the hypothesis that public appearances
increase support for certain presidential policy items. Again, experiments
offer researchers an opportunity to improve the quality of causal inferences
while avoiding reliance on assumptions made by multivariate regression, which addresses spuriousness by introducing control variables.
The randomization process allows me to isolate the impact of the first
lady while holding potentially confounding factors constant. Because

random assignment of treatment assures that, in expectation, the treatment and control groups will have identical levels of all pretreatment covariates, we can be confident that any observed differences in response between the two groups are due to the treatment. Some confounders (i.e., group attributes) that may have a strong influence on individuals' assessments of presidential policy include party affiliation, educational attainment, and gender. Scholars who have used experiments to assess the impact of candidate gender have likewise noted that observational studies are ill suited for this task because gender interacts with so many other forces in the political environment, such as the candidate's party affiliation, ideology, and past experience.[6]

In addition, blind survey experiments allow researchers to assess subconscious effects or prejudice held by respondents in a way that cannot be achieved by asking direct questions about female candidates or the first lady because of social desirability bias. An example of a subconscious effect might be the "humanizing" effect of the first lady often mentioned by interview participants and cited by journalists.[7] Survey respondents may not be aware of these psychological processes and their potential impact on political views, but a lack of awareness does not deny the existence of a cause. Previous experimental work on gender stereotyping actually shows that sex stereotypes benefit female politicians in some issue areas. For example, a series of experiments conducted by Kim Kahn demonstrated that subjects who read news coverage of female candidates found their candidates to be more honest, more compassionate, and better equipped to deal with health care issues than subjects who read news coverage about male candidates.[8] Finally, compliance is more probable in a survey experiment than it is in the aforementioned observational studies or even in field experiments. Even if there are some individuals in the treatment group who did not receive the treatment (e.g., respondents who click through survey questions without paying very much attention), no one in the control group can possibly receive the treatment by accident. Therefore, any observed difference in responses between the treatment and control units is likely an *underestimate* of the treatment effect.

Experimental Design

In one version of the experiment I conducted to inform the research in this book, I showed 2,000 respondents brief excerpts (five sentences or less) from presidential and first lady speech transcripts concerning policies frequently discussed by both principals during the Clinton, Bush, and Obama administrations and manipulated whether the speech was attributed to the president or the first lady. After answering a series of demographic questions, respondents were randomly routed to one of the three administrations, at which point they either saw a speech attributed to the first lady, a speech attributed to the president, or saw no speech and were routed directly to the dependent variable questions. Among these standard demographic questions were questions about partisanship. I used block random assignment to partition respondents into subgroups based on their party identification, and complete random assignment then occurred within these blocks. There are a few reasons that motivate the use of blocks. First, if I relied on complete random assignment, there is a greater chance that unequal number of Democrats and Republicans would be assigned to the treatment groups. Second, block randomizing can help reduce sampling variability because it ensures that respondents in each block have similar potential outcomes.[9] Finally, blocking promises that certain subgroups (in my case, Democrats and Republicans) are available to analyze separately, guaranteeing that a specific proportion of Democrats and Republicans will be assigned to the treatment.[10] Because partisanship strongly predicts attitudes toward the president, as we observed in Chapter 3, I wanted to compare the average treatment effect of the first lady among Democrats to the average treatment effect of the first lady among Republicans. For subgroup sizes, see Table A.5 in the Appendix.

Also randomly assigned were the topics of speeches. If a respondent received a speech made in the Clinton administration, it was either about health care reform or about the economy; if a respondent received a speech made during the Bush administration, it was either about education reform or about foreign policy; and if a respondent received a speech from the Obama administration, it was either about health care reform or about veterans. I chose speeches on a variety of topics that were discussed frequently by both the first lady and president in a particular administration (i.e., signature agenda items) and made sure that supposedly "soft" (i.e., health care and education) and "hard" (i.e., foreign policy and economy) issue areas were represented in each administration. I then asked respondents a series of evaluative questions about the president, how they thought he was handling (or handled) certain issues, and their support for specific policies. Dependent variables varied slightly for each administration, so if respondents were routed into the Clinton control or treatment condition, they were only asked questions about President Clinton and policies debated during his administration. Here is an example of a speech excerpt to which a respondent may have been routed:

Below is part of a speech recently made by [President Barack Obama/ First Lady Michelle Obama] regarding the Affordable Care Act. After reading it, you will be asked a series of questions about your political views.

And thankfully, because we fought for health reform, today our parents and grandparents on Medicare are paying hundreds less for their prescription drugs; our young people can stay on our parent's insurance until they're 26 years old. Insurance companies now have to cover basic preventive care—things like contraception, cancer screenings—with no out-of-pocket cost. They won't be able to discriminate against you because you have a preexisting condition like diabetes or asthma. And if you get a serious illness—let's say breast cancer—and you need expensive treatment, they can no longer tell you, sorry, you've hit your lifetime limit and we're not covering a penny more—no more. That is illegal because of health reform.

The key dependent variable of interest in this case was support for the Affordable Care Act. The question was worded in this way (adopted from the 2012 ANES): "Do you generally approve or disapprove of the 2010 Affordable Care Act, signed into law by President Obama, that restructured the U.S. health care system? [Approve/Disapprove/Neither]." I was particularly interested in the possibility that some respondents might be more supportive of a policy if they thought the first lady made the speech than respondents who thought the president made the speech. I also expected this support to strengthen in certain issue areas but not in others, for example, on the compassion issues mentioned earlier such as health care and education; issues first ladies are expected to discuss more frequently; and women are often deemed more credible. To be more specific, I expected to see a positive boost in support for the Affordable Care Act among respondents who received the Michelle Obama Affordable Care Act speech, relative to those who received the Barack Obama speech, and I expected to see a positive effect on support for No Child Left Behind among respondents who received a Laura Bush speech on No Child Left Behind, relative to respondents who received the George W. Bush speech on No Child Left Behind, for example. Although some respondents were also routed into a Clinton condition and received a speech on the Health Security Act of 1993, attributed either to Hillary Clinton or to Bill Clinton, I did not expect to see a strong positive Hillary Clinton effect here. Unlike Mrs. Bush and Mrs. Obama, Mrs. Clinton's subsequent career as a senator, presidential candidate, and secretary of state has probably rendered nonpartisan evaluations of her rare, or at least, rendered them indistinguishable from evaluations of Bill Clinton. I also did not expect first lady speeches to have a strong impact on opinions of "harder" issues such as foreign policy or the economy, although as I discussed in Chapters 4 and 5, the pet projects adopted by Mrs. Bush and Mrs. Obama were often intended to frame public opinion of serious foreign policy objectives.

In another version of the experiment, I showed 1,954 respondents brief video clips (45 seconds or less) of convention speeches made by presidents and first ladies in the last three administrations and manipulated whether the respondent was assigned a video of the first lady or a video of the president (Bill and Hillary Clinton's DNC speeches in 1996, George and Laura Bush's RNC speeches in 2004, and Barack and Michelle Obama's DNC speeches in 2012). Like the speech excerpt experiment, the video experiment showed clips of the president or first lady speaking about the same topics and respondents were randomly assigned the topic they received or routed directly to the dependent variable questions. In the Clinton administration, speeches either pertained to health care reform or education; in the Bush administration, the topics included the War on Terror or education; and in the Obama administration, the topics included health care or the economy. Other than the obvious differences in medium and content, the speech and video versions of the experimental design were alike, including in my use of randomized block assignment.

The importance of administering both a speech and video version of the experiment can be explained in terms of the trade-off between internal and external validity. The speech version of the experiment scores well on internal validity; it optimizes the investigator's ability to achieve confidence that changes in the dependent variable truly resulted from manipulation of the independent variable.[11] In other words, precision is high. Because presidential and first lady speech excerpts are identical (save for the speaker's name), we can be confident that any differences in respondent support for presidential policy items between the treatment and control groups are attributable to the speaker alone. Although I pulled excerpts from real remarks delivered by presidents and first ladies, the speech version of the experiment is low on external validity; it lacks realism. People do not often read transcripts of speeches made by presidents and first ladies—they usually watch them online or on television. The visual experience of watching a speech made by a first lady versus that by a president is also an important distinction. The content and rhetorical style of convention speeches made by first ladies and presidents differ, as well as the body language and appearance of the speakers. Yet, what the video version of the experiment gains from external validity it lacks in internal validity. Although the videos undoubtedly provide the respondent a more representative or generalizable experience, mimicking a real-world situation, generalizability can only occur to the extent that extraneous or confounding hypotheses can be eliminated.[12] Unlike the speech excerpt experiment, there are many ways in which the various treatment conditions differ, besides the identity of the speaker. *If* we observe differences in responses between treatment and control groups, we can still be confident that it was due to receipt of the treatment, but isolating which particular facet of the treatment is responsible for the effect is more challenging in this setting.

It is imperative to remember that all causal inference involves assumptions, even experiments. The fundamental problem of causal inference is that we cannot observe the expected value of Y_{1i} and Y_{0i} for a single unit. Because a single unit can never receive both the treatment and the control, we are always attempting to compare something we observe with something we do not. Thus, if there are baseline differences in the treatment and control groups, even experiments require researchers to make some assumptions, namely, that there is only one form of treatment and control, and units are independent.[13]

To recruit subjects for both experiments, I posted an online survey using Amazon's Mechanical Turk. Studies that compare the internal and external validity of experiments conducted using Mechanical Turk have found that samples of subjects drawn from the site are more representative of the U.S. population than convenience samples drawn in person.[14] Tables A.5 and A.6 in the Appendix display summary demographics of both samples attained, as well as demographic comparisons of the treated and control groups for each condition to convey balance. We can generally see from the balance tables that randomization worked. Key demographic indicators appear to be similar across treatment and control groups.[15] This assures us, among other things, that we are comparing apples to apples; in other words, that respondents assigned to a presidential speech or video are comparable to respondents assigned to a first lady speech or video, and are also comparable to those respondents who received no speech or video at all, on average.[16]

Results

Figures 6.1–6.3 illustrate the impact of receiving a first lady treatment in the form of a speech excerpt, relative to receiving no treatment at all. These graphics help us assess whether respondents who read a first lady

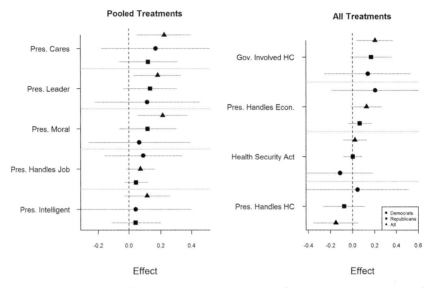

Figure 6.1   Effect of Hillary Clinton Speech (Relative to No Speech)

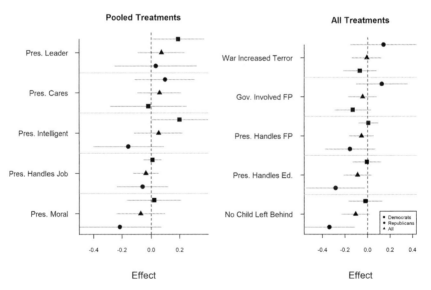

Figure 6.2   Effect of Laura Bush Speech (Relative to No Speech)

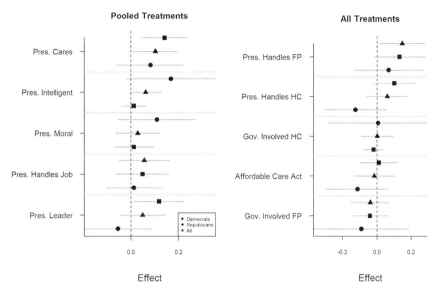

Figure 6.3   Effect of Michelle Obama Speech (Relative to No Speech)

speech before answering a series of questions about their political views evaluated the president differently than those respondents who were routed directly to questions about their political views without first receiving a treatment. I hypothesized in Chapter 3 that presidential spouses have a positive effect on public opinion of certain presidential policy items such as education and health care (i.e., "women's issues" or "soft" issues in the literature). I did not expect to find a corresponding positive effect in "hard" issue areas such as foreign policy or the economy. Although Laura Bush and Michelle Obama championed projects that strategists suggest were intended to soften the hard image of the wartime presidents and their foreign policy objectives, we also saw in Chapter 3 that Americans typically expect first ladies to go public on education, health care, and issues like fair pay, but not on foreign policy or the economy, issues they more often attribute to presidents. I also hypothesized that spouses have a positive effect on public opinion of the president himself. This expectation was sustained among interview participants who recounted the unique ability of spouses to sway public perceptions of what kind of person the president is. The range of dependent variables displayed in these graphs is relevant to both sets of hypotheses.

Overall, the coefficients on Hillary Clinton are weak and positive, a few of which are statistically distinguishable from zero at the 95 percent confidence level. These include the effect of receiving either a Hillary Clinton speech treatment on whether respondents agreed with the statements "Bill Clinton cares about people like me," "Bill Clinton is a strong leader," and "Bill Clinton is moral." The effect of receiving a health care speech attributed to Hillary Clinton on whether respondents agreed with the statement "the government in Washington should help people get doctors and health care at a low cost" was also significant. The dependent variables are coded dichotomously, so, for example, a positive effect of 0.2 can be read as a 20 percentage point increase in agreement with the statement. The results for the video experiment (Figures A.1–A.3 in the Appendix) are not as robust, although we do see fairly strong results among Democrats who were more supportive of the Health Security Act after watching a clip of Mrs. Clinton discussing health care during her 1996 convention speech, as well as Democrats who were more supportive of the way in which Bill Clinton handled health care after watching the same portion of Mrs. Clinton's convention speech. It is important to keep in mind that although some of the confidence intervals shown in Figures 6.1–6.3 and A.1–A.3 barely overlap zero, at a lower threshold for statistical significance, such as the 90 percent confidence level used by many researchers, many of these results would easily stand out.

Figures 6.2 and A.2 reflect some of the same themes depicted in Figures 6.1 and A.1 (Hillary Clinton). Only a few of the Laura Bush speeches and video effects are statistically distinguishable from zero. Interestingly, both Mrs. Clinton and Mrs. Bush appear to have persuaded members of the president's opposing party more effectively than their own base when some of the president's personal qualities are under question. In Hillary Clinton's case, Republicans who received Hillary's speech about health care or education agreed more strongly with the statement that Bill Clinton "is moral" than respondents who received no speech, and Democrats who received either an education or a foreign policy speech by Mrs. Bush more strongly agreed with the statements "George Bush is a strong leader" and "George Bush is intelligent" than those who received no speech. Democrats who watched Laura Bush's War on Terror video were also significantly more supportive of U.S. interventions in foreign conflicts than those who saw no video. However, Democrats who watched convention clips of Laura Bush *disagreed* strongly with the statement "George Bush is a strong leader" and disapproved of the way in which George Bush handled his job as president compared to Democrats who saw no video. These divergent results are perhaps suggestive of the disparate content of speeches and videos. While speech excerpts and video clips pertained to the same policy topics, they appear to have elicited very different reactions from similar groups.

It does seem, however, that when the content of the speech or video most closely matches the dependent variable of interest, the responses are the strongest in the directions we expect. Prompts that directly pertain to a policy area have stronger effects than prompts on slightly more nebulous topics. Moreover, prompts that address an issue closely associated with a presidency appear to have strong effects. This may be why, for example, strong positive reactions among Democrats who watched Hillary Clinton's health care videos are evident in items about whether the government should be involved in the provision of health care at a lower cost and in the Health Security Act item, but not in items related to education, a policy area that was often discussed by the Clintons but did not have a prominent place on the administration's policy agenda.

Written speech and video results for Michelle Obama (Figures 6.3 and A.3) appear to leave intact the prospect that first ladies can effectively rally the president's base on specific policy issues and convince his enemies that he is a decent person and leader, at least compared to groups who received no such appeal from the first lady. Looking more closely, we can see that similarly to Hillary Clinton, reading a speech excerpt attributed to Michelle Obama on either health care reform or veterans prompted significant positive responses among all groups, who agreed with the statements that the president "cares about people like me." A strong effect among Democrats is also evident on the "strong leader" coefficient in the speech condition for Michelle Obama as well as the "is intelligent" coefficient among Republicans. None of the Michelle Obama video treatments yielded significant positive results among Republicans, perhaps somewhat diluting the popular notion that Hillary Clinton is the most polarizing of the last three first ladies. However, Michelle Obama video treatments did draw strong support from Democrats in some cases, who rated the president's economic performance and government involvement in health care reform significantly higher than those who did not receive a video. Partisans of all groups were also significantly more supportive of the way in which President Obama handled foreign affairs after reading a speech on veterans by Michelle Obama, which reinforces the theory that pet projects can be effectively used by first ladies to boost public opinion of related presidential policies. Indeed, Mrs. Obama's focus on military families and Laura Bush's emphasis on Afghan women in international affairs speeches may have been well-calculated presidential messaging tactics.

The next set of tests holds the same written speech and video treatments to a much tougher standard: the effects of written speeches and videos attributed to first ladies are compared to the effects of written speeches and videos attributed to the president of the United States (rather than to the control condition). There are perhaps two ways to digest the results displayed in Figures 6.4–6.6 and Figures A.4–A.6 in the Appendix. On one hand, the results appear inconclusive, evidenced by the crowding of coefficients around the line indicating an effect size of zero; evidence is scarce in most issue areas that the first lady's effect on public opinion is markedly smaller or larger than the effect of the president. On the other hand, the nearly indistinguishable nature of effect sizes belonging to the first lady and president is quite remarkable. In the video experiment, in particular, it is somewhat impressive that televised appeals made by first ladies and presidents motivate similar evaluations of presidents and their policy agendas. While we should be careful not to "embrace the null hypothesis" of no difference in effect, given that survey experiments are stacked in favor of such null results, these results do reaffirm to some extent the status of spouses as serious political players and debunk myths espoused by some historians and journalists that Americans are uncomfortable with presidential spouses who discuss policy in public. In light of these results, the strategic deployment of spouses on the campaign trail and during the administration makes sense, especially when the goal is to reinforce the president's message or redouble

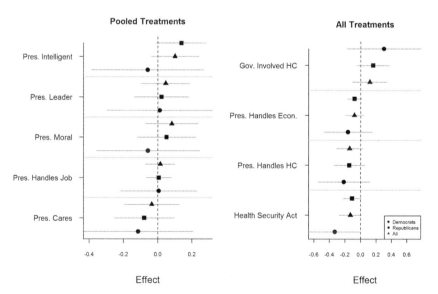

Figure 6.4   Effect of Hillary Clinton Speech (Relative to Bill Clinton Speech)

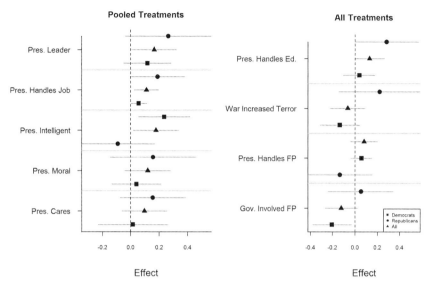

Figure 6.5   Effect of Laura Bush Speech (Relative to George Bush Speech)

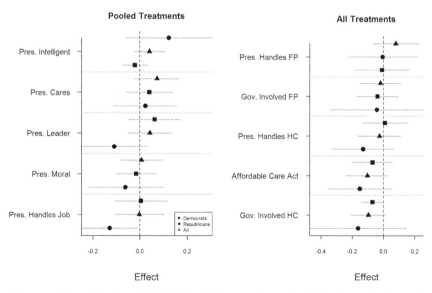

Figure 6.6   Effect of Michelle Obama Speech (Relative to Barack Obama Speech)

his efforts to meet public demands for a visible and responsive White House. Let us take a closer look at the few cases where first ladies were actually more influential than their presidential counterparts.

In Figure 6.4 we can see that Hillary Clinton has a substantially larger effect than Bill Clinton on the extent to which respondents agree with the statement "Bill Clinton is intelligent," but not among Republicans, perhaps not a surprising finding. However, the same figure reveals that reading a speech attributed to Hillary Clinton elicited less support for the way in which the president handled the economy and health care than reading the same speech by Bill Clinton; respondents claimed Bill Clinton did a *worse* job on the economy and health care after reading a Hillary Clinton speech on either issue. The results for Laura Bush are more potent. All partisans assigned to a Laura Bush speech were significantly more supportive of the notions that George Bush "is a strong leader," "is intelligent," and answered that he "handled his job as president" significantly more favorably than partisans who read the same speech by George Bush. It also appears from the results that partisans who received a written speech on education attributed to Laura Bush were much more supportive of No Child Left Behind and the way in which the president handled education, in some cases accounting for a 20 to 40 percentage point bump in support (Figure 6.5). Notwithstanding the relatively uniform education results, partisan responses to foreign policy appeals made by Mrs. Bush varied substantially. Once more, we see that compared to Democrats who received a written foreign policy speech attributed to President Bush or a foreign policy video of President Bush, Democrats who received a written or televised Laura Bush foreign policy treatment often rated the president's foreign affairs performance more favorably and the notion that President Bush's foreign policy increased terror abroad more negatively. Democrats' positive evaluations of the president's performance in response to the Laura Bush conditions often trumped those of Republicans; Democrats in the Laura Bush written speech condition even claimed that terrorism decreased as a result of President Bush's efforts. To review, the text provided in the written foreign policy prompt attributed to Laura Bush was excerpted from a speech by Mrs. Bush that connected the War on Terror to the well-being of Afghan women, a prevailing argument made by administration officials in 2003 and 2004. It is possible that these speeches were well received among Democrats who thought that Mrs. Bush delivered it because it made the war a women's issue, or at least a human rights issue, as opposed to one of terrorism.

A useful extension of the foreign policy speech effect observed in the Laura Bush condition is the effect of receiving a foreign policy speech attributed to Michelle Obama, the text of which in this case discussed the importance of assisting veterans when they return home from Iraq and Afghanistan, a strategic approach designed to frame President Obama's campaign promise to withdraw troops from the Middle East. Like Laura Bush's Afghan women's initiatives, aimed to publicize the humanitarian incentives for the U.S. War in Afghanistan, Joining Forces, a project shared by Michelle Obama and Jill Biden, can be viewed as a soft frame for foreign policy decisions made early in the Obama administration. As Figure 6.6 illustrates, Michelle Obama's speech positively but weakly affected respondent evaluations of the president's handling of foreign policy compared to the president's speech. In fact, few tests provide evidence that Michelle Obama was more effective than her husband in any case. Republican respondents who received a Michelle Obama speech treatment disagreed with the statement Barack Obama "is a strong leader" and more negatively evaluated his handling of the presidency compared to those who received a speech by President Obama, and all partisans who watched a video clip of Michelle Obama speaking about the economy at the 2012 DNC were significantly less supportive of the way in which the president handled economic issues than those who watched a clip of the president's DNC speech on the economy (Figure A.6).[17]

Another set of results that should be inspected briefly includes the effects of first lady written speech and video treatments on respondent evaluations compared to the effects of presidential written speech and video treatments on respondent evaluations, among women. Although I did not have a strong theoretical hunch about the way in which respondent gender might condition the effect of reading or watching a speech made by a spouse versus that by a president, instead focusing on the strong role of respondent partisanship, I acknowledged the possibility that women might be more receptive of certain messages conveyed by female surrogates, such as issues related to women's health or children. Many interview participants attributed the public relations prowess of the first lady to her innate ability to communicate the president's message to women and families, perhaps even more effectively than male surrogates or the president himself. For this reason, strategists encourage first ladies to adopt pet projects that contain "the appropriate quotient of femininity," as one expert explained, and that can be seamlessly integrated into the president's policy agenda. Examples include Hillary Clinton's advocacy of the State Children's Health Insurance program late in her husband's second term and Michelle Obama's town hall speeches on the ways in which the Affordable Care Act helps women and young adults.

However, like the results uncovered before, effect sizes of first lady treatments among women are small and mixed, hardly distinguishable from the effects of presidential treatments among women in many cases. On some items though, first ladies do appear to be more convincing among women than among their presidential counterparts (Figures A.7–A.12). Nearing statistical significance are the effects of a Hillary Clinton speech treatment on the statements Bill Clinton "is intelligent" and "is moral," and the effect of a Michelle Obama speech treatments on the statements Barack Obama "is a strong leader" and "is intelligent." Women who received a Laura Bush speech treatment were significantly more approving of the way in which George W. Bush "handled his job as president" than women who read the same speech by George W. Bush. In Figure A.12 we can also see that the video clip of Michelle Obama discussing health care reform was more effective among women than the clip of the president discussing health care reform among women, despite its poor reception amid partisans.

To be thorough, I also examined the effects of the first lady treatments among female respondents compared to those among male respondents. On some of the same character measures such as intelligence, leadership, and morality and in the issue areas where spouses outperform their presidential counterparts among women, first ladies appear to influence women significantly more effectively than they influence men. I conducted difference-in-differences tests comparing the treatment effects of first ladies among women to those among men in order to verify this. For example, a reasonable question might be whether the significant positive effect portrayed in Figure A.9 of reading Michelle Obama's speech on either health care or veterans on whether women think Barack Obama "is a strong leader" (an effect size of 13.47 percent, compared to women who read the same speeches attributed to the president) is a product of respondent gender, or whether the same effect exists among men. Interestingly, the same effect does not exist among men, and the difference between message impact among men ($\beta = -0.03$) and among women ($\beta = 0.14$) is significant at the 95 percent confidence level. Other first lady treatments that appeared to be significantly more effective among women than among men included the effect of Laura Bush's written speeches on how George Bush handled his job as president, whether the War in Afghanistan increased terror, and No Child Left Behind. The video of Michelle Obama's health care remarks at the DNC was also more effective among women than among men, who were more supportive of government involvement in health care. Women who received either of Hillary Clinton's written speeches claimed Bill Clinton was more intelligent than men claimed, and women who received either of Hillary Clinton video clips claimed Bill Clinton was more moral than men claimed.

Overall, we may conclude that the first lady can have a significant positive impact on public opinion of the president and his performance in certain issue areas—at times even surpassing the impact of the president himself—but that these effects only appear in some situations and before certain audiences. There is evidence that some messages transmitted by first ladies are in fact more effective among audiences of women than among audiences of men. Moreover, these opportunities appear to be very different for each first lady, making it difficult for experimental research of this kind to inform a general playbook or overarching communications strategy for spouses. The potential, however, is certainly within reach. The apparent ability of spouses in the last three administrations to compete squarely with presidents on the national playing field of strategic political communications is no small feat.

Evidence from a follow-up survey experiment I conducted shows that the public appeals of spouses regarding the president's agenda are also at least as effective as the public appeals of *vice presidents*. Because measuring the first lady's ability to sway Americans' opinions of the president and his policy agenda against the president's ability to sway the public on his own leadership qualities and policy agenda is indeed a very tough test, there is reason to believe the vice president may make for a more apt comparison. Using the same experimental design comparing the effect of a written speech attributed to our most recent three first ladies to that of the same written speech attributed to our most recent three presidents, I compared the effect of a written speech attributed to Hillary Clinton, Laura Bush, or Michelle Obama to that of the same written speech attributed to Al Gore, Dick Cheney, or Joe Biden among 2,215 survey respondents hired through Amazon's Mechanical Turk service. Again, the written speech displayed to respondents who were routed into the Clinton administration either pertained to the economy or to health care, the speech displayed to respondents who were routed into the Bush administration either pertained to education or to foreign policy, and the speech displayed to respondents routed into the Obama administration either pertained to health care or to veterans. To refresh our memory, let us look again at an example of a speech excerpt to which a respondent may have been routed:

Below is part of a speech made by [former Vice President Dick
Cheney/former First Lady Laura Bush] regarding the War on Terror.
After reading it, you will be asked a series of questions about your
political views.

   Afghan women know, through hard experience, what the rest of
the world is discovering: The brutal oppression of women is a central goal of the terrorists. Long before the current war began, the
Taliban and its terrorist allies were making the lives of children and
women in Afghanistan miserable. Seventy percent of the Afghan
people are malnourished. One in every four children won't live past
the age of five because health care is not available. Because of our
recent military gains in much of Afghanistan, women are no longer
imprisoned in their homes. They can listen to music and teach their
daughters without fear of punishment. Yet the terrorists who helped
rule that country now plot and plan in many countries. And they
must be stopped. The fight against terrorism is also a fight for the
rights and dignity of women.

One of the dependent variables of interest in this case was perception of
the war in Afghanistan, which was worded in this way (adopted from
the 2012 ANES): "As a result of the United States' war in Afghanistan, do you think the threat of terrorism against the United States has
increased, decreased, or stayed about the same? [Increased/Decreased/
Stayed about the same]" Just the same as the speech experiment that
compared presidents to first ladies, we were interested in whether a simple
name switch (the perception that Laura Bush made the speech rather
than Dick Cheney) produced more positive evaluations of George Bush's
foreign policy initiatives. The results for all of the tests that compare the
effectiveness of policy appeals in speeches attributed to first ladies to
those made in speeches attributed to vice presidents are displayed in
Figures A.13–A.15. Regarding the question about the war in Afghanistan
already mentioned, we can see in Figure A.14 that Republicans who
thought the speech was made by Laura Bush were more likely to report
that the threat of terrorism had *decreased* because of the war compared
to those Republicans who thought Dick Cheney made the speech (an
effect size of about $\beta=-0.5$ on a three-point scale), but that Democrats
who received the Laura Bush treatment largely reported terrorism has
increased compared to Democrats who received the Dick Cheney speech.
This is atypical, considering that first ladies often produce more positive
responses among survey participants who do not belong to the presi-

dent's party. However, the results of tests that compare Laura Bush's to Dick Cheney's effectiveness on questions of the president's character were even stronger in the directions we can expect, based on some of the results we observed when comparing Laura Bush to George Bush. On the left side of Figure A.14, the results of interest are those estimating the impact of a "pooled treatment effect," the effect of receiving *either* of the speeches attributed to Laura Bush (the War on Terror speech quoted before or a speech about education policy) compared to the effect of *either* of the speeches attributed to Dick Cheney on assessments of George Bush's personality and leadership qualities. We see the same pattern in nearly every one of these categories (i.e., how George Bush handled his job as president, and whether George Bush "is honest," "is moral," "cares about people like me," and "is a strong leader"), which is one where Laura Bush produces more positive evaluations of George Bush than does Dick Cheney. The results in favor of Laura Bush among Republicans are particularly strong, clearly meeting standards for statistical significance in the case of "George Bush cares" and "George Bush is moral." The results given in Figure A.14 are consistent with the slightly positive effect we detected for Laura Bush shown in Figure 6.5 among the same dependent variables, suggesting that Laura Bush clearly tops Dick Cheney's ability to persuade the public on George Bush's character, at least among Republicans, but our best guess is that she probably only slightly surpasses the president's ability to do this on his own behalf, if at all.

We see a similar story in Figure A.15 if we look at survey respondents' reactions to reading a speech attributed to Michelle Obama instead of the same speech attributed to Joe Biden. Again, there is one policy area where Michelle Obama appears to have a much more positive impact than the vice president on respondent support for the president's policy initiatives: Republican respondents who read a health care speech attributed to Michelle Obama reported much more support for the Affordable Care Act than Republicans who read the same health care speech attributed to Joe Biden. And again on the left side of Figure A.16, we can see that receiving either a speech about health care or a speech about veterans attributed to Mrs. Obama prompted more favorable evaluations of President Obama's character (i.e., "is moral," "cares about people like me," and "is honest,") than the same speeches attributed to Vice President Biden, although not by much. What is more surprising is that Joe Biden outperformed Michelle Obama on the questions of how well President Obama is handling foreign policy and health care, among all partisans. As we can see by looking at Figures A.13–A.15 collectively, Joe

Biden was the *only* vice president of our last three to produce more positive evaluations of the president than first ladies when directly compared.

The trade-off between Hillary Clinton and Al Gore as surrogates for President Clinton is again a cloudy one (Figure A.13 in the Appendix). Democratic survey respondents who received a speech about health care attributed to former first lady Hillary Clinton posted significantly more positive assessments of the Health Security Act of 1993 than respondents who read the same health care speech attributed to Al Gore. But respondents who received either a health care or an economy speech attributed to Hillary Clinton only slightly more positively evaluated President Clinton on personal qualities like leadership and morality than respondents who thought Al Gore made the same appeals.

I can practically hear the voices of the political practitioners I interviewed in my head as I contemplate these results. They would remind me that Bill Clinton did *not* require the same kind of help from Hillary Clinton to get people to like him when he was president as George Bush did from Laura Bush in the later years of his presidency, so it would make sense that Laura Bush is consistently more effective than Dick Cheney in this regard to strategists, not to mention that Joe Biden and Al Gore are pretty likable guys and very talented orators. Yet, I would be negligent not to stress once more the toughness of these tests and to emphasize all of the processes that must take place for a statistically significant result to emerge in a presidential spouse's favor. The ideal test that could tell us which of the three speakers in each administration is most successful at driving positive evaluations of policy items and the president himself would require filling three auditoriums with 2,000 people of the exact same demographic background and asking First Lady Michelle Obama, Vice President Joe Biden, and President Barack Obama, for example, to deliver the same speech to the audience in one room, and then ask audience members to evaluate President Obama and his policy agenda. Detecting an effect in the experiments we implemented is so much more difficult than this. Survey respondents reading a brief excerpt from a speech on a computer may not be paying very close attention, and aside from that, the oratorical skills of the person to which the speech is attributed are undetectable, because the only information from which respondents in the control and treatment groups can draw separate conclusions is the text bearing the speaker's name. Put differently, what respondents are reacting to in our version of the experiment is the mere *idea* of Michelle Obama delivering remarks on health care reform compared or the mere *idea* of Barack Obama delivering the same remarks on health care reform, or the mere *idea* of Joe Biden delivering the same remarks on health care reform. Whatever image of the president is brought forth in a respondent's mind by simply seeing Michelle Obama's name is the only driving force between any detectable differences between the evaluations of treatment and control group members, so for the experiment to yield statistically significant results, that image must be very powerful. As I mentioned before, substantial differences detected between the evaluations of the treatment and control groups, despite the ability of respondents to idly click through the surveys, suggest that the results are probably even stronger than what we can see, and the statistically significant results I am reporting are those that would hold up in 95 percent of the cases if we sampled the data over and over again. The results for Laura Bush are particularly impressive because asking survey respondents about past presidential administrations necessitates their recollection of the president during those years. It is plausible that respondents have more relevant and more immediately accessible opinions of President Obama than they do of President Clinton and President Bush. As we can also see from the remaining tables in the Appendix (Tables A.5–A.7), the treatment and control groups were balanced on all covariates, on average, that we expect to play a role in the formation of political opinion, such as education, age, partisanship, and gender, so we know the differences we detected between the treatment and control groups were in fact due to the name of the speaker and not some other factor.

Because this kind of research has not been conducted on president's spouse before, the best application of these results, at least for political practitioners, would be to focus on the few areas where first ladies appear to be more effective leaders of public opinion than presidents and vice presidents and to look for applications of those results, as I discuss further in Chapters 7 and 8. For political scientists, the best next steps would entail replications of the experiments that yielded these particular results, in order to make sure the results reappear in multiple tests conducted among multiple samples, and to explore the strength of these results among specific groups.

For example, in the vice presidential experiment, we did find a few strong results among women and also among certain partisan groups. Naturally, large enough samples should be gathered in the future to warrant an investigation into the interaction between gender and party. We see, for instance, that among women, the economy speech attributed to Hillary Clinton (compared to the same speech attributed to Al Gore) had a small ($\beta = 0.18$ on a three-point scale) but statistically significant impact on respondent evaluations of how former president Clinton handled the economy when he was president [Approve, Disapprove, Neither]. Also among women, Laura Bush's foreign policy speech (compared to the same speech with Dick Cheney's name attached instead) had a strong impact on whether respondents thought terrorism increased or decreased as a result of the war in Afghanistan; responses of survey participants were about 16 percent lower on the scale of whether terrorism has increased or decreased than the responses of participants who thought Dick Cheney uttered the speech. And finally, women who read either a foreign policy appeal or an education appeal thought to be uttered by Laura Bush reported that President Bush was a significantly more honest president than women who received either of the speeches attributed to Dick Cheney.

CHAPTER 7

Modernizing Our Perspectives on Presidential Spouses

It has become something of a scholastic convention for political scientists to prescribe the direction of future research at the end of their projects. Even books that have succeeded in the toilsome endeavor of disrupting an established body of literature often fall short of answering all of the new questions generated during that journey. As Sniderman, Brody, and Tetlock put it, "There are two quite different ways of determining if a research program is making headway: One is if old questions are being disposed of, the other if new questions are cropping up."[1]

The first contribution this book makes to the academic study of presidential spouses is an attempt to shift the prevailing focus among political scientists, historians, and journalists away from first ladies as personal confidantes and advisors to presidents of the United States to spouses as instruments of the highly professionalized White House public relations and communications operation. West Wing and East Wing staffs alike decry oversimplified and unsophisticated depictions of first ladies as "private," "behind-the-scenes," or "secret" power brokers. This book makes the case that the influence of first ladies on U.S. politics is exercised most palpably in plain view, before cameras and microphones, rather than in pillow talk with the president, a form of influence that surely exists but cannot be measured. As a top communications strategist for Michelle Obama expressed: "I think there's a big myth to dispel, because [journalists and academicians] refer to the spouse as 'the secret weapon'. They're not the secret weapon because we all know the value of the spouse . . . they're deployed in every single campaign." In the process of dismantling typological analyses of first ladies that confine them to the categories of "traditional" and "active" spouses, I demonstrate, through the use of speech frequencies as a proxy for public activity, that presidential spouses have become consistently more active over the last three presidential administrations, regardless of their party affiliation or personality-based stereotypes promulgated by scholars. The aggressive pace with which first ladies make public appearances has even surpassed that of vice presidents in most years of the last three decades. Not only has the volume of these appearances increased overall but also the content of remarks made by these first ladies has changed, as I illustrated through a careful content analysis of their almost 1,700 speeches. It appears that the scope of campaign appearances made by spouses has exploded. While only a small number of speeches on the White House Briefing Room web sites in the 1990s were campaign remarks attributed to Hillary Clinton, more than a third of Michelle Obama's total remarks were delivered on the campaign trail.

The Office of the First Lady has also expanded and carefully honed its use of pet projects, which over the course of the last three presidential administrations have become highly organized and fully staffed initiatives that favorably frame and reinforce the president's policy agenda. As I learned from analyzing speeches and from interviews with former White House staff, pet projects are ideal vehicles for the promotion of administration-sponsored policies because they protect first ladies from the negative public attention Hillary Clinton garnered when she chaired the president's task force on health care reform by somewhat buffering them from the policy-making process. For this reason, pet projects often address a small, uncontroversial, portion of a presidential policy initiative, usually the portion that most directly affects families or women. Hillary Clinton charted the waters with CHIP late in the Clinton administration, a modified version of the Health Security Act of 1993 expressly aimed at helping children. Laura Bush's role as an ardent advocate of the War on Terror was fulfilled largely through her efforts to expose Americans to the plight of Middle Eastern women living under extremist regimes, and her literacy initiatives provided her with a logical platform from which to promote the authorization and reauthorization of the No Child Left Behind Act. Michelle Obama has similarly sought public support for the Obama administration's signature legislative accomplishment, the Affordable Care Act, through Lets Move! an initiative centered on the obesity epidemic in the United States, and Mrs. Obama's military families cause is an optimal frame for the president's removal of troops from Iraq and Afghanistan.

There is much more to the strategic communications theory of presidential spouses, however, than the adherence of pet projects to presidential agenda items. The extent to which first ladies have emerged as the most visible presidential surrogates is clarified by their unique qualifications to be messengers-in-chief. In other words, presidential spouses bring assets to the bully pulpit that are unobtainable to other surrogates. Most of these assets relate to the ability of the first lady to go personal. Armed with the knowledge I gleaned from statistical analyses of existing opinion surveys and descriptive information extracted from speeches and elite interviews, I proposed several reasons why presidential spouses might be effective communicators. First, I demonstrated that in almost every year of the last three administrations, first ladies have had higher favorable ratings than presidents and vice presidents, that their favorable ratings often rise when presidential favorability falls, and that even if these favorability scores are highly dependent on the partisanship of survey participants asked to rate political figures, partisanship plays a much *less* central role in the way first ladies are evaluated compared to the way presidents are evaluated. Also relevant is my finding that survey respondents recognize the first lady's name at higher rates than they recognize the vice president's. Second, first ladies benefit from different rules of engagement concerning the mass media. Unlike the West Wing, the East Wing is not subject to the customs of the press room rotation, and thus has more opportunities to pursue positive forms of coverage such as women's magazines and daytime television interviews. East Wing staff can also better control the narrative in these alternative settings. Journalists are not in the habit of asking first ladies tough policy questions (though spouses are often very capable of answering them) and first ladies often decline to respond to such inquiries, a luxury rarely afforded to presidents, vice presidents, and cabinet secretaries.

Third, when first ladies make public appearances on behalf of the White House or on the presidential campaign trail, they overemphasize their status as humble outsiders—ever appreciative of the chances they have to connect with Americans, and lacking a pronounced professional stake in the outcomes of elections or political conflicts. Barbara Bush, Laura Bush, and Michelle Obama have mastered this kind of self-deprecation. Spouses can shed light on the character of the president and can convey the attributes that make him fit to lead more authentically than Capitol Hill colleagues and official running mates. Fourth, perhaps because presidential spouses have been women so far, Americans seem to expect them to go public on certain issues but not on others. In one of the surveys I conducted through Mechanical Turk, I observed that when

I asked respondents to guess whether the speech provided in the prompt was made by a president or first lady, they overwhelmingly answered that speeches on the economy and foreign policy belonged to presidents and speeches on women's issues such as equal rights and fair pay, as well as health care and education, belonged to first ladies. Finally, when the first lady travels, she is not hindered by the same security concerns and time constraints faced by the president and other high-ranking officials. Spouses are advantaged by the flexibility a small staff and Secret Service detail permits and can interact more intimately with groups and individuals at home and abroad. The White House welcomes the favorable press coverage that comes with the first lady's goodwill tours to food banks, women's shelters, and military hospitals.

The second major contribution this book makes is an effort to empirically test the theory it introduces in Chapter 3. Although elite interviews provided crucial evidence that the proliferation of public appearances by first ladies in the last three administrations is an outgrowth of White House communications strategy, it remained unclear whether this strategy is effective. It is not a requirement for academics to test the new theories they propose. Strong works of political science customarily pursue only one of four types of missions: theory proposing, theory testing, theory applying, or literature assessing.[2] However, online survey design tools like Qualtrics and marketplaces such as Amazon's Mechanical Turk where researchers can easily and relatively inexpensively recruit thousands of study participants have made it possible to conduct experiments like those in Chapters 6 and 8, leaving political scientists little excuse to kick the methodological can down the road. We have entered the Data Age, and the drumbeat that drives the march of quantification, as Harvard Government professor Gary King calls it, grows louder everyday as it demands responsible parties remove the guesswork from their prognoses when possible.

Randomized experiments are more rigorous empirical tests than those implemented through multiple regression, which at best mimics an experimental setting by holding observable confounders constant. The experiments I used provided important preliminary insight into the questions elite interview subjects could not answer without bias. I tested the assertions that first, presidential spouses can increase public evaluations of the president and second, that presidential spouses can increase public evaluations of certain policies, especially those policies women are expected to be more qualified to deal with such as education and health care.

By showing approximately 5,000 respondents speech excerpts and manipulating whether the speech was attributed to a first lady, vice president, or a president, or video clips of speeches made by first ladies or presidents at the Democratic and Republican National Conventions, then gauging their support for a number of policies and the president himself, compared to respondents who received no speech or video, I achieved a much more accurate test of the first lady's effect on public opinion than what the existing literature on presidential spouses proffers. The experiments revealed that compared to respondents who received no treatment (i.e., neither a speech excerpt nor a video clip), respondents who read or watched a speech made by the president's spouse were quite supportive of the presidential agenda items discussed in those speeches and video clips, and that first ladies are sometimes quite capable of convincing respondents that the president is a strong leader, cares about Americans, is moral, or is intelligent. Yet, when compared to respondents who received a vice presidential treatment (i.e., a speech excerpt attributed to the vice president or a video clip of the vice president), some of these effects are diluted, and they were understandably even more diluted than a presidential treatment.

Suggestions for Future Research

The abated strength and magnitude of coefficients made apparent in comparisons of the effects of written presidential speeches and video clips to the effects of written first lady speeches and video clips are not cause for abandonment of the experimental study of the strategic mobilization of spouses. After all, the notion that first ladies can elicit *more* enthusiastic responses to their policy appeals than the originators of these policies is a very tall order. However, it is a good starting place. What we can say with reasonable confidence is that in the majority of scenarios, in a wide variety of policy areas such as foreign affairs, veterans affairs, education, health care reform, and the economy, first ladies are adequate presidential replacements, garnering similar levels of support for the policies they discuss on the campaign trail and in other public settings. As Edwards concludes in *On Deaf Ears*, the fact that presidents usually fall short of changing public opinion on an issue does not mean they should stop going public. He instead suggests that presidents should stop basing their governing strategies on the premise of growing the size of their public support. The permanent campaign, Edwards argues, is actually antithetical to governing, because governing requires presidents to use the bully pulpit to intimidate opponents by increasing the political costs of opposition rather than attracting them with benefits.[3] If going public has become a fundamentally coercive exercise for presidents, as Edwards urges, then presidential spouses are in an ideal position to balance tough talk emitted from the West Wing with positive messages on which presidents do not have the luxury of focusing.

Summary of Experimental Findings in Chapter 6

Because we estimated many statistical models in Chapter 6, examining the impact of three different principals on evaluations of the president, including the president himself, across two different mediums, four issue areas, and three administrations, it may be helpful to review some of the circumstances in which first ladies produced notable opinion results among individuals in our experiment in a clear and succinct manner.

Hillary Clinton

1. Compared to the control condition where no speech was shown, Hillary Clinton's speeches positively and statistically significantly impacted respondents' perceptions of President Bill Clinton when the question was whether Bill Clinton cares about people "like me," is a good leader, is honest, is moral, is intelligent, and handled the presidency well. Hillary Clinton's policy speeches also produced positive evaluations of the way in which President Clinton handled health care reform and handled the economy, among all partisans.

2. Compared to the condition where a speech was attributed to President Clinton (rather than Hillary Clinton), Hillary Clinton's speeches performed worse than President Clinton's speeches on health care and the economy, producing significantly more negative evaluations of the way in which President Clinton handled health care reform, handled the economy, and of the Health Security Act of 1993, among all partisans. Hillary Clinton outperformed President Clinton when the question was whether President Bill Clinton is intelligent, and her health care speech slightly outperformed his when the question was whether the U.S. government should be involved in health care reform.

3. Compared to the control condition where no video was shown, the video clip of Hillary Clinton speaking about health care reform at the 1996 DNC increased respondent evaluations of President Clinton when the question was whether the government should be involved in health care reform, as well as support for the Health Security Act of 1993, among all partisans. Hillary Clinton's 1996 DNC speeches also enhanced respondent evaluations of President Bill Clinton when the question was whether the former president is moral, among Republicans. However, when the

effects produced by the health care and education portions of Hillary Clinton's 1996 DNC speech are compared to those produced by the health care and education portions of Bill Clinton's 1996 DNC speech, Hillary Clinton's speeches do no better nor worse on average than the president's except in one question area: whether former President Clinton cares about people "like me," where the video clips of President Clinton's speech produced significantly more positive scores than Hillary Clinton's speech. The DNC video clips and written speech excerpts attributed to Hillary Clinton appear to do slightly better than the video clips and written speech excerpts attributed to President Clinton, among women, on the question of whether President Bill Clinton is moral, but she does not produce better or worse evaluations of the president among women on average than the president himself.

4. Compared to the condition where a health care speech was attributed to Al Gore (rather than Hillary Clinton), Hillary Clinton produced substantially more positive evaluations of Bill Clinton when the question was support for the Health Security Act of 1993, among Democrats, and whether the U.S. government should be involved in health care reform, among Republicans. Hillary Clinton also produced more positive evaluations of President Clinton than Al Gore among Republicans on the question of whether Bill Clinton is a good leader. Finally, Hillary Clinton produced significantly more positive evaluations of President Clinton than Al Gore among women when the question was how well President Clinton handled the economy.

Laura Bush

1. Compared to the control condition where no speech was shown, Laura Bush's speeches positively and statistically significantly impacted respondent perceptions of President George W. Bush when the question was whether George Bush is intelligent and whether George Bush is a good leader, among Democrats. However, Laura Bush's education speech negatively impacted the perceptions Republican respondents had of No Child Left Behind and the way in which George Bush handled education reform. Her foreign policy speech also produced strong negative results among Democrats who claimed they disagreed with U.S. involvement in foreign conflicts.

2. Compared to the condition where a speech was attributed to George Bush (rather than Laura Bush), Laura Bush's speeches on education and foreign policy produced more positive evaluations of George Bush than George Bush's speeches, particularly when the question was how the

president handled education, support for No Child Left Behind, and again, when the question was whether the U.S. war in Afghanistan had increased terror, or how the president handled foreign affairs. Laura Bush also outperformed President Bush among all partisans when the question was whether George Bush is intelligent, whether George Bush is a strong leader, and how George Bush handled his job as president.

3. Compared to the control condition where no video was shown, the video clip of Laura Bush speaking about the War on Terror during the 2004 RNC increased respondent evaluations of President Bush among Democrats when the question was whether the United States should be involved in foreign conflicts and decreased the evaluations of Republicans on the same question. Laura Bush's 2004 RNC speeches also enhanced respondent evaluations of President Bush when the question was whether the former president is a good leader, among Republicans; however, the speeches decreased the evaluations of Democratic respondents on the same question. The written speech excerpts attributed to Laura Bush appear to do much better than the written speech excerpts attributed to President Bush among women on the question of whether President Bush is a strong leader and slightly better on the questions concerning his handling of education and No Child Left Behind.

4. Compared to the condition where speeches about the War on Terror and education were attributed to Dick Cheney (rather than Laura Bush), Laura Bush produced substantially more positive evaluations of George Bush among Republicans on every character question, including whether George Bush is moral, a question where she even more powerfully swayed Democrats, whether George Bush is intelligent, is honest, is a strong leader, and cares about people "like me." Laura Bush also outperformed Dick Cheney among Republicans who disagreed that the U.S. war in Afghanistan increased terror; however, she produced stronger responses than Dick Cheney in the other direction among Democrats who thought terror had increased. Finally, Laura Bush produced more positive evaluations of President Bush than Dick Cheney among women when the question was whether the U.S. war in Afghanistan increased terror and whether George Bush is honest.

Michelle Obama

1. Compared to the control condition where no speech was shown, Michelle Obama's speeches positively and statistically significantly impacted respondents' perceptions of President Obama when the question was whether Barack Obama cares about people "like me," is a good

leader, and is intelligent, among all partisans. Michelle Obama's policy speeches also produced positive evaluations of the way in which President Obama handled foreign policy, among all partisans, and handled health care reform, among Democrats.

2. Compared to the condition where a speech was attributed to President Obama (rather than Michelle Obama), Michelle Obama's speeches performed slightly worse than President Obama's speeches on health care and foreign policy, producing more negative evaluations of the Affordable Care Act, and on the question of whether the government should be involved in health care, and how Barack Obama is handling his job as president, among all partisans.

3. Compared to the control condition where no video was shown, the clips of Michelle Obama speaking about the economy and health care during the 2012 DNC increased respondent evaluations of President Obama among Democrats when the question was how well President Obama has handled the economy and whether President Obama is a strong leader; however, the health care clip decreased evaluations of the Affordable Care Act. The video clips of Michelle Obama's speech at the DNC appear to do about as well as the video clips of President Obama's DNC speech on most measures, except on questions of whether Barack Obama is moral, and how President Obama handled the economy, where the president outperforms her among all partisans. However, the health care portion of Michelle Obama's DNC speech substantially outperformed the health care portion of President Obama's DNC speech among women, and the written speeches attributed to Michelle Obama significantly improve women's evaluations of President Obama when the questions are whether he is a strong leader and whether he is intelligent.

4. Compared to the condition in which speeches about health care and veterans were attributed to Joe Biden (rather than Michelle Obama), Michelle Obama produced significantly more positive evaluations of the Affordable Care Act among Republicans, but worse evaluations than Joe Biden on the question of how President Obama handled foreign policy. Among Democrats, Michelle Obama outperforms Joe Biden on the question of whether Barack Obama is moral.

There are several adjustments that can be made to the existing experimental design that would paint a more complete picture of the first lady's efficacy as a presidential surrogate. First, the control condition in the speech experiment can be modified, which is currently the condition in which respondents receive no speech or video. Instead of routing respondents in the control condition directly to a set of dependent variable questions, the survey flow should perhaps route respondents in the control group to the same speech text with no attribution (i.e., a speech excerpt that does not bear the president's or the first lady's name). This adjustment would allow me to more accurately ascertain whether some of the strong first lady effects identified in comparisons of the control group to the treatment group were attributable to the first lady's name or to the content of the speech.

The second adjustment that can be made is the addition of other surrogates to the experiment that would perhaps be fairer matches for the first lady. Even though I added the vice president to the mix to combat this, another spokesperson such as the White House Press Secretary, a prominent congress member, or a party leader such as the DNC or RNC chair could be a good choice. On the presidential campaign trail, staff and advisors must often choose among several top-tier surrogates available for deployment in battleground states. As I learned in elite interviews, first ladies are often more popular than vice presidential running mates, but are often mobilized based on the best guesses and hunches of strategists, for example: states where principals are polling more or less successfully, states with high volumes of requests for certain principals, states where the women's vote is critical, and states where first ladies raise the most funds. The experimental comparison of first ladies to other surrogates besides the vice president would provide for better informed choices. Finally, especially if additional speakers are added, a larger sample should be obtained for future research and the data should be used more efficiently. With larger sample sizes, we could also take a closer look at the way in which survey participants respond to the president's spouse by gender *and* by party, rather than either of these, an exercise that would have required the data to be spliced too finely in this chapter for us to accurately estimate the effects. However, after reviewing some of the areas where first ladies outperform their vice presidential and presidential colleagues on certain questions of character and in certain issue areas among women and among members of the opposite party, gender and party should surely be examined in conjunction in the future. Although it has no impact on the validity of the results or soundness of the experimental design, in the first round of the experiment, a disproportionately high number of respondents were routed into the control condition, with about a 33 percent probability compared to a 17 percent probability of being routed into each of the two first lady speech (or video) topics and a 17 percent probability of being routed into each of the two presidential speech (or video) topics. This simply means that treatment groups were generally smaller than control groups and there may have been less statistical sensitivity underlying these estimates, although this does not appear to be the case. If larger samples are attained in the future, I will also be able to compare the effect of first lady speeches and videos to presidential and vice presidential speeches and videos among independents, a group that may be more receptive to the appeals of first ladies, but that was untenably small in my sample.

As better data become available for the study of presidential spouses, the quality of research will also improve. As I mentioned in Chapter 3, when the daily schedules of Mrs. Bush and Mrs. Obama are eventually released as a result of FOIA requests for these materials, they will provide invaluable additions to the database of speeches I created and will facilitate the incorporation of other types of public appearances, such as television and radio interviews, into tabulations of public remarks. Research should also be conducted on the communications roles of gubernatorial and congressional spouses. Studying spouses in other facets of the U.S. government and in other countries with female leaders can help us begin to address the looming question of what the East Wing will look like under the occupation of a male spouse. Perhaps until then we will not truly understand the importance of gender in the communications roles of presidential spouses.

A plausibility probe I conducted in 2012 for the further study of congressional spouses yielded several remarkable findings, including that the spouses of Senate candidates are more involved in campaigns than the spouses of House candidates, that spouses of male House and Senate candidates appear more frequently on the campaign trail than the spouses of their female counterparts, that spouses are most frequently present in the campaigns of successful challengers who beat incumbents, and that party does not appear to be a powerful predictor of the frequency with which spouses appear in videos and photographs. Percentage of Facebook and campaign web page videos and photos featuring the candidate's spouse was used as a proxy for spouse involvement, and candidates for the study were randomly selected from a CQ database of 2012 congressional races. Although I found substantial and interesting variation in the frequency of spouse appearances by gender, institution, and levels of electoral success, spouse involvement in congressional campaigns appears to be relatively infrequent in general. Yet, the substantial gap in levels of spouse involvement in winning versus losing campaigns begs questions regarding the potential measurable impact of spouses on electoral outcomes. This study should be replicated in future elections and experiments should be used to measure the effect of spousal participation on the congressional campaign trail. As Hillary Clinton navigates the waters of another presidential run, the serious treatment of the study of presidential spouses in political science has become painfully overdue— not only because of the political careers spouses may pave for themselves from the prominent role of presidential spokesperson but also because of the window spouses provide into White House and presidential campaign communications strategy. Public appearances of first ladies are indicative of the priorities, goals, weaknesses, and fears of the president of the United States.

CHAPTER 8

Epilogue: An Operative's Guide to Spouse Mobilization in 2016

It is a common grievance of people who work in politics or study politics for a living that it is probably one of the most difficult professions to profess in a social setting. No matter how advanced the science behind our discipline becomes, nonpolitical scientists feel much more at home making policy recommendations, prognosticating election results, and diagnosing the major ills facing modern democracies than nonheart surgeons feel discussing heart surgery and nonengineers feel contemplating building design. First ladies, I have found along this journey, are an especially alluring topic to the everyday emissaries among us. Maybe it is because even if we do not follow politics, we are likely to consume some form of nonpolitical coverage of the first lady that we discussed in Chapter 3, the easier forms of coverage being actively pursued by the White House—a talk show appearance, a magazine interview, or a guest spot on our favorite television shows. And in this vein, in order to have an opinion about the first lady, we do not have to know much about current events. Or maybe it is because, as we also discussed, the president and the president's spouse have become cultural symbols and gender role models in the United States.

I have also learned that individuals' opinions of the first lady of the United States are often more revealing about the person in possession of the opinion than the president's spouse. People seem to project their own insecurities, beliefs, and feelings about themselves on to presidential spouses in a way that I have not observed with many other political figures. One woman I met, for instance, told me, about Hillary Clinton,

"Well I don't like her because she's done nothing on her own. Everything she has and all of the success she enjoys is because of her husband." Eventually, I asked the woman about her own occupation and she said, "I'm in business with my husband." Another gentleman I encountered to whom I told I was writing a book about presidential spouses was a stay-at-home dad and was also highly sensitive to the topic of first ladies. Unprompted, he shared, "Well they are just *so* much more than spouses! I mean, I hope you put that in the book. Being first spouse is a huge job, there is so much involved that the president doesn't even appreciate. It's all the work behind the scenes that makes the place run and so many sacrifices." And finally, as one of Michelle Obama's former communications staffers shared with me, unsolicited comments on the state of the president's marriage are *even* rampant if the commenter knows that *you* personally know and work with the president and the first lady. The likes of "Of course they live separately!" or "Everyone knows they aren't together in real life" have been spouted often about Bill and Hillary Clinton and Barack and Michelle Obama to their staff members.

Although the public images of our three most recent presidents and their spouses have been refined and solidified in the minds of Americans for years, election 2016 brings a new crop of candidates and candidate spouses who remain fairly blank slates. We even saw a Republican primary candidate, Senator Lindsey Graham, face questions last summer from reporters about who would occupy the East Wing if he was elected because he is not married. Senator Graham replied "Well, I've got a sister. She could play that role if necessary" and later, "I've got a lot of friends, we'll have a rotating first lady."[1] The year 2016 also brings a few candidates and candidate spouses who we know quite well: former First Lady, U.S. Senator, and Secretary of State Hillary Clinton; brother of former President George W. Bush; son of former President George H.W. Bush; and former Florida Governor Jeb Bush. In this chapter, I examine one last set of results from a novel experiment that tests the effect of appearing on the presidential campaign trail alongside a spouse on respondent favorability toward that presidential candidate compared to the effect of appearing alone on the campaign trail. I examine the contributions of the spouses of two prominent candidates for the presidency on the likability of their spouses: former President Bill Clinton, and Columba Bush, wife of former Florida Governor Jeb Bush.[2] Based on these results, I strategize about the best way forward for campaigns interested in capitalizing on the potential appeal of a candidate's spouse in 2016 and avoiding the negative projections onto spouses that often arise out of a lack of positive information circulating about them, and I explain why it is so important to share information with the public at an early stage.

Readers who navigate this chapter will have a much more educated take on the role of spouses in presidential election 2016 than the talking heads who are starting to make predictions about the effect the spouses of primary candidates will have on the electability of their partners. The "Bill Clinton Question" has been a universal thread in political talk shows and newspapers of late. As recently as June 2015 when Hillary Clinton announced her candidacy, Bill Clinton claimed that his role on the campaign should be one of a "backstage advisor" to his wife "until we get much, much closer to the election."[3] However, journalists have closely covered the campaign events where Bill Clinton has already started to stump for Hillary, such as one of the first in Des Moines where he joked "There's been a lot of talk about breaking the glass ceiling, and I want to talk about one barrier that has not been broken. I want you to support Hillary for me too, because I want to break a ceiling. I am tired of the stranglehold that women have had on the job of presidential spouse."[4] The media has been looking for clues about how President Clinton's involvement might affect the Clinton campaign. If his first appearances are any indication, the aim of the appearances seems to be to explain the policies underlying Hillary Clinton's campaign in terms voters can understand, and to offer a personal perspective on the kind of president Hillary Clinton would be based on the observations of someone who has been married to her for 40 years.[5] The problem is that whether these efforts influence voters is difficult to measure in the aggregate, and campaign operatives looking at polling numbers in key states like Iowa before and after Bill Clinton gave a speech and attempting to ascertain whether the speech caused the increase are engaged in an impossibly endogenous endeavor. Even the effect of big televised campaign speeches can be muddled or strengthened by the newspaper and 24-hour news cycle analysis that supplements them, and prospective voters polled over the phone, if they read or watched the speech at all, likely also read or saw other political coverage about the Clintons and other presidential candidates in the same time, fundamentally interfering with the "treatment" of watching a stump speech by Bill Clinton and sharing an opinion with a pollster about Hillary Clinton. In the world of constant campaign coverage and thousands of different places to absorb it, pollsters cannot reliably tell us what exactly is causing a candidate to rise or fall in the polls.

Another haphazard polling approach that has been applied to identifying the "Bill Clinton Effect" is asking Americans whether *they* believe

Bill Clinton, if involved in Hillary Clinton's campaign, would have a positive or a negative effect on the outcome. A Reuters poll that was conducted in October 2015, for example, found that 40 percent of independent voters were unsure about whether Bill Clinton's involvement in Hillary Clinton's presidential campaign would help or hurt her campaign (35 percent of Democrats were unsure), 55 percent of Democratic poll respondents thought Bill Clinton would help the campaign, and 35 percent of Republican poll respondents thought Bill Clinton would hurt the campaign (34 percent of Republicans were unsure).[6] The article unpacking the Reuters poll concluded that Bill Clinton could help in the primary, but should take a step back in the general election; however, a Democratic strategist quoted in the same article claimed having Bill Clinton on the campaign trail "is a good thing, but needs to be done carefully." In another place in the article, the authors said, "the poll underscores the challenges of figuring out how to deploy Bill Clinton." It is not surprising that a survey conducted in this manner would yield such inconclusive results, with the vast majority of nonpresidential campaign strategists claiming that they were unsure about the impact of including Bill Clinton in Hillary Clinton's campaign communications strategy would have on her success. The question requires survey respondents to jump through multiple hoops by first contemplating their own opinion of Bill Clinton, then imagining how millions of other voters perceive Bill Clinton, in an effort to predict whether Bill Clinton's involvement in Hillary Clinton's presidential run would hurt or help the campaign overall. This is a strange ask for U.S. voters, especially when their unvarnished opinions of the candidates are probably what pollsters are seeking in the end.

But even seasoned political experts who have designed and implemented the very strategies that depend on spouses are torn on the question of whether Bill Clinton will help or hinder Hillary Clinton's presidential bid. David Axelrod, a well-known Democratic strategist and Obama campaign veteran, told the *Washington Post* in May that "It's hard to shine when you're standing next to the sun," and that ". . . it is diminishing to have him out there by her side."[7] In a similar vein, former presidential candidate and Democratic National Committee chairperson Howard Dean said the best role for Bill Clinton would be "to raise a bit of money and let Hillary speak for herself," doubting that Bill Clinton would be as involved as he once was in Hillary Clinton's 2008 campaign.[8] However, other insiders like Paul Begala, a former Clinton White House advisor, said that "it would be malpractice" not to use Bill Clinton on the campaign trail, and the Clinton campaign's own communications director

Jennifer Palmieri has said of Bill Clinton, "We're going to use him when we need him."[9]

Columba Bush, the Republican spouse I chose to include in the experiment, has at least one thing in common with Bill Clinton, a recognizable last name in U.S. politics. Unlike him, Mrs. Bush reportedly has very little desire to be active on the campaign trail, a factor that experts say could be tragic at the early stages of a campaign. In an *Atlantic* piece published in June titled "The Mysterious Columba Bush," Hannah Rosin emphasized Columba Bush's dislike of public life and the lack of involvement she has had in Jeb Bush's previous campaigns. At one point, Rosin even describes Columba as the "anti-Bill Clinton" due to her disinterest in electoral politics. Nonetheless, there are some signs that Mrs. Bush could become a more dominant player in the campaign, for example, a heartfelt speech she delivered in October at a domestic violence fundraiser in Florida where she was introduced by Governor Bush. She sincerely admitted, "Like most of you, I like to communicate one-on-one . . . without the glare of the public light. Most of you have never heard me give a speech before."[10] Yet, as the small handful of articles about Columba Bush reveal, she is an admirable and fascinating person who has experienced the challenges faced by many Mexican American immigrants firsthand as well as a childhood shaped by poverty and domestic violence in León, Mexico. If any surrogate could shape Jeb Bush's image in a different or more positive way than he can on his own, Columba Bush might be a solid bet.

Does Spouse Involvement on the 2016 Presidential Campaign Trail Improve Public Perceptions of the Candidates?

In order to assess the impact Columba Bush and Bill Clinton have on the favorability of their spouses, I designed a basic survey experiment that compares the perceptions Americans have of both presidential contenders when they appear *alone* on the campaign trail to the perceptions of Americans when presidential candidates appear *alongside their spouses* on the campaign trail.[11] Instead of showing survey respondents speech excerpts and changing the name of the speaker, as we did in Chapter 6, 1,099 survey respondents were randomly routed into either the Clinton or the Bush version of the experiment. Within the Clinton experiment, respondents were randomly shown either a picture of Hillary and Bill Clinton together (the treatment condition) or the same picture with Bill Clinton cropped out (the control condition where Hillary Clinton appears alone). Within the Bush experiment, respondents were either randomly shown a picture of Jeb and Columba Bush together (the treatment condition) or the same picture with Columba Bush removed (the control condition where Jeb Bush appears alone). The text that flanked the picture was a variant of the following:

> As you may know, the 2016 elections are coming up. Below is a picture of presidential candidate [Jeb Bush/Hillary Clinton] and [his wife Columba Bush/her husband former President Bill Clinton]. In the next section we'll ask you a few questions about the candidates and your political views.

Figures 8.1A and 8.1B simulate the way in which the pictures in the survey were presented to participants.[12] As you can see, because a cropped image was used, we can ensure that there were no differences between the treatment and control conditions other than the inclusion or exclusion of the candidate's spouse from the shot.

Before the pictures were displayed, respondents were asked demographic questions, allowing me to ensure that the treatment and control groups were balanced on demographic covariates such as age, race, gender, and partisanship. After the pictures were displayed, respondents were

Figure 8.1A   Example of Campaign Experiment Control Condition

Figure 8.1B   Example of Campaign Experiment Treatment Condition

asked to rate Jeb Bush or Hillary Clinton on a feeling thermometer, and were also asked whether the candidate pictured "is honest," whether the candidate "cares about people like me," and whether the candidate is "down to earth," some of the same questions we used in the experiments in Chapter 6 to address the question of presidential character. For more information about the sample of respondents that participated in the survey, see Table A.8 in the Appendix. Respondents were also asked four policy qualification questions about the candidates intended to gauge perceptions of the candidate's ability to improve our nation's schools if elected, improve our nation's economy, and how well the candidate would handle immigration and handle foreign policy. To be clear, only respondents who received the Jeb Bush treatment or control conditions were asked about Jeb Bush, and only respondents who received the Hillary Clinton treatment or control conditions were asked about Hillary Clinton.

To boil this down even further before we examine the results, consider that the beauty of an experiment like this is its ability to cut through the multiple treatment and contamination problems inherent to the polls we dissected earlier by empirically focusing on one question: On average, do people rate Jeb Bush higher when he is pictured with his wife Columba Bush, do they rate him lower, or do they rate him the same? On average, do people rate Hillary Clinton higher when she is pictured with her husband Bill Clinton, do they rate her lower, or do they rate her the same? Because there is only one form of treatment (i.e., spouse with candidate) and one form of control (i.e., candidate alone) and because randomization ensures each group of people receiving each version of the treatment is demographically comparable, we know that the differences in how respondents evaluate Jeb Bush can *only be explained* by the fact that Columba was either in the picture or out of the picture, and the only differences in how respondents evaluate Hillary Clinton can *only be explained* by the fact that Bill Clinton was in the picture or out of the picture.

Figure 8.2 is a great starting place for us to delve into questions about the impact Bill Clinton and Columba Bush could have on Hillary Clinton's and Jeb Bush's favorability, respectively. Favorability was measured with a feeling thermometer, so respondents in each group were asked to rate Hillary Clinton or Jeb Bush on a scale of 0 to 100, where ratings between 50 and 100 degrees mean that the respondent feels favorable and warm toward the person, ratings between 0 and 50 degrees mean the respondent does not feel favorable toward the person and does not care too much for that person, and ratings at the 50 degree mark indicate the respondent does not feel particularly warm or cold toward the person. At the time the experiment was conducted in August 2015, the mean feeling thermometer for Jeb Bush was 31.1 among all respondents (mean scores were 25.1 among all Democrats, 46.0 among all Republi-

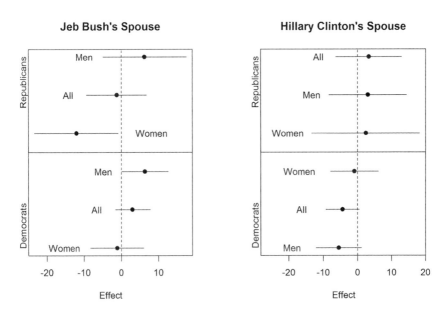

Figure 8.2   Effect of 2016 Presidential Candidate Spouses on Candidate Favorability

cans, 25.0 among Democratic men, 44.4 among Republican men, 48.1 among Republican women, and 25.2 among Democratic women). The mean feeling thermometer for Hillary Clinton was 49.1 among all respondents (mean scores were 59.6 among all Democrats, 26.3 among all Republicans, 55.5 among Democratic men, 20.6 among Republican men, 65.1 among Democratic women, and 33.5 among Republican women).

As we can see in Figure 8.2, men and women of both parties responded disparately to Columba Bush. On one hand, Republican women who received the picture of Columba Bush with Jeb Bush rated Jeb Bush more than 12 points *lower* on average than Republican women who received the same picture where Jeb Bush appeared alone ($\beta = -12.06$), a very strong statistically significant difference. However, Republican men who received the picture of Columba Bush with Jeb Bush rated Jeb Bush a few points *higher* on average than Republican men who received the same picture where Jeb Bush appeared alone, although this effect is not nearly as strong and in repeated sampling could have been zero or negative. On the other hand, seeing Columba Bush with Jeb Bush has a significant positive effect on the feeling thermometer ratings *Democratic* men gave Jeb Bush, which averaged 6.5 points higher than the ratings Democratic men gave Jeb Bush when he was pictured alone. In fact, our best guess is that Columba Bush has a positive impact overall on Democratic favorability toward Jeb Bush, after examining these tests.

Regarding the right side of Figure 8.2, where we can observe feeling thermometer results for Hillary Clinton, we see some similar themes, where men and women of each party respond differently to seeing Bill Clinton pictured with Hillary Clinton. Seeing Bill Clinton pictured with Hillary Clinton appears to have a slightly positive effect on Republicans' feeling thermometer ratings of Hillary Clinton, among men and women. However, when Democrats see Bill Clinton pictured alongside Hillary Clinton, they rate Hillary Clinton significantly lower on the feeling thermometer scale (for Democratic men, $\beta = -5.5$ among Democratic men, and $\beta = -4.3$ among all Democrats) than those Democrats who see the same picture where Hillary appears alone. These results may suggest that strategists who warn about the dangers of mobilizing Bill Clinton too early in the primary are on track when it comes to Hillary Clinton's favorability. Regarding Jeb Bush's campaign, Columba Bush could prove to be a great asset in the general election if Jeb wins the Republican nomination, but it appears she needs to overcome the negative image she bears among Republican women.

Favorability is a key ingredient in the electability recipe and has also been shown to be an important factor in a president's ability to get his agenda passed in Congress. However, other metrics I measured have been watched closely in the 2016 presidential election so far, such as perceptions of candidate honesty, relatability, and compassion. In addition to whether spouses have an impact on these perceptions, I measured whether spouses shape our perceptions of a candidate's ability to deal with particular policy challenges, namely the economy, immigration, education, and foreign policy. Let us start by inspecting the effect of Columba Bush on perceptions of Jeb Bush in Figure 8.3.

The areas where Columba Bush appears to have a strong positive impact on respondent perceptions of Jeb Bush are again most numerous among Democrats. In particular, Democrats who saw a picture of Columba Bush with Jeb Bush before being asked to evaluate Jeb Bush reported that Jeb Bush was honest at significantly higher rates than Democrats who saw a picture of Jeb Bush alone ($\beta = 0.14$), a result that was even stronger among Democratic men ($\beta = 0.21$). Democratic men in the Columba Bush treatment group also rated Jeb Bush's ability to deal with immigration reform substantially higher than those Democratic men in the control condition who viewed a picture of Jeb Bush alone, an effect size of 0.27. To be clear, all of the variables in Figures 8.3 and 8.4 are coded dichotomously, so an increase among Democratic men on the question of how well Jeb Bush would handle immigration if elected of 0.27 can be understood as an increase in support of 27 percent on that

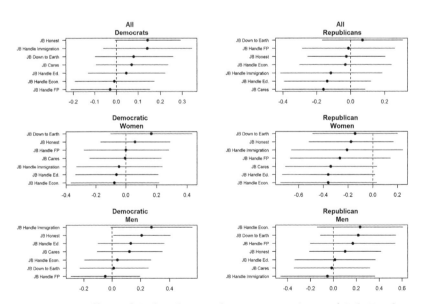

Figure 8.3   Effect of Columba Bush on Perceptions of Jeb Bush

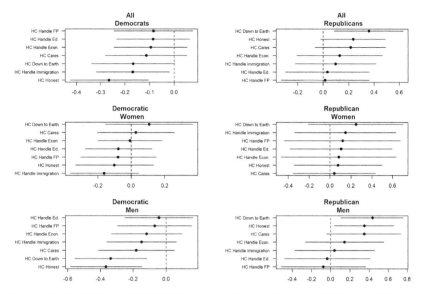

Figure 8.4   Effect of Bill Clinton on Perceptions of Hillary Clinton

measure, something strategists looking for ways to capitalize on Jeb Bush's appeal among out-party members would be wise to examine more closely. Among Republicans, however, Columba Bush does not do nearly as well. The Republican women problem we detected in the favorability test appears to translate to other dependent variables, and in fact, there was no metric (policy related *or* character related) where seeing Columba Bush pictured alongside Jeb Bush produced more positive results among Republican women than seeing Jeb Bush alone. There is also some limited evidence that seeing Columba Bush pictured alongside the candidate hurts Jeb Bush among *all* Republicans on the question of whether he is equipped to handle immigration and on the question of whether Jeb Bush "cares about people like me." Some of these effects disappear among Republican men, though, among whom seeing Columba Bush has largely positive effect on perceptions of Jeb. These mixed results underscore the notion that Mrs. Bush has the potential to greatly enhance her husband's image among Democrats on a number of different fronts, but that Republican men and Republican women have dissimilar reactions to her campaign presence.

The results shown in Figure 8.4 estimating the effect of seeing Bill Clinton pictured alongside Hillary Clinton are admittedly fascinating against a backdrop of media fixation on the "Bill Question" and the problems Hillary was facing in summer and fall 2015 surrounding her public perceptions of her honesty and trustworthiness, a character gap Bill Clinton has addressed on her behalf by telling audiences "She's still got the best friends she had in grade school."[13] The former secretary of state has also tackled her honesty deficit directly in statements like one from a recent interview: "People should and do trust me."[14] Figure 8.4 suggests that among Democrats (recall Democrats in our sample were quite supportive of Hillary Clinton, assigning her a mean feeling thermometer of about 60 percent), seeing Bill Clinton pictured alongside Hillary Clinton actually hurts Hillary Clinton in every single issue area and on character questions, most notably whether Hillary Clinton is down to earth ($\beta = -0.11$) and whether Hillary Clinton is honest ($\beta = -0.27$). Bill Clinton's negative effect on assessments of Hillary Clinton's honesty is particularly robust, making for a discrepancy of almost 28 percent between Democrats who saw a picture of Bill Clinton with Hillary Clinton and those who saw the same picture where Hillary appeared alone. The mean score among all Democrats in the sample on the question of Hillary Clinton's honesty (where 1 = Disagree, 2 = Neither, 3 = Agree) was 2.11, so seeing Bill Clinton produced a strong enough negative impression among Democrats to bring mean responses close to the "Disagree" range of the scale. The negative honesty effect detected among all Democrats is even stronger among men (a 38 percent drop in agreement with the statement that Hillary Clinton "is honest" compared to a 30 percent drop among all Democrats) and Democratic men who saw a picture of Bill and Hillary Clinton together before evaluating Hillary Clinton also claimed they disagreed more strongly with the statement Hillary Clinton is "down to earth" (a 35 percent drop in agreement with the statement compared to 30 percent among all Democrats).

However, if we look at the same measures among Republicans, heeding the responses of Republican men, in particular, seeing Bill Clinton with Hillary Clinton has a very strong *positive* impact on perceptions of her. Republicans who saw a picture of Bill Clinton with Hillary Clinton agreed much more strongly with the statements Hillary Clinton "is honest" (+24 percent), "is down to earth" (+36 percent), and "cares about people like me" (+22 percent) than Republicans who saw a picture of Hillary Clinton alone. Again, these effects are clearest and most pronounced among Republican men, for whom Bill Clinton appears to make powerful difference in evaluations of Hillary Clinton's character, and a slight positive difference in evaluations of Hillary Clinton's ability to deal with immigration, foreign policy, education, and the economy. Although the results are largely inconclusive among Republican women, the point estimates for these estimations are all positive as shown in Figure 8.4.

Summary of Experimental Findings in Chapter 8

Overall, the results in this chapter suggest that candidate spouses, based on tests that posit Bill Clinton and Columba Bush as cases, have the clear potential to influence public perceptions of the candidates for president in 2016. Hereunder are some of the effects we discovered summarized in what may be a more accessible manner:

1. Columba Bush helps Jeb Bush's favorability among Democratic men, but hurts his favorability among Republican women.
2. Columba Bush has a strong positive effect on evaluations of Jeb Bush among Democrats when the questions are whether Jeb Bush is honest and whether Jeb Bush would do a good job handling immigration if elected. These effects are strongest among Democratic men.
3. Columba Bush has a strong negative effect on evaluations of Jeb Bush among Republican women when the questions are whether Jeb Bush cares "about people like me," whether Jeb Bush would do a good job handling education, and whether Jeb Bush would do a good job handling the economy.
4. Bill Clinton may help Hillary Clinton's favorability among Republicans, but hurts Hillary Clinton's favorability among Democrats, especially among Democratic men.
5. Bill Clinton has a strong positive effect on evaluations of Hillary Clinton among Republicans when the questions are whether Hillary Clinton is down to earth, whether Hillary Clinton is honest, and whether Hillary Clinton cares "about people like me." These effects are strongest among Republican men.
6. Bill Clinton has a strong negative effect on evaluations of Hillary Clinton among Democrats when the questions are whether Hillary Clinton is down to earth and whether Hillary Clinton is honest, negative effects that are most pronounced among Democratic men.

Concluding Remarks

For too long and for too many weak reasons, presidential spouses have been the third rail of the field of presidential communications. As I mentioned earlier, empirically trained presidential scholars wary of upsetting the status quo and risking their standing in the research community by attaching themselves to the study of an unelected, unappointed government official have excluded the president's spouse from their considerations of the factors that influence public opinion of presidents of the United

States and the policies they propose. But political operatives, concerned with winning elections and passing the legislation they want with whatever political capital they can muster, have increasingly made presidential spouses a centerpiece of their communications efforts on the campaign trail and in the White House, and the evidence in this book shows that those efforts have not been expended in vain. Here are some ground rules for mobilizing candidate spouses in general election 2016 based on the scientific results we grappled throughout the book.

Deploy the Spouse Early

The importance of giving a presidential candidate's spouse adequate support and staff as early in the campaign as possible cannot be understated. Many of the interview subjects we heard from in Chapters 4 and 5 opined that spouses most often make gaffes that draw media attention at the early stages of the general election or at the late stages of the primary election before spouses recognize the persistent need to be careful and to stay on message. Some of the campaign insiders I consulted also stated the importance of projecting an image of strong family support as early as possible, urging that while spouses may not be the reason presidents get elected, they can certainly be the reason presidential candidates do not. Even for experienced political spouses who have accompanied their partners on the congressional and statewide campaign trail, fielding constant inquiries from the most practiced journalists is an art that requires preparation to master. In other words, major media attention requires major media training.

In addition to avoiding mistakes, introducing the candidate's spouse at the primary stage of a campaign may help fill a vacuum of information about the candidate's family, personality, and background, if pertinent. Some strategists have claimed recently that introducing a spouse too early could take attention away from a candidate who may still be unknown to most of the public, a topical concern in a primary field as large as the Republican starting lineup in 2016. Even so, releasing positive information about the candidate's spouse that is handpicked by the campaign should be considered an attractive alternative to the background exploration that is conducted by journalists in the absence of such information, a search that will be unsanctioned and unchecked by the campaign when it happens. Presidential campaigns should take the responsibility of controlling the pervading narrative about the candidate's spouse as seriously as journalists take the obligation of providing information to the U.S. public about the personal lives of our presidential candidates. The findings in this book suggest that, if anything, spouses could help an unknown candidate get more attention, since Americans usually show more interest in spouses than other elected officials.

Although we identified some pitfalls associated with deploying Columba Bush in the Republican primary, it should be clarified that we do not know whether the hesitation that is activated when Republican women see a picture of Jeb Bush with Columba is due to a lack of public information about her or the limited public information that already exists. Something that can be included in future experiments involving presidential spouses is a knowledge test, in which survey respondents are asked to describe or name a spouse, or are offered information about the spouse en route to the treatment that they will be asked to recall later. For example, if survey respondents were informed about Columba Bush's personal background or the philanthropic causes she patronizes in Florida, it is possible seeing Columba Bush with Jeb Bush could have produced more positive responses among Republicans or among women. Similarly in the case of Bill Clinton, we cannot identify the reason he deflated evaluations of Hillary Clinton among Democrats, although Americans are probably more acquainted with Bill Clinton than with Columba Bush on average. In late fall 2015, only two candidates for the presidency devoted a separate section of their campaign web sites to spouses: Rand Paul's wife Kelley Paul was prominently featured and introduced on his campaign web site and Marco Rubio's wife Jeanette Rubio was also introduced on a section of the campaign's web site, although most other candidates display their family prominently in the first or second photograph in the "About" sections of their sites.

Deploying spouses at the primary stage of a campaign, although it may seem risky and expensive, is a decidedly less risky setting than the general election. Message content and style can be tried and perfected in the primary when media attention is distributed over a larger number of candidates and is not quite as arduous. As Laura Bush's staff shared, Mrs. Bush was originally uncomfortable speaking in front of large crowds, so she started campaigning by speaking to small groups of women and families in their homes about her husband during the 2000 primary, graduating slowly to larger venues until she felt she gained a command of the message she wanted to share and could deliver it smoothly in high-profile stump speeches.

Deploy the Spouse Often

In combination with efforts to control the personal narrative of presidential candidates through a preemptive approach to media preparation and the information disclosure regarding candidate spouses, campaigns should remember that even positive impressions of presidential candidates evaporate quickly from the minds of voters, and that voters who consume political news are constantly bombarded with new information from different sources. That is why political scientists have focused on the timing of political advertisements and important campaign events such as rallies and television appearances as close to Election Day as possible, when voters are paying the most attention to political coverage. Campaign operatives should not be as worried about overexposing a notoriously great communicator like former President Bill Clinton, for example, as they should be about carefully timing his most concentrated appearances, and placing him in front of the audiences where he is likely to make the biggest difference.

Deploy the Spouse Separately

Another reoccurring theme of the interviews I conducted with White House insiders was the importance of deploying the president's spouse to interest groups and to geographic regions where the president is not popular. Even though general elections demand all well-liked surrogates to be mobilized on the president's or candidate's behalf because there is so much ground to cover, the public perceives spouses very differently than presidents and vice presidents. The general election is a golden opportunity for campaigns to capitalize on the ability of spouses to convert new audiences. We saw examples in some administrations of policy areas where first ladies are stronger messengers than vice presidents and even presidents, but what we observed more impressively in every administration was the first lady's ability to convince members of the opposite party about what kind of person the president is. We then observed the same phenomenon in this chapter, where Bill Clinton had a strong impact on Republican favorability of Hillary Clinton and Republican impressions of her as honest, down to earth, and caring. Lastly, we observed the powerful effect of Columba Bush on Democratic perceptions of Jeb Bush's ability to deal with immigration if elected and his honesty.

Another possibility that should be considered is that when presidential candidates are pictured with their spouses, as they were in the 2016 experiments, those images convey a different message than if the spouses of candidates were pictures alone on the campaign trail, which we did not explore. Pictures of Hillary Clinton with Bill Clinton and Columba Bush with Jeb Bush were used primarily to ensure that when the pictures were cropped, the only difference between the control and treatment conditions would be the presence or absence of the spouse, but it is not improbable that the image of Bill Clinton and Hillary Clinton together summoned something negative in the minds of Democrats, perhaps reminiscent of the scandals that plagued the Clinton White House, for example, so a picture of Bill Clinton alone may have prompted more positive evaluations of Hillary Clinton.

In Chapter 3 we considered the possibility that when presidential spouses (and perhaps candidate spouses too) interact with voters independently of the president, they appear to transcend partisan politics. In other words, voters have the opportunity to consider the first lady's message in a context separate from the presidency. This opportunity for the first lady to resemble an outsider is one East Wing staffs have recognized over the years, and precisely for this reason, the number of first lady speeches that are delivered in nonpolicy-oriented settings but contain policy plugs has risen. Even if the message itself is not overtly political, presidential spouses and presidential candidate spouses open themselves to better framing opportunities for their messages and more receptive audiences when they appear separately from the president or candidate in venues that seem apolitical, such as late-night talk shows. To summarize, spouses can be very effective *replacements* for presidents, presidential surrogates, and presidential candidates in public settings, in addition to presidential *companions*.

Appendix: Supplemental Figures and Tables

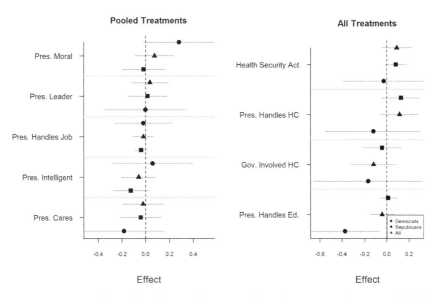

Figure A.1 Effect of Hillary Clinton Video (Compared to No Video)

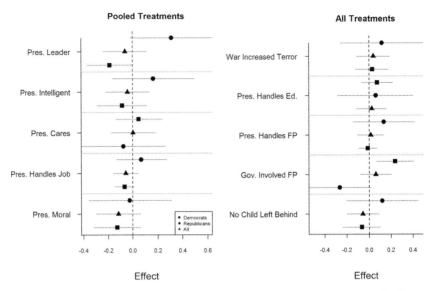

Figure A.2   Effect of Laura Bush Video (Compared to No Video)

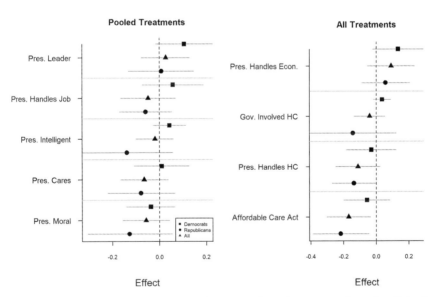

Figure A.3   Effect of Michelle Obama Video (Compared to No Video)

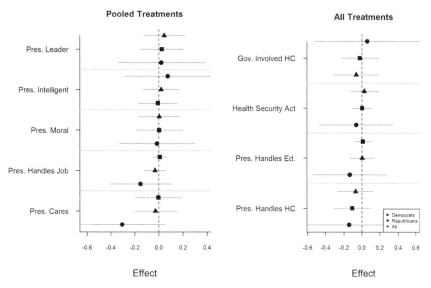

Figure A.4   Effect of Hillary Clinton Video (Compared to Bill Clinton Video)

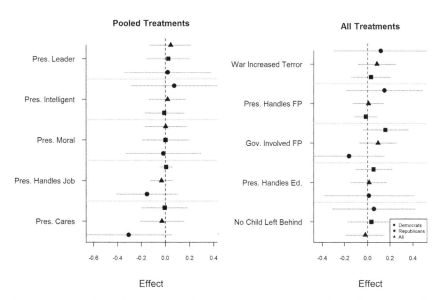

Figure A.5   Effect of Laura Bush Video (Compared to George Bush Video)

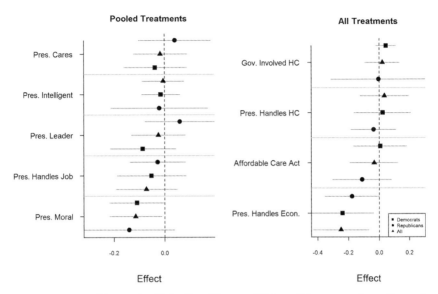

Figure A.6   Effect of Michelle Obama Video (Compared to Barack Obama Video)

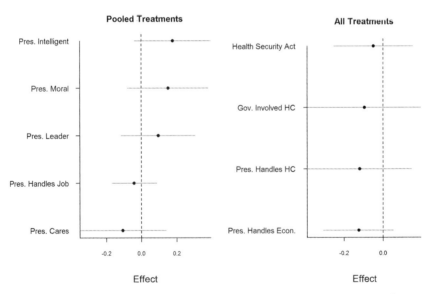

Figure A.7   Effect of Hillary Clinton Speech Among Women (Compared to Bill Clinton Speech Among Women)

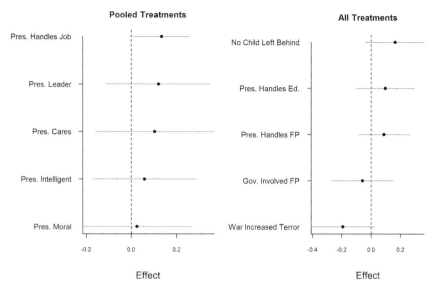

Figure A.8   Effect of Laura Bush Speech Among Women (Compared to George Bush Speech Among Women)

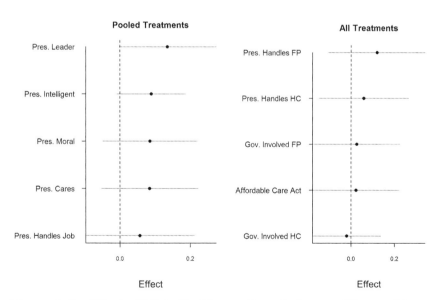

Figure A.9   Effect of Michelle Obama Speech Among Women (Compared to Barack Obama Speech Among Women)

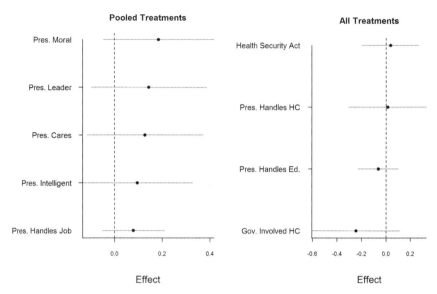

Figure A.10   Effect of Hillary Clinton Video Among Women (Compared to Bill Clinton Video Among Women)

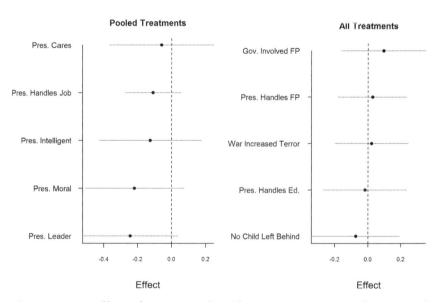

Figure A.11   Effect of Laura Bush Video Among Women (Compared to George Bush Video Among Women)

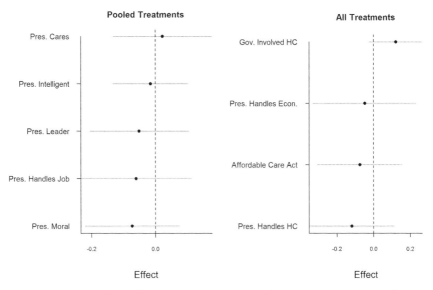

Figure A.12   Effect of Michelle Obama Video Among Women (Compared to Barack Obama Video Among Women)

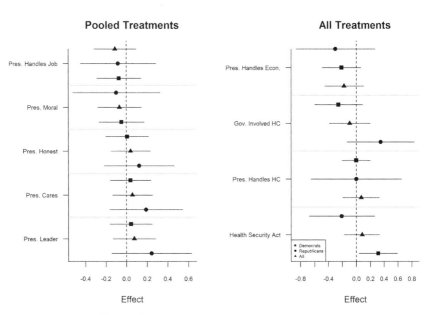

Figure A.13   Effect of Hillary Clinton Speech Compared to Al Gore Speech

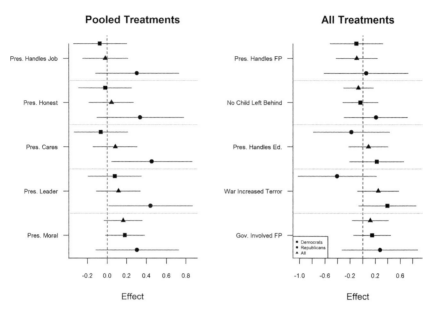

Figure A.14 Effect of Laura Bush Speech Compared to Dick Cheney Speech

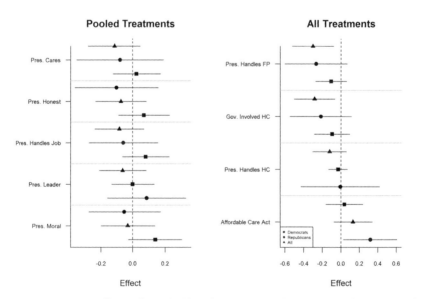

Figure A.15 Effect of Michelle Obama Speech Compared to Joe Biden Speech

Table A.1 Effect of Respondent Partisanship on Favorability Toward the President and First Lady (1992–1995)

	1992 HC	1992 BC	1993 HC	1993 BC	1994 HC	1994 BC	1995 HC	1995 BC
Party ID	-2.136***	-3.660***	-4.301***	-5.765***	-4.455***	-5.718***	-4.570***	-5.011***
	(0.687)	(0.710)	(0.602)	(0.612)	(0.556)	(0.495)	(0.821)	(0.802)
Ideology	-4.438***	-3.153***	-1.664***	-2.008***	-7.494***	-5.388***	-5.756***	-6.652***
	(0.851)	(0.877)	(0.463)	(0.465)	(0.874)	(0.777)	(0.982)	(0.959)
Women's Place	-0.784	-1.278*	-2.016***	-0.709	7.781***	3.925	-2.444***	-1.373*
	(0.679)	(0.708)	(0.564)	(0.558)	(2.885)	(2.590)	(0.803)	(0.784)
Male	-5.007**	-5.706**	2.312	-0.710	-4.137**	0.799	-9.481***	-2.755
	(2.199)	(2.289)	(1.811)	(1.839)	(2.009)	(1.799)	(2.509)	(2.449)
Religious	1.770**	3.056***	0.829	1.800**	-0.143	-0.644	2.398**	0.922
	(0.866)	(0.907)	(0.755)	(0.770)	(0.763)	(0.681)	(0.963)	(0.940)
Married	1.327	-4.007*	0.598	1.150*	0.989	-1.199	-0.581	0.533
	(2.155)	(2.243)	(0.627)	(0.630)	(2.010)	(1.797)	(2.498)	(2.438)
Age	0.0689	0.110	0.0814	0.103*	0.124**	0.175***	-0.0854	-0.0480
	(0.0657)	(0.0692)	(0.0567)	(0.0574)	(0.0601)	(0.0533)	(0.0778)	(0.0759)
African American	10.31***	14.19***	3.952	9.329***	13.16***	13.85***	8.849	9.101
	(3.698)	(3.818)	(2.706)	(2.688)	(3.322)	(2.980)	(5.908)	(5.766)
Hispanic	12.31	30.90*	-9.164	3.574	—	—	8.510	9.916
	(18.18)	(18.65)	(6.894)	(7.183)			(9.490)	(9.263)
Education	-0.365	-0.360	-0.0193	0.142	0.368	-1.240**	-0.879	-0.977*
	(0.481)	(0.502)	(0.404)	(0.405)	(0.618)	(0.551)	(0.566)	(0.552)
Constant	66.18***	63.94***	43.51***	39.81***	77.93***	91.59***	83.77***	84.80***
	(10.24)	(10.59)	(7.285)	(7.339)	(8.177)	(7.318)	(12.02)	(11.73)
Observations	297	288	5.54	582	560	566	294	294
R-squared	0.245	0.316	0.207	0.297	0.438	0.484	0.408	0.406

Standard errors in parentheses.
*p<0.1, **p<0.05, ***p<0.01.

Table A.2 Effect of Respondent Partisanship on Favorability Toward the President and First Lady (1996–2000)

	1996		1997		1998		2000	
	HC	BC	HC	BC	HC	BC	HC	BC
Party ID	-6.586***	-7.971***	-6.540***	-8.174***	-4.766***	-3.109***	-7.318***	-7.611***
	(0.373)	(0.343)	(0.651)	(0.596)	(0.788)	(0.769)	(0.413)	(0.378)
Ideology	-4.060***	-3.394***	-5.096***	-3.107***	-7.278***	-7.405***	-3.055***	-3.126***
	(0.589)	(0.541)	(1.040)	(0.949)	(0.680)	(0.667)	(0.598)	(0.544)
Women's Place	-1.438***	-0.612	-0.134	0.341	-0.342	-0.704	-0.953	-0.772
	(0.429)	(0.393)	(0.787)	(0.719)	(0.581)	(0.571)	(0.754)	(0.684)
Male	-5.322***	-1.439	-7.278***	-3.609*	-4.567**	2.707	-4.684***	1.355
	(1.332)	(1.225)	(2.360)	(2.154)	(1.777)	(1.741)	(1.434)	(1.311)
Religious	0.275	0.750	0.844	0.476	0.135	0.797	-0.0437	0.875*
	(0.519)	(0.477)	(0.946)	(0.861)	(0.695)	(0.682)	(0.544)	(0.498)
Married	-0.675	-2.015*	-2.814	-4.344**	1.179	1.257	-5.058***	-4.018***
	(1.296)	(1.192)	(2.290)	(2.087)	(1.751)	(1.719)	(1.425)	(1.304)
Age	0.0896**	0.0478	0.0671	0.0684	0.123**	0.159***	0.0497	0.0723*
	(0.0387)	(0.0356)	(0.0699)	(0.0637)	(0.0528)	(0.0517)	(0.0434)	(0.0397)
African American	12.85***	10.64***	8.541	10.91**	18.52***	26.38***	8.864***	11.15***
	(2.318)	(2.132)	(5.182)	(4.731)	(3.019)	(2.955)	(2.793)	(2.559)
Hispanic	7.853***	4.735**	6.364	4.291	11.41***	17.29***	6.915**	6.538**
	(2.443)	(2.216)	(4.405)	(3.962)	(3.005)	(2.941)	(3.049)	(2.793)
Education	0.0912	-0.255	0.499	0.0633	-1.126***	-2.109***	0.554	0.271
	(0.277)	(0.254)	(0.498)	(0.453)	(0.367)	(0.360)	(0.453)	(0.414)
Constant	91.70***	103.5***	88.41***	98.43***	110.2***	109.1***	91.29***	90.02***
	(5.459)	(5.019)	(10.01)	(9.107)	(7.279)	(7.177)	(4.396)	(4.021)
Observations	1,265.00	1,274	409	409	937	956	1,146	1,151
R-squared	0.462	0.533	0.489	0.559	0.238	0.276	0.439	0.497

Standard errors in parentheses.
$*p<0.1$, $**p<0.05$, $***p<0.01$.

160

Table A.3 Effect of Respondent Partisanship on Favorability Toward the President and First Lady (2002–2012)

	2002		2004		2008		2012	
	LB	GB	LB	GB	MO	BO	MO	BO
Party ID	2.168***	5.203***	4.591***	9.257***	-4.667***	-5.249***	-6.296***	-8.468***
	(0.541)	(0.608)	(0.440)	(0.482)	(0.556)	(0.561)	(0.387)	(0.392)
Ideology	3.405***	3.403***	3.182***	4.364***	-0.905	-3.004***	-3.022***	-3.220***
	(0.762)	(0.848)	(0.698)	(0.761)	(0.718)	(0.730)	(0.498)	(0.505)
Women's Place	0.00150	-1.312*	-0.558	0.751	-0.657	-0.443	1.145***	1.022**
	(0.691)	(0.777)	(0.532)	(0.583)	(0.648)	(0.661)	(0.443)	(0.448)
Male	-4.646**	0.0747	-4.043***	0.402	-6.192***	-4.611*	-4.144***	-1.351
	(1.951)	(2.191)	(1.465)	(1.608)	(1.909)	(1.935)	(1.270)	(1.288)
Religious	-1.480*	-1.575	-0.758	-0.960	2.038**	1.956**	-1.434***	-0.373
	(0.889)	(0.999)	(0.563)	(0.622)	(0.837)	(0.846)	(0.480)	(0.485)
Married	4.014**	4.043*	2.538*	2.261	-0.419	-2.635	-1.627	-1.304
	(2.012)	(2.251)	(1.485)	(1.639)	(1.931)	(1.953)	(1.284)	(1.300)
Age	0.145**	0.0252	0.251***	0.0737	-0.00271	0.0273	0.0293	-0.00440
	(0.0619)	(0.0689)	(0.0449)	(0.0492)	(0.0581)	(0.0586)	(0.0376)	(0.0382)
African American	-0.878	-3.595	-1.759	1.298	25.47***	19.48***	14.96***	16.00***
	(3.999)	(4.470)	(2.475)	(2.693)	(2.571)	(2.609)	(1.745)	(1.763)
Hispanic	0.567	0.943	-0.693	3.853	10.92***	11.38***	6.076***	3.740**
	(3.548)	(3.893)	(2.851)	(3.166)	(2.443)	(2.483)	(1.829)	(1.843)
Education	0.816	-0.729	-0.349	-2.234***	-0.189	-0.990	0.538**	0.234
	(0.704)	(0.787)	(0.465)	(0.512)	(0.621)	(0.627)	(0.256)	(0.257)
Constant	36.91***	40.64***	30.29***	7.626	76.52***	95.60***	94.95***	97.24***
	(6.840)	(7.640)	(4.461)	(4.880)	(6.522)	(6.590)	(4.518)	(4.537)
Observations	329	343	797	817	450	461	1,167	1,176
R-squared	0.265	0.397	0.375	0.592	0.498	0.517	0.495	0.583

Standard errors in parentheses.
$*p<0.1$, $**p<0.05$, $***p<0.01$.

Table A.4 Speech Topics Attributed to First Ladies vs. Presidents by Survey Respondents

Issue

	Education			Health care			Foreign Affairs			Economy		
	HC Speech (%)	BC Speech (%)	Avg. (%)	HC Speech (%)	BC Speech (%)	Avg. (%)	HC Speech (%)	BC Speech (%)	Avg. (%)	HC Speech (%)	BC Speech (%)	Avg. (%)
Hillary Clinton	51	52	51	60	55	58	69	37	53	45	39	42
Bill Clinton	49	48	49	40	45	43	31	63	47	55	61	58
Difference			2			15			6			16
n=628												

	Education			Health care			Foreign Affairs			Economy		
	LB Speech (%)	GB Speech (%)	Avg. (%)	LB Speech (%)	GB Speech (%)	Avg. (%)	LB Speech (%)	GB Speech (%)	Avg. (%)	LB Speech (%)	GB Speech (%)	Avg. (%)
Laura Bush	53	53	53	59	53	56	46	41	44	39	33	36
George W. Bush	47	47	47	41	47	44	54	59	56	61	67	64
Difference			6			12			12			28
n=628												

	Education			Health care			Foreign Affairs			Economy		
	MO Speech (%)	BO Speech (%)	Avg. (%)	MO Speech (%)	BO Speech (%)	Avg. (%)	MO Speech (%)	BO Speech (%)	Avg. (%)	MO Speech (%)	BO Speech (%)	Avg. (%)
Michelle Obama	46	45	46	53	38	46	46	39	43	37	36	37
Barack Obama	54	55	55	47	62	55	54	61	58	63	64	64
Difference			9			9			15			27
n=628												

	Women (Afghanistan)		
	LB Speech (%)	GB Speech (%)	Avg. (%)
Laura Bush	63	35	49
George W. Bush	37	65	51
Difference			2
n=628			

	Women (Fair Pay)		
	MO Speech (%)	BO Speech (%)	Avg. (%)
Michelle Obama	55	56	56
Barack Obama	45	44	45
Difference			11
n=628			

Table A.5 Relationship Between Treatment Group Assignment and Covariates in Speech Experiment (Means)

	Control	HC Health care	BC Health care	HC Economy	BC Economy	LB Education	GB Education	LB War	GB War	MO Health care	BO Health care	MO Veterans	BO Veterans
Male	0.56	0.55	0.55	0.51	0.63	0.50	0.58	0.52	0.51	0.62	0.52	0.52	0.57
Age (Years)	33.9	33.9	35.6	33.9	34.2	33.1	33.5	33.6	33.3	33.4	33.5	34.1	35.7
Democrat	0.53	0.68	0.54	0.65	0.61	0.64	0.66	0.66	0.69	0.63	0.59	0.69	0.53
Republican	0.25	0.21	0.40	0.21	0.27	0.24	0.22	0.26	0.18	0.24	0.24	0.20	0.32
Education (Years)	15.4	15.4	15.6	15.3	15.1	15.7	15.4	15.7	15.8	15.5	15.5	15.4	15.5
Income (Thousands)	48.8	48.7	51.8	50.1	48.8	48.1	47.9	50.3	49.8	45.9	47.4	49.8	45.3
Non-Hispanic Black	0.07	0.06	0.10	0.06	0.06	0.09	0.05	0.10	0.06	0.11	0.08	0.14	0.04
Non-Hispanic White	0.77	0.81	0.81	0.81	0.84	0.77	0.84	0.80	0.87	0.80	0.84	0.78	0.90
N =	661	87	101	91	103	121	108	125	111	115	101	110	117

Table A.6 Relationship Between Treatment Group Assignment and Covariates in Video Experiment (Means)

	Control	HC Health care	BC Health care	HC Education	BC Education	LB Education	GB Education	LB War	GB War	MO Health care	BO Health care	MO Economy	BO Economy
Male	0.51	0.50	0.63	0.50	0.34	0.66	0.55	0.60	0.54	0.57	0.50	0.52	0.58
Age (Years)	34.0	32.2	33.2	33.3	33.0	33.5	34.6	32.1	32.4	31.3	33.7	33.3	33.2
Democrat	0.58	0.62	0.61	0.65	0.60	0.66	0.58	0.74	0.68	0.57	0.57	0.58	0.61
Republican	0.22	0.24	0.27	0.26	0.29	0.19	0.30	0.21	0.27	0.29	0.31	0.26	0.29
Education (Years)	15.4	15.7	15.2	15.4	15.4	15.3	15.6	15.7	15.3	15.3	15.5	15.5	15.5
Income (Thousands)	48.1	51.7	48.0	46.9	47.8	45.3	46.3	54.0	52.0	53.6	50.0	48.2	49.9
Non-Hispanic Black	0.07	0.10	0.04	0.06	0.12	0.11	0.08	0.09	0.03	0.07	0.07	0.07	0.05
Non-Hispanic White	0.80	0.80	0.87	0.83	0.78	0.82	0.78	0.79	0.85	0.85	0.81	0.82	0.82
N =	884	93	75	82	73	85	86	87	93	93	93	89	77

Table A.7 Relationship Between Treatment Group Assignment and Covariates in Vice President Speech Experiment (Means)

	HC Health care	AG Health care	HC Economy	AG Economy	LB Education	DC Education	LB War	DC War	MO Health care	JB Health care	MO Veterans	JB Veterans
Female	0.40	0.46	0.46	0.41	0.46	0.49	0.45	0.45	0.44	0.46	0.53	0.51
Age (Years)	34.3	34.5	36.7	33.6	35.6	34.7	35.7	34.6	34.2	34.1	34.9	36.9
Democrat	0.68	0.62	0.57	0.61	0.54	0.55	0.60	0.61	0.52	0.68	0.61	0.62
Republican	0.21	0.28	0.30	0.28	0.27	0.30	0.28	0.24	0.33	0.26	0.31	0.29
Education	3.66	3.63	3.59	3.40	3.45	3.61	3.64	3.47	3.60	3.64	3.64	3.62
Income	3.38	3.69	3.67	3.34	3.52	3.57	3.73	3.40	3.39	3.34	3.64	3.41
Non-Hispanic Black	0.05	0.06	0.03	0.08	0.10	0.07	0.05	0.05	0.07	0.05	0.08	0.06
Non-Hispanic White	0.74	0.79	0.83	0.75	0.75	0.76	0.77	0.76	0.76	0.77	0.78	0.77
N =	145	144	135	152	137	127	154	148	123	129	135	154

Table A.8   Relationship Between Treatment Group Assignment and Covariates in Candidate Picture Experiment (Means)

	Jeb Alone (Control)	Jeb w/ Spouse (Treatment)	Hillary Alone (Control)	Hillary w/ Spouse (Treatment)
Female	0.40	0.44	0.45	0.40
Age (Years)	33.8	34.7	34.8	34.0
Democrat	0.55	0.63	0.64	0.67
Republican	0.32	0.25	0.23	0.21
Education	3.51	3.56	3.60	3.66
Income	3.37	3.36	3.30	3.45
Non-Hispanic Black	0.07	0.06	0.06	0.08
Non-Hispanic White	0.76	0.76	0.77	0.78
$N =$	268	254	283	259

Notes

Preface

    1. Calao 2012.
    2. Tracey 2012; Jansen 2012; Winfield 2010.
    3. Hillygus and Jackman 2003: 583.
    4. See Gallup 2006; Gallup 2009; and Gallup Historical Trends 2014.

Chapter 1

    1. Center for American Women and Politics 2015.
    2. Fehrman 2010.
    3. Boyd Caroli 2003.

Chapter 2

    1. Winter 2000: 1, 2.
    2. Watson 2000: 54–56.
    3. Ibid.: 93–98.
    4. Campbell and McCluskie in Watson 2003: 179; Schepsle and Weingast 1987: 85.
    5. Campbell and McCluskie in Watson 2003: 174; Gutin in Watson 2003: 280.
    6. O'Connor, Nye, and Assendelft 1996: 835.
    7. Greenstein 1994; Hadstedt in Watson 2003: 195, 197; Eksterowicz and Paynter 2000: 547.
    8. Hadstedt in Watson 2003: 205.
    9. Sulfaro 2007: 489; Eksterowicz and Sulfaro 2002; ed. Watson 2001; Watson 2003: 169.
    10. Sulfaro 2007: 490.

11. Ibid.: 508.
12. Anthony 2012.
13. Watson 2000: 84.
14. Schneider and Schneider 2001: 150.
15. National First Ladies Library.
16. Schneider and Schneider 2001: 204, 205.
17. National First Ladies Library.
18. Schneider and Schneider 2001: 267.
19. Gould 1996.
20. Watson 2000: 86.
21. Grimes 1990: 24; Beasley 2005: 157; Burns 2008: 153.
22. Beasley 2005: 19–20.
23. Watson 2003: 215–216; Beasley 2005: 74.
24. Grimes 1990: 25.
25. Mueller 2008: 51, 55.
26. Ibid.: 103–104.
27. Watson 2003.
28. Ibid.: 210.
29. Beasley 2010; Burns 2008; ed. Wertheimer 2005; Grimes 1990.
30. Gains in Grimes 1990: 328.
31. Ed. Wertheimer 2005: xiii, xix, xx; Medhurst 1996: 179; Campbell 1990: 1.
32. Godbold 2010: 212–223; Blair and Perry-Giles in ed. Wertheimer 2005: 144, 148.
33. Heclo 1977: 71–74; Wyzomerski 1982: 448; eds. Chubb and Peterson 1985: 239; eds. Chubb and Peterson 1999: 193; eds. Aberbach and Peterson 2005: 143, 145; eds. Krause and Meier 2005: 235–236; OMB 2013.
34. Eds. Chubb and Peterson 1985; eds. Chubb and Peterson 1989; eds. Aberbach and Peterson 2005.
35. Frederickson and Smith 2003: 26–27, 40.
36. Eds. Watson and Eksterowicz 2003: 215.
37. Zaller 1992; Blumler and Kavanagh 1999; eds. Entman and Bennett 2000.
38. Eds. Carroll and Fox 2006; Macmanus and Quecan 2008: 337.
39. Ed. Weisberg 1995; Burrell 2001: 112.
40. Allgor 2012.
41. Borrelli 2011: 3.
42. Sulfaro 2007: 501.
43. Ibid.: 500.
44. Smith and Caporimo 2013.
45. Borrelli 2011: 5.
46. Shapiro and Mahajan 1986; Huddy and Tirkildsen 1993: 120–122; Kahn 1996; McDermott 1997; Winter 2008.

Chapter 3

1. Goldstein 2008: 374.

2. Freedom of Information Act requests for both sets of schedules were made in 2014 and these documents will be incorporated into future analysis of pubic activity should they become available.

3. Kernell 1997.

4. Sulfaro 2007: 486; Eksterowicz and Sulfaro 2002: 307; Watson 2000: 93–98.

5. For a complete list of issue categories and subcategories that were used to determine whether an appearance qualified as a pet project speech, see the Office of the First Lady page of the archived and/or current White House web sites (http://clinton4.nara.gov/, http://georgewbush-whitehouse.archives.gov/, http://www.whitehouse.gov/).

6. For a complete list of legislation signed in each administration, see the presidential library web sites (http://www.clintonlibrary.gov/, http://www.georgewbushlibrary.smu.edu/), the archived and/or current White House web sites, (http://clinton4.nara.gov/, http://georgewbush-whitehouse.archives.gov/, http://www.whitehouse.gov/), or the American Presidency Project at UCSB (http://www.presidency.ucsb.edu/), which contains comprehensive lists of signing statements and statements of administration policy for each of the last three presidential administrations.

7. Watson 2014: 119–120.

8. Corrigan 2000: 157–159.

9. Burrell 2001; Corrigan 2000: 149; Cohen 2000: 575; Burden and Mughan 1999: 237.

10. In an effort to present a complete timeline, during years in which the ANES was not conducted or did not ask the feeling thermometer question, Gallup feeling thermometers serve as a replacement (1999, 2001, 2003, 2005, 2006, 2009, 2010), and in the years in which neither an ANES nor Gallup poll was conducted, Pew feeling thermometers serve as a replacement (2007, 2011, 2013, 2014). These are mean annual feeling thermometers, meaning that if the same questions were asked over several months in the Gallup or Pew survey, the number is an average over those months.

11. Sulfaro 2007: 486.

12. Sulfaro 2007: 488.

13. Questions about the president's spouse were included in the 1992, 1993, 1994, 1995, 1996, 1997, 1998, 2000, 2002, 2004, 2008, and 2012 American National Election Studies.

14. Another way to configure the findings shown in Figure 3.7 might be to plot the actual differences in effects of partisanship on first lady and presidential favorability along with confidence intervals on those differences, allowing us to more clearly ascertain whether the differences themselves are statistically distinguishable from zero. However, this sort of presentation automatically obscures

the effect sizes, detracting from our ability to interpret the impact of party identification on respondent evaluations of presidents and first ladies by simply
looking at the picture. It is difficult to convey units of analysis with a difference-
in-differences plot.

15. Surveys were designed in Qualtrics and administered through Amazon's
Mechanical Turk, the same online tools used to design and administer the survey
experiments in Chapter 6. See Chapter 6 for more details on Mechanical Turk and
Internet survey respondents. In the Bush and Obama administrations, I also asked
respondents to guess whether speeches about women's rights in Afghanistan and
equal pay for women were made by the president or first lady. I was careful to
select speeches about each topic that sounded as if they could have been made
by either a president or first lady and contained no rhetorical clues or identifying information about the speaker so that the only perceptible difference among
speeches was topic.

Chapter 4

1. In an earlier phase of this project, as a preliminary test for my hypothesis
regarding strategic appearances, I examined the relationship between public
approval ratings of the president and number of first lady speeches using part of
the public appearances data set I constructed, which included average presidential job approval ratings for each month from 1992 to 2012 and first lady speech
frequencies per month collected from the White House Briefing Room web sites.
Although I found convincing evidence that presidential approval ratings do not
have a strong effect on the frequency with which first ladies speak in public, the
results clearly showed that the strength and direction of the relationship between
approval and speeches varies substantially by administration, even controlling
for factors unique to each administration using fixed effects. More specifically,
the relationship between speeches and approval ratings in the Clinton administration appears to be very different from that in the Bush and Obama administrations. The significant relationship between approval ratings and speech
frequencies identified in the Clinton administration suggests that first lady activity cannot be studied separately from the president and his agenda.

2. Because the White House and the East Wing, especially, have such small
numbers of staff and have become very exclusive groups, most of my interviews
were attained through snowball sampling. Very few were achieved through the
so-called cold calls to White House staff whose contact information was provided through a presidential library or retrieved from the Internet, although I
made plenty of these calls. Of the 87 total preliminary conversations I had with
potential interview participants, 54 interviews were scheduled, recorded, and
transcribed (see previous footnote), a response rate of about 65%. The majority
of interviews were conducted in person in California, Texas, and the Washington, DC metro area, although several were also conducted over the phone.
Almost all of the interviews were successfully recorded and transcribed excepting

a few interviews that were conducted in loud public places, rendering portions of the interview recording unusable. In these cases, notes were used as a substitute. None of the interview participants refused to be recorded. The entire elite interview process, including the informed consent document and a list of interview questions, was formally approved by the Georgetown University Institutional Review Board (IRB) under Study Identification Number 2013-1063. Because interviews were conducted with many officials and staff members still involved in politics, participants were granted privacy and anonymity during the interviews, meaning no identifying information will be provided in the discussion of my results. By guaranteeing participants that information collected during the interviews would not be attributed to them, I found that participants felt freer to answer questions in the most honest and valid manner possible, without fear that their relationship with a president, first lady, or another staff member could be tarnished. A list of people who were consulted as part of the research for this book is provided in the Appendix.

Although I did not read from a script during the interviews, eventually becoming so familiar with my questions that I did not need one, I kept a list of possible questions with me for reference. A list of interview questions was only provided to interview participants in three cases where elite participation in the interview process was made conditional on the ability to review a list of possible questions ahead of time. I did not find in these cases that showing the interview participant a list of questions diminished or improved the general quality of the interview in any way, compared to those participants who did not ask me for a list of questions beforehand. Interviews ranged from 15 minutes to 1.5 hours, although most interviews lasted roughly 30 minutes.

3. Public Law 95–750 was enacted in 1978.

4. Clinton, August 27, 1996: Chicago, IL. The full text transcript of Hillary Clinton's remarks at the 1996 DNC in Chicago as well as transcripts of other public speeches cited in this dissertation can be found on the Clinton Library's web site. For the DNC speech, on the First Lady's Press Office page, see Box 19 under "FLOTUS Statements and Speeches 5/1/96–1/22/97 [Binder]."

5. Clinton, November 1, 1993: Washington, DC.

6. Clinton, July 23, 1994: Seattle, WA.

7. Clinton, October 9, 1998: Little Rock, AK.

8. Carter 1994.

9. Kelly 1993.

10. Texas State Archives 2008.

11. Bush, February 26, 2001: Hyattsville, MD.

12. National First Ladies Library 2015.

13. Bush, November 17, 2001: Washington, DC.

14. National First Ladies Library 2015.

15. Obama, September 18, 2009: Washington, DC.

16. Obama, December 14, 2011: Fort Bragg, NC.

17. Blumenthal 1982; Klein 2005.

Chapter 5

1. Williams 1992.
2. Shapiro 2004.
3. Frederick 2008; CBS News/AP 2008.
4. Wolffe 2008.
5. The Economic Growth and Tax Reconciliation Relief Act (EGTRRA) of 2001 and the Jobs and Growth Tax Relief Reconciliation Act (JGTRRA) of 2003 are often now referred to together as "the Bush tax cuts."
6. Obama, September 4, 2012: Charlotte, NC.
7. Bush 2010: 386.
8. Kessler 2007.
9. Garofoli 2008.
10. Bush, September 25, 2008: Washington, DC.
11. Butterfield 1990.
12. Bush, June 1, 1990: Wellesley, MA.
13. West 2004.
14. Toner and Kornblut 2006; Hernandez and Healy 2005.
15. Bumiller 2002.

Chapter 6

1. Kernell 2007; Cohen 2004; Edwards 2003; Corrigan 2000; Cohen 1995.
2. Woessner 2005; Cohen and Hamman 2003; Shaw 1999.
3. Edwards 2003: 207.
4. Gerber and Green 2012: 3.
5. Gerber and Green 2012: 4.
6. Druckman et al. 2011: 290; Iyengar et al. 1997.
7. Sapiro 1981: 63.
8. Kahn 1994: 181.
9. Gerber and Green 2012: 72.
10. Ibid.: 73.
11. McDermott in Druckman et al. 2011: 38.
12. McDermott 2011.
13. Sekhon in Box-Steffensmeier, Brady, and Collier 2007: 5.
14. Berinsky et al. 2012.
15. I conducted paired Welch two-sample t-tests to assess whether differences in means between groups given in Tables A.5 and A.6 were statistically significant. Paired two-sample t-tests can be considered a simplified form of analysis of variance (ANOVA), which generalizes t-tests of a population parameter such as the mean of more than two groups. Of 480 pairwise comparisons conducted on the groups in the written speech balance table (Table A.5), only 3.1% of the means were statistically significantly different. Of 480 pairwise comparisons conducted on the groups in the video balance table (Table A.6), less than 1.9% of

the means were statistically significantly different. I conducted a similar exercise to ensure that balance was achieved for respondents in the treatment groups in the vice presidential experiments discussed in Chapter 6 and the candidate spouse experiments discussed on Chapter 8 (Tables A.7 and A.8, respectively). Here, I used an F-test, rather than a t-test, to assess whether a group of respondent characteristics was capable of predicting the assignment of individuals to a given treatment condition. If the respondents in various treatment groups are the same on average, characteristics such as their age, partisanship, race, and gender should not be able to predict the treatment group to which they were assigned. In statistical terms, this means that if we estimated a regression where respondent characteristics predicted assignment to treatment, the coefficients on these characteristics should all be zero (i.e., these variables have no systematic relationship with treatment assignment). An F-test posits the null hypothesis that all of these coefficients are jointly zero. After estimating regressions of this form for each treatment assignment indicator, I was unable to reject this null hypothesis in any case, indicating that respondents in various treatment groups were balanced on pretreatment characteristics.

16. Angrist and Pischke 2009: 17, 12–15, 22.

17. Power analyses were conducted on all of the statistically significant ($\alpha = 0.05$) results reported in this chapter, to ensure that sample sizes were large enough to properly determine statistical significance. These results met or surpassed the default power criteria of 0.90 used in STATA and other software packages, which can be understood as the probability that a statistical test correctly rejects the null hypothesis when it is false (UCLA). Power analyses are typically conducted at the beginning of a research project to determine the minimal sample size required to detect an effect of a given size. I recruited as many subjects as possible for my written speech and video experiments ($N = 6,169$), given financial and time-related constraints.

Chapter 7

1. Sniderman et al. 1991: 261.
2. Van Evera 1997: 93.
3. Edwards 2003: 246–248.

Chapter 8

1. Gass 2015.
2. At the time this experiment was designed in late June 2015, Hillary Clinton and Jeb Bush were each the respective front-runners in the Democratic and Republican primary contests (see Agiesta 2015a; Todd and Murray 2015 for polls that were frequently cited at the time, or RealClearPolitics for a good historical snapshot of all Republican polls over the summer). Hillary Clinton and

Jeb Bush were chosen for the experiment based on these polls, as well as their scores on other variables that political scientists use to predict election outcomes at early stages such as name recognition, fundraising, and endorsements. To be clear, the purpose of the experiment is not to predict the outcome of the 2016 presidential primaries, but to estimate the hypothetical impact a spouse could have on a candidate's image in 2016. Only one candidate could be chosen from each party due to the financial and time-related restrictions associated with including more candidates.

3. Pilkington and Stafford 2015.

4. Collinson 2015.

5. Haberman 2015.

6. Lopez 2015.

7. Rucker 2015.

8. Przybyla 2015.

9. Frizell 2015.

10. Portal 2015.

11. The basic setup of the 2016 candidate spouse experiment was the same as the written speech and video experiments detailed in Chapter 6. This includes the implementation of the experiment through Amazon's Mechanical Turk using Qualtrics survey software, the randomization procedures used including the application of block random assignment by party to ensure equal or near equal number of Republican and Democratic respondents in each block, and measures taken to ensure a high enough number of respondents were recruited in each cell, to ensure the tests were adequately statistically powered, and to ensure the respondents in each condition (i.e., Clinton treatment group, Clinton control group, Bush treatment group, and Bush control group) were balanced on all pretreatment covariates, including age, party identification, gender, education, income, and race. All of the results were also estimated in the same way as the results of the experiments in Chapter 6 were estimated, using differences in means tests.

12. Permission to use the images of Hillary and Bill Clinton and Jeb and Columba Bush that appeared in the survey experiment in this book was not granted by the web sites that originally published the images, but the images were similar to those in Figure 8.1A and 8.1B purchased from a stock photo web site. In the real images shown to respondents in the experiment, both candidates and spouses were standing rather than sitting and both spouses appeared to the right of their partners in the chosen images. Specifically, the image used in the Clinton version of the experiment was of Hillary Clinton waving and smiling after she exited a vehicle with Bill Clinton, also smiling, whose hand rested on her back as they proceeded away from the vehicle. The image chosen for the Bush version of the experiment was of Jeb and Columba Bush holding hands standing slightly apart, also both smiling, as they exited an event.

13. Agiesta 2015b.

14. A separate section of Rick Santorum's web site is devoted to "The Santorum Family," although not immediately visible on the home page. Although the

spouses of every married presidential candidate are mentioned at least once in the biography posted on their campaign sites, only 8 candidates in the field of 13 Republican presidential candidates and 4 Democratic presidential candidates use a picture with their spouse or with their family as the main picture in the "About" section of the campaign web sites, and none of them are Democrats: Marco Rubio, Rick Santorum, Bobby Jindal, Ted Cruz, Ben Carson, Jeb Bush, Rand Paul, and Chris Christie.

Bibliography

Aberbach, Joel and Mark Peterson, eds. *Institutions of American Democracy: The Executive Branch* (New York: Oxford University Press, 2005).

Aday, Sean and James Devitt. *Newspaper Coverage of Female Candidates: Spotlight on Elizabeth Dole.* Paper presented at the National Press Club as part of the White House Project Education Series, 2000.

Adler, Scott, Chariti Gent, and Cary Overmeyer. "The Home Style Homepage: Legislator Use of the World Wide Web for Constituency Contact." *Legislative Studies Quarterly* 4(1998): 585–595.

Agiesta, Jennifer. "How Another Clinton Overcame an Honesty Defecit." *CNN*, accessed July 8, 2015. http://www.cnn.com/2015/07/08/politics/hillary-clinton -honest-trustworthy-empathy-poll/.

Agiesta, Jennifer. "Poll: Bush, Trump Rising Nationally for GOP, but Both Rrail Clinton." *CNN*, accessed July 1, 2015. http://www.cnn.com/2015/07/01 /politics/donald-trump-poll-hillary-clinton-jeb-bush/.

Alexander, Deborah and Kristi Anderson. "Gender as a Factor in the Attribution of Leadership Traits." *Political Research Quarterly* 1(1993): 527–545.

Allgor, Catherine. "What Candidates' Wives Are Telling Us." *CNN*, accessed September 5, 2012. http://www.cnn.com/2012/09/04/opinion/allgor-wives -convention-speeches/index.html.

Ansolabehere, Stephen and Shanto Iyengar. *Going Negative: How Political Advertisements Shrink and Polarize the Electorate* (New York: The Free Press, 1995).

Anthony, Carl. "The First First Lady's First Day." *Carl Anthony Online*, accessed May 27, 2012. http://carlanthonyonline.com/2012/05/27/the-first-first-ladys -first-day/.

Anthony, Carl. *First Ladies: The Saga of the Presidents' Wives and Their Power 1789–1961* (New York: William Morrow, 1990).

Anthony, Carl. *First Ladies: The Saga of the Presidents' Wives and Their Power 1961–1990* (New York: William Morrow, 1991).

Anthony, Carl. "When Spouses Talk, Voters Listen." *The New York Times*, accessed November 9, 2013. http://www.nytimes.com/roomfordebate/2012/09/04/do -we-need-to-hear-from-the-candidates-spouse/when-spouses-talk-voters-listen.

Banwart, Mary Christine, Dianne Bystrom, and Terry Robertson. "From the Primary to the General Election: Comparative Analysis of Candidate Media Coverage in Mixed-Gender 2000 Races for Governor." *American Behavioral Scientist* 5(2003): 658–676.

Beasley, Maurine. *First Ladies and the Press* (Evanston, IL: Northwestern University Press, 2005).

Beasley, Maurine. "The Rhetorical Presidency Meets the Unitary Executive: Implications for Presidential Rhetoric on Public Policy." *Rhetoric and Public Affairs* 1(2010): 7–35.

Beck, James, et al. "What Have You Done for Me Lately? Charisma Attenuates the Decline in U.S. Presidential Approval over Time." *The Leadership Quarterly* 5(2012): 729–992.

Bennett, Andrew, et al. *Friends in Need* (New York: St. Martin's Press, 1997).

Berinsky, Adam, et al. "Evaluating Online Labor Markets for Experimental Research: Amazon.com's Mechanical Turk." *Political Analysis* 1(2012): 351–368.

Blumler, Jay G. and Dennis Kavanaugh. "The Third Age of Political Communication: Influences and Features." *Political Communication* 1(2012): 209–230.

Borrelli, MaryAnne. *The Politics of the President's Wife* (College Station: Texas A&M University Press, 2011).

Box-Steffensmeier, Janet, Henry Brady, and David Collier. *The Oxford Hand book of Political Methodology* (New York: Oxford University Press, 2007).

Boyd Caroli, Betty. *First Ladies* (New York: Oxford University Press, 2003).

Bumiller, Elisabeth. "The First Lady's Mideast Sandstorm." *The New York Times*, accessed June 6, 2005. http://www.nytimes.com/2005/06/06/politics/06letter .html?_r=0.

Bumiller, Elisabeth. "Teach the Children Well, First Lady Urges." *The New York Times*, accessed January 25, 2002. http://www.nytimes.com/2002/01/25/us /teach-the-children-well-first-lady-urges-senators.html.

Burden, Barry and Anthony Mughan. "Public Opinion and Hillary Rodham Clinton." *Public Opinion Quarterly* 2(1999): 237–250.

Burns, Lisa. *First Ladies and the Fourth Estate* (DeKalb: Northern Illinois Press, 2008).

Burrell, Barbara. *Public Opinion, the First Ladyship, and Hillary Rodham Clinton* (New York: Garland, 2001).

Bush, Barbara. *A Memoir* (New York: Scribner, 1994).

Bush, Laura. *Spoken from the Heart* (New York: Scribner, 2010).

Bystrom, Dianne, et al. *Gender and Communication: VideoStyle, WebStyle, NewStyle* (New York: Routledge, 2004).

Calao, J.J. "Michelle Obama's Speech Gets More Views Than the Entire RNC Convention." *Forbes*, accessed September 7, 2012. http://www.forbes.com

/sites/jjcolao/2012/09/07/michelle-obamas-speech-gets-more-online-views
-than-the-entire-rnc/.

Campbell, Karlyn. *Deeds Done in Words* (Chicago: Chicago University Press, 1990).

Carroll, Joseph. "Americans' Ratings of Dick Cheney Reach New Lows." *Gallup*, accessed July 18, 2007. http://www.gallup.com/poll/28159/Americans
-Ratings-Dick-Cheney-Reach-New-Lows.aspx.

Carroll, Susan and Richard Fox. *Gender and Elections: Change and Continuity Through 2004* (New York: Cambridge University Press, 2006).

Carter, Rosalynn. *First Lady from Plains* (Boston: Houghton Mifflin, 1984).

CBS News. "Michelle Obama Retools 'I'm Proud' Remark" accessed February 20, 2008. http://www.cbsnews.com/news/michelle-obama-retools-im-proud
-remark/.

Center for American Women and Politics. "Gender Differences in Voter Turnout" accessed May 2014. http://www.cawp.rutgers.edu/sites/default/files/resources
/genderdiff.pdf.

Chubb, John and Paul Peterson. *Can the Government Govern?* (Washington, DC: The Brookings Institution, 1989).

Chubb, John and Paul Peterson. *The New Direction in American Politics* (Washington, DC: The Brookings Institution, 1985).

Clinton, Hillary Rodham. *Living History* (New York: Scribner, 2003).

Cohen, Jeffrey. "If the News Is So Bad, Why Are Presidential Polls So High?" *Presidential Studies Quarterly* 3(2004): 493–515.

Cohen, Jeffrey. "The Polls: Public Favorability Toward the First Lady 1993–1999." *Presidential Studies Quarterly* 3(2000): 575–585.

Cohen, Jeffrey. "Presidential Rhetoric and the Public Agenda." *American Journal of Political Science* 1(1995): 87–107.

Cohen, Jeffrey and John Hamman. "Can Presidential Rhetoric Affect the Public's Economic Perceptions?" *Presidential Studies Quarterly* 2(2003): 408–422.

Collinson, Stephen. "Bill Clinton Stumps for Hillary in First 2016 Campaign Appearance." *CNN*, accessed October 25, 2015. http://www.cnn.com/2015
/10/24/politics/jefferson-jackson-dinner-bill-clinton/.

Corrigan, Matthew. "The Transformation of Going Public: President Clinton, the First Lady, and Healthcare Reform." *Political Communication* 2(2000): 149–168.

Denton, Robert. *The 1992 Presidential Campaign: A Communication Perspective* (Westport, CT: Praeger, 1994).

Denton, Robert. *The 2000 Presidential Campaign: A Communication Perspective* (Westport, CT: Praeger, 2002).

Devitt, James. "Framing Gender on the Campaign Trail: Female Gubernatorial Candidates and the Press." *Journalism and Mass Communication Quarterly* 1(2002): 445–463.

Dodd, Lawrence and Bruce Oppenheimer. *Congress Reconsidered* (Washington, DC: CQ Press, 1993).

Druckman, James, et al., eds. *Cambridge Handbook of Experimental Political Science* (New York: Cambridge University Press, 2011).

Edwards, George. *On Deaf Ears* (New Haven, CT: Yale University Press, 2003).

Eksterowicz, Anthony and Valerie Sulfaro. "The Presidential Partnerships of First Ladies and Their Influence on Public Policy." *Current Politics and Economics of the United States* 4(2002): 307–328.

Elman, Colin. "Explanatory Typologies in Qualitative Studies of International Politics." *International Organization* 2(2005): 293–326.

Entman, Robert and Lance Bennett. *Mediated Politics* (New York: Cambridge University Press, 2000).

Fehrman, Craig. "First Lady Lit." *The New York Times*, accessed May 23, 2010. http://www.nytimes.com/2010/05/23/books/review/Fehrman-t.html?_r=0.

Ford, Betty. *The Times of My Life* (New York: Ballantine Books, 1978).

Frederick, Don. "Michelle Obama's 'Proud' Remark Draws Conservative Fire." *Los Angeles Times*, accessed February 19, 2008. http://latimesblogs.latimes.com/washington/2008/02/michelle-obama.html.

Frederickson, H. George and Kevin Smith. *The Public Administration Theory Primer* (Cambridge, MA: Westview Press, 2003).

Freedman, David, et al. *Statistics* (New York: W.W. Norton and Company, 1998).

Frizell, Sam. "Hillary Clinton Aides Shed Light on Bill's Role in Her Campaign." *Time*, accessed June 12, 2015. http://time.com/3920153/bill-clinton-hillary-campaign-adviser/.

Gallup. "Presidential Job Approval Center" accessed August 21, 2015. http://www.gallup.com/poll/124922/Presidential-Approval-Center.aspx.

Gallup. "Presidential Ratings—The First Lady" accessed August 21, 2015. http://www.gallup.com/poll/3340/Presidential-Ratings-First-Lady.aspx.

Garofoli, Joe. "Why Do Political Wives Stand by Their Men?" *San Francisco Chronicle*, accessed March 12, 2008. http://www.sfgate.com/news/article/Why-do-political-wives-stand-by-their-men-3223202.php.

Gass, Nick. "Bachelor Lindsey Graham Promises a 'Rotating First Lady'." *Politico,* accessed June 9, 2015. http://www.politico.com/story/2015/06/lindsey-graham-rotating-first-lady-bachelor-president-118783.

Geertz, Gary and James Mahoney. *A Tale of Two Cultures* (Princeton, NJ: Princeton University Press, 2012).

Gelman, Andrew and Jennifer Hill. *Data Analysis Using Regression and Multilevel/Hierarchical Models* (New York: Cambridge University Press, 2007).

George, Alexander and Andrew Bennett. *Case Studies and Theory Development in the Social Sciences* (Cambridge: Belfer Center for Science and International Affairs, 2005).

Gerhart, Ann. *The Perfect Wife* (New York: Simon & Schuster, 2004).

Gerth, Jeff and Don Van Natta. *Her Way* (New York: Little, Brown and Company, 2007).

Godbold, Stanley. *Jimmy and Rosalynn Carter* (New York: Oxford University Press, 2010).

Goldstein, Joel. "The Rising Power of the Modern Vice Presidency." *Presidential Studies Quarterly* 3(2008): 374–389.

Gould, Lewis. *American First Ladies: Their Lives and Their Legacy* (New York: Garland, 1996).

Greenstein, Fred. *The Hidden-Hand Presidency* (Baltimore, MD: The Johns Hopkins University Press, 1994).

Grimes, Ann. *Running Mates: The Making of a First Lady* (New York: William Morrow and Company, 1990).

Haberman, Maggie. "Bill Clinton Rallies Iowa for Hillary Clinton as 'Honest and Trustworthy'." *New York Times*, accessed October 24, 2015. http://www.nytimes.com/politics/first-draft/2015/10/24/bill-clinton-rallies-iowa-for-hillary-clinton-as-honest-and-trustworthy/.

Heclo, Hugh. *A Government of Strangers: Executive Politics in Washington* (Washington, DC: The Brookings Institution, 1977).

Hernandez, Raymond and Patrick Healy. "The Evolution of Hillary Clinton." *The New York Times*, accessed July 13, 2005. http://www.nytimes.com/2005/07/13/nyregion/13hillary.ready.html?_r=0.

Herrnson, Paul. *Congressional Elections: Campaigning at Home and in Washington* (Washington, DC: CQ Press, 2004).

Hillygus, D. Sunshine and Simon Jackman. "Voter Decision Making in 2000: Campaign Effects, Partisan Activation and the Clinton Legacy." *American Journal of Political Science* 4(2003): 583–596.

Holbrook, Thomas. *Do Campaigns Matter?* (Thousand Oaks, CA: Sage, 1996).

Huddy, Leonie and Tony Carey. "Group Politics Redux: Race and Gender in the 2008 Democratic Presidential Primaries." *Politics and Gender* 1(2009): 81–96.

Huddy, Leonie and Nayda Terkildsen. "Gender Stereotypes and the Perception of Male and Female Candidates." *American Journal of Political Science* (1993): 119–147.

Iyengar, Shanto, Nicholas Valentino, Stephen Ansolabehere, and Adam Simon. "Running as a Woman: Gender Stereotyping in Political Campaigns," in *Women, Media and Politics*, ed. Pippa Norris (New York: Oxford University Press, 1997), 77–98.

Jacobson, Gary. "The Marginals Never Vanished." *American Journal of Political Science* 1(1987): 126–141.

Jansen, Lesa. "The First Lady and the Kid's Choice Awards." *CNN*, accessed March 31, 2012. http://whitehouse.blogs.cnn.com/2012/03/31/the-first-lady-and-the-kids-choice-awards/.

Johnson, Lady Bird. *A White House Diary* (New York: Holt, Rinehart and Winston, 1970).

Jones, Jeffrey. "Americans Laud Kerry's Efforts as Secretary of State." *Gallup*, accessed September 16, 2013. http://www.gallup.com/poll/164411/americans-laud-kerry-efforts-secretary-state.aspx.

Jones, Jeffrey. "VP Favorable Ratings: Gore Down, Cheney, Biden Flat." *Gallup*, accessed July 14, 2010. http://www.gallup.com/poll/141269/Favorable -Ratings-Gore-Down-Cheney-Biden-Flat.aspx}.

Kahn, Kim. "Does Gender Make a Difference? An Experimental Examination of Sex Stereotypes and Press Patterns in Statewide Campaigns." *American Journal of Political Science* 54(1994): 162–195.

Kahn, Kim. *The Political Consequences of Being a Woman* (New York: Columbia University Press, 1996).

Kelly, Michael. "THE INAUGURATION; The First Couple: A Union of Mind and Ambition." *The New York Times,* accessed January 20, 1993. http://www .nytimes.com/1993/01/20/us/the-inauguration-the-first-couple-a-union-of -mind-and-ambition.html.

Kernell, Samuel. *Going Public: New Strategies of Presidential Leadership* (Washington, DC: CQ Press, 1997).

Kessler, Ronald. *Laura Bush* (New York: Random House, 2006).

King, Gary, et al. *Designing Social Inquiry* (Princeton, NJ: Princeton University Press, 1994).

Koch, Jeffrey. "Gender Stereotypes and Citizens' Impressions of House Candidates' Ideological Orientations." *American Journal of Political Science* 2(2007): 453–462.

Krause, George and Kenneth Meier. *Politics, Policy and Organizations* (Ann Arbor: University of Michigan Press, 2005).

Kriner, Douglas and Liam Schwartz. "Partisan Dynamics and the Volatility of Presidential Approval." *British Journal of Political Science* 3(2009): 609–631.

Lopez, Luciana. "Will Bill Clinton Be a Boon to Hillary's White House Campaign?" *Reuters*, accessed October 23, 2015. http://www.reuters.com/article /2015/10/23/us-usa-election-clinton-bill-idUSKCN0SH0YT20151023.

Macmanus, Susan and Andrew Quecan. "Spouses as Campaign Surrogates: Strategic Appearances by Presidential and Vice Presidential Candidates' Wives in the 2004 Election." *PS* 2(2008): 337–348.

Mahoney, James. "After KKV: The New Methodology of Qualitative Research." *World Politics* 1(2010): 120–147.

Marton, Kati. *Hidden Power: Presidential Marriages That Shaped Our Recent History* (New York: Pantheon Books, 2001).

McCallops, James. *Edith Bolling Galt Wilson: The Unintended President* (New York: Nova History Publications, 2003).

McDermott, Monika. "Voting Cues in Low-Information Elections: Candidate Gender as a Social Information Variable in Contemporary United States Elections." *American Journal of Political Science* (1997): 270–283.

Means, Marianne. *The Woman in the White House* (New York: Random House, 1963).

Mechanical Turk. "About" accessed August 21, 2015. https://www.mturk.com.

Medhurst, Martin. *Beyond the Rhetorical Presidency* (College Station: Texas A&M University Press, 1996).

Milton, Joyce. *The First Partner* (New York: William and Morrow, 1999).

Mueller, James. *Tag Teaming the Press: How Bill and Hillary Work Together to Handle the Media* (New York: Rowman & Littlefield, 2008).

Mundy, Alicia. "Mate Check: As Americans Consider the Right Spouse for the White House, the More Things Change, the More They Stay the Same." *American Demographics* 8(2004): 21–23.

National First Ladies Library. "First Ladies Library Blog" accessed August 21, 2015. http://www.firstladies.org/blog/.

National First Ladies Library. "First Lady Biography: Florence Harding" accessed October 30, 2015. http://www.firstladies.org/biographies/firstladies.aspx?biography=30.

O'Connor, Karen, et al. "Wives in the White House: The Political Influence of First Ladies." *Presidential Studies Quarterly* 3(1996): 835–853.

Office of Management and Budget. "Historicals" accessed August 21, 2015. https://www.whitehouse.gov/omb/budget/Historicals.

Parry-Giles, Shawn and Diane Blair. "The Role of the Rhetorical First Lady: Politics, Gender, Ideology, and Women's Voice." *Rhetoric and Public Affairs* 4(2002): 565–600.

Pew Research Center. "In Gun Control Debate, Several Options Draw Majority Support" accessed January 14, 2013. http://www.people-press.org/2013/01/14/in-gun-control-debate-several-options-draw-majority-support/.

Pew Research Center. "Laura Bush's Declining Favorability" accessed January 24, 2008. http://www.people-press.org/2008/01/24/laura-bushs-declining-favorability/2/.

Pew Research Center. "Obama in Strong Position at Start of Second Term" accessed January 17, 2013. http://www.people-press.org/2013/01/17/section-1-obama-job-rating-personal-traits-views-of-michelle-obama/.

Pilkington, Ed and Zach Stafford. "Hillary Clinton Campaign Deploys Not-So-Secret Weapon: Bill." *The Guardian,* accessed September 18, 2015. http://www.theguardian.com/us-news/2015/sep/18/hillary-clinton-campaign-bill-not-so-secret-weapon.

Portal, Pedro. "Columba Bush Steps Out, Gingerly, into the Political Spotlight." *Miami Herald*, accessed October 17, 2015. http://www.miamiherald.com/news/politics-government/elections-2016/jeb-bush/article39645780.html.

Przybyla, Heidi. "Bill Clinton Comes off the Sidelines of 2016 Campaign." *USA Today*, accessed October 8, 2015. http://www.usatoday.com/story/news/politics/elections/2015/10/08/bill-hillary-clinton-2016-campaign/73508638/.

Rabe-Hesketh, Sophia and Anders Skrondal. *Multilevel and Longitudinal Modeling Using Stata* (College Station, TX: Stata Press, 2012).

Ragin, Charles. *Redesigning Social Inquiry* (Chicago: University of Chicago Press, 2008).

Reagan, Nancy. *My Turn* (New York: Random House, 1989).

Real Clear Politics. "All Republican Presidential Nomination Polling Data." *RealClearPolitics,* accessed October 26, 2015. http://www.realclearpolitics .com/epolls/2016/president/us/2016_republican_presidential_nomination -3823.html#polls.

Rucker, Philip. "Clinton Campaign's Dilemma: What to Do with Bill?" *The Washington Post*, accessed May 10, 2015. https://www.washingtonpost.com /politics/for-the-clintons-a-big-question-what-to-do-with-bill/2015/05/10 /1f5b6212-f4db-11e4-bcc4-e8141e5eb0c9_story.html.

Saad, Lydia. "Pre-Debate, Biden, Ryan Share Lackluster Favorable Ratings." *Gallup,* accessed October 11, 2012. http://www.gallup.com/poll/158009/pre -debate-biden-ryan-share-lackluster-favorable-ratings.aspx.

Sanbonmatsu, Kira. "Gender Stereotypes and Vote Choice." *American Journal of Political Science* 46(2002): 20–34.

Sapiro, Virginia. "If U.S. Senator Baker Were a Woman." *Political Psychology* 1(1981): 61–83.

Schepsle, Kenneth and Barry R. Weingast. "The Institutional Foundations of Committee Power." *American Political Science Review* 1(1987): 85–104.

Schneider, Dorothy and Carl Schneider. *First Ladies: A Biographical Dictionary* (New York: Facts on File, 2001).

Schroeder, Jim. *Confessions of a Political Spouse* (Golden, CO: Fulcrum Publishing, 2009).

Shapiro, Laura. "The Great Bush-Kerry Bake-Off." *The Boston Globe*, accessed July 11, 2004. http://www.boston.com/news/globe/ideas/articles/2004/07/11 /the_great_bush_kerry_bake_off/.

Shapiro, Robert and Harpreet Mahajan. "Gender Differences in Policy Preferences and Priorities." *Public Opinion Quarterly* 1(1986): 42–61.

Shaw, Daron R. "The Effect of TV Ads and Campaign Events on Statewide Presidential Votes." *American Political Science Review* 1(1999): 345–361.

Smith, Courtenay and Allison Caporimo. "Reader's Digest Trust Poll." *Reader's Digest*, accessed June 2013. http://www.rd.com/slideshows/readers-digest -trust-poll-the-100-most-trusted-people-in-america/.

Sniderman, Paul, Richard Brody, and Phillip Tetlock. *Reasoning and Choice: Explorations in Political Psychology* (New York: Cambridge University Press, 1991).

Stolz, Elizabeth. "Beyond Pillow Talk: How Gender, Media and Politics Shape the Role and Legacy of First Ladies." Paper presented at NCUR, 2013. http://www .ncurproceedings.org/ojs/index.php/NCUR2013/article/viewFile/472/433.

Sulfaro, Valerie. "Affective Evaluations of First Ladies." *Presidential Studies Quarterly* 3(2007): 486–514.

Todd, Chuck and Mark Murray. "Jeb Bush Surges to Lead GOP Pack in New 2016 Poll." *MSNBC,* accessed June 22, 2015. http://www.msnbc.com/msnbc /jeb-bush-surges-lead-gop-pack-new-2016-poll.

Toner, Robin and Anne Kornblut. "Wounds Salved, Clinton Returns to Health Care." *The New York Times,* accessed June 10, 2006. http://www.nytimes .com/2006/06/10/washington/10hillary.html?ei=5070.

Tracey, Bree. "Michelle Obama Becoming the Most Televised First Lady." *Fox News,* accessed April 22, 2012. http://www.foxnews.com/politics/2012/04/22/michelle-obama-becoming-most-televised-first-lady/.

UCLA Statistical Consulting Group. "Introduction to Power Analysis" accessed August 22, 2015. http://www.ats.ucla.edu/stat/seminars/Intro_power/default.htm.

U.S. Department of Transportation. "How the Highway Beautification Act Became a Law" accessed October 17, 2013. http://www.fhwa.dot.gov/infrastructure/beauty.cfm.

Van Evera, Stephen. *Guide to Methods for Students of Political Science* (Ithaca, NY: Cornell University Press, 1997).

Watson, Robert. *American First Ladies* (Pasadena, CA: Salem Press, 2001).

Watson, Robert. "The First Lady Reconsidered: Presidential Partner and Political Institution." *Presidential Studies Quarterly* 1(1997): 805–818.

Watson, Robert. *The Presidents' Wives: Reassessing the Office of the First Lady* (Boulder, CO: Lynne Reiner, 2000).

Watson, Robert. "Ranking the Presidential Spouses." *Social Science Journal* 1(1999): 117–136.

Watson, Robert. "Source Material Toward the Study of the First Lady: The State of Scholarship." *Presidential Studies Quarterly* 2(2003): 423–441.

Watson, Robert. "The White Glove Pulpit." *OAH Magazine of History* 3(2001): 9–14.

Watson, Robert and Anthony Eksterowicz, eds. *The Presidential Companion* (Columbia: University of South Carolina Press, 2003).

Watson, Robert, et al. *The Obama Presidency: A Preliminary Assessment* (Albany, NY: Albany University Press, 2012).

Weisberg, Herbert. *Democracy's Feast* (Chatham, NJ: Chatham House, 1995).

Wertheimer, Molly. *Leading Ladies of the White House* (Lanham, MD: Rowman & Littlefield, 2005).

West, Cassandra. "Her Plan Went Awry, but Michelle Obama Doesn't Mind." *The Chicago Tribune,* accessed September 1, 2004. http://articles.chicagotribune.com/2004-09-01/features/0408310383_1_michelle-obama-sidley-austin-brown-best-laid-plans/2.

West, Darrell. "Television and Presidential Popularity in America." *British Journal of Political Science* 2(1991): 199–214.

Williams, Marjorie. "Barbara's Backlash." *Vanity Fair,* accessed August 1992. http://www.vanityfair.com/magazine/archive/1992/08/williams199208.

Winfield, Betty. "The Making of an Image: Hillary Rodham Clinton and American Journalists." *Political Communication* 2(2010): 241–253.

Winter, Nicholas. *Dangerous Frames: How Ideas About Race and Gender Shape Public Opinion* (Chicago: University of Chicago Press, 2008).

Winter, Nicholas. "Gendered and Re-Gendered: Public Opinion of Hillary Rodham Clinton." Paper presented at the Annual Meeting of the Midwest Political Science Association, 2000.

Woessner, Matthew. "Scandal, Elites and Presidential Popularity." *Presidential Studies Quarterly* 1(2005): 94–115.

Wolffe, Richard. "Who Is Michelle Obama?" *Newsweek*, accessed February 16, 2008. http://www.newsweek.com/who-michelle-obama-94161.

Wyzomirski, Margaret. "The De-Institutionalization of Presidential Staff Agencies." *Public Administration Review* 1(1982): 448–458.

Zaller, John. *The Nature and Origins of Mass Opinion* (New York: Cambridge University Press, 1992).

Index

Absent Spouses period, 10
accolades, 62
Adoption and Safe Families Act, 33
"Affective Evaluations of First Ladies" (Sulfaro), 38
Affordable Care Act, 70, 93, 94, 103, 114, 122
Afghan women's issues, 64
aggregated polling data, 99, 100
Allgor, Catherine, 19
"all hands on deck" approach, 7, 71–74
American National Election Studies (ANES), 35–36, 37, 39, 103, 116
analysis of variance (ANOVA), 174
apolitical venues, 149
"appropriate quotient of femininity," 113
approval ratings and speech frequencies, 172
Arkansas Rural Health Advisory Committee, 61
Aspiring Spouses period, 10
Association of American Physicians and Surgeons v. Hillary Rodham Clinton, 11, 52
aversion to presidential spouses as policy makers, 60
Axelrod, David, 136

Ball, Andi, 60
Beasley, Maurine, 14
beautification, 95
Beck, Glenn, 66
Begala, Paul, 136
belief approach to gender stereotypes, 20
Biden, Jill, 70, 113
Biden, Joe, 24 (table), 117–118, 158 (figure)
Biggest Loser, 73
"Bill Clinton Question," 135, 143
bivariate regression, 39, 40
Blair, Diane, 17
blind survey experiments, 101. *See also* randomized survey experiments
block random assignment, 102, 105, 176
Blue Goose, 83
Borrelli, MaryAnne, 20
Briefing Room web sites. *See* White House Briefing Room web sites
Brody, Richard, 121
bully pulpit, 58, 73, 88, 123, 125
Burma, 43, 91
Burns, Lisa, 14

Bush, Barbara: covert vs. overt power,
    17; Desert Storm, 58–59;
    Grandma's House, 58; hostile
    crowd, 92; humanizing president's
    image, 59; instant popularity, 59;
    invaluable campaign commodity,
    15; negative press attention, 79;
    Salvation Army bell ringers, 58
Bush, Columba, 134, 137. *See also*
    candidate spouse experiment
Bush, Jeb, 134, 177. *See also*
    candidate spouse experiment
Bush, Laura: 2004 election, 89, 90;
    Afghan women's issues, 64;
    alternative media outlets, 66;
    breast cancer in the Middle East,
    91; Burma, 43, 91; campaign
    speeches, 44; Clinton, Hillary,
    compared, 96; "Comforter in
    Chief," 60; continuation of her
    work in Texas, 60; East Wing staff,
    56, 60, 63; East Wing-West Wing
    tradeoff, 81; educational
    attainment, 38; effect of speech/
    video, 106 (figure), 108–109, 152
    (figure); familiarity with White
    House from father-in-law's time in
    office, 60; favorability ratings,
    36–37; first lady speech vs.
    husband's speech, 111 (figure),
    112; first lady speech vs. vice
    president, 116–117, 118, 120, 158
    (figure); focus on children, 94;
    foreign policy, 64–65, 83–84,
    96–97; foreign policy speech, 112,
    120, 158 (figure); governor's wife,
    as, 92–93; Hurricane Katrina, 65;
    literacy initiatives, 6, 61, 62, 122;
    media strategists, 67; midterm
    elections, 90; No Child Left
    Behind Act, 60–61;
    noncontroversial and "private"
    policy agenda, 12; offensive vs.
    defensive communications strategy,
    60; older voters, 20; pet projects,
    28; pet projects as soft frames for
    husband's domestic policies,
    93–94; politicized pet project
    speeches, 34; positivity, 62; public
    opinion, 61; public speeches, 24
    (table); public sphere work as
    extension of private sphere
    priorities, 20; reserved mannerism,
    91; speaking in front of large
    crowds, 147; speeches by type and
    topic, 30 (figure), 31; *Spoken
    From the Heart*, 86; strategy shift,
    60; summary of experimental
    findings, 126–127; supporting
    president's policy initiatives, 63;
    swing districts (2004 election),
    89; traditional first lady, 12;
    traveling abroad, 90–91; voter
    indifference, 12; War on Terror,
    43, 122. *See also* spouses of
    last three presidential
    administrations

campaign appearances, 32
campaign speeches, 29
campaign trail, 71–72
Campbell, Colton, 11
candidate spouse experiment: Bush
    experiment, 138; Clinton
    experiment, 137–138; control
    condition, 138 (figure);
    favorability, 140–141, 141 (figure);
    methodology, 138–140, 176;
    negative honesty effect, 143
    (figure), 144; perceptions of
    Hillary Clinton, 143–144, 143
    (figure); perceptions of Jeb Bush,
    142–143, 142 (figure); summary of
    experimental findings, 145;
    treatment condition, 139 (figure);
    treatment group assignment/
    covariates, 167 (table); underlying
    purpose, 175–176

Carson, Ben, 177
Carter, Rosalynn, 11, 56–57, 85, 95
causal inference, 105
"celebrity-fication" of political
    figures, 72
ceremonial first lady, 11
ceremonial speeches, 27
Cheney, Dick, 24 (table), 116–117,
    118, 120, 158 (figure)
Cheney, Liz, 91
Children's Health Insurance Program
    (CHIP), 95, 113, 121
Christie, Chris, 177
Cleveland, Frances, 13, 14
Cleveland, Grover, 13
Clinton, Bill, 15, 86–87, 134–137,
    148. *See also* candidate spouse
    experiment
Clinton, Hillary, 134; 1992 campaign
    trail, 15; 1996 DNC speech, 53,
    54; activist, as, 12; Bush, Laura,
    compared, 96; candidate picture
    experiment (*see* candidate spouse
    experiment); CHIP, 95, 113, 121;
    congressional testimony/legislative
    workshops, 11; controversial and
    "public" policy agenda, 12;
    convention speech (1996), 31–32;
    covert political cues, 61, 71;
    damage control capacity, 65–66;
    economy speech, 119–120, 157
    (figure); effect of speech/video, 106
    (figure), 107–108, 151 (figure);
    female voters, 20; first lady speech
    vs. husband's speech, 110 (figure),
    112; first lady speech vs. vice
    president, 118, 157 (figure);
    foreign policy activities, 11;
    governor's wife, as, 92–93; health
    care reform, 28–29, 33, 34, 45–46,
    53, 55, 56, 62, 94–95; honesty
    deficit, 144; human rights abroad,
    11; image softening, 54;
    involvement in policy making

    process, 61, 75; joint appearances
    with husband, 33–34; legislation
    which she supported, 33;
    negative honesty effect, 143
    (figure), 144; negative press
    attention, 79–80; negative
    reaction to her support of Health
    Security Act, 7, 75; nonpartisan
    evaluations, 103–104; pet
    projects, 27–28; polarizing
    activist figure, 12; policy-free
    speeches, 32, 55; politically
    charged policy speeches, 32, 43;
    public opinion, 61, 75; public
    speeches, 24 (table); shift in
    strategy, 53, 54–55, 92, 94–95;
    speeches by type and topic, 30
    (figure), 31; "stand by her man,"
    66, 87; summary of experimental
    findings, 125–126; traveling
    overseas, 91, 92; "two for the
    price of one" slogan (1992), 75;
    "Women's Rights are Human
    Rights," 92. *See also* spouses of
    last three presidential
    administrations
"Comforter in Chief," 60
committee hearings, 11
compassion issues, 20, 21
complete random assignment, 102
confidence level, 50
confounders, 100, 101
congressional campaigns, 131
congressional spouses, 131
congressional testimony, 11
conservation, 95
controversial comments/statements,
    79–80
convention speeches, 32. *See also*
    Democratic National Convention
    (DNC) speeches
correlation, 39, 100
Corrigan, Matthew, 33
covert policy cues, 35 (figure)

criticism, 62
Cruz, Ted, 177
Curry, Ann, 64

daily schedules, 25, 131
damage control, 65–66, 87
Data Age, 124
Dean, Howard, 136
Dean, Judith Steinberg, 79
demand-side explanations, 5, 49
Democratic National Convention
    (DNC) speeches: Clinton, Hillary,
    53, 54; Obama, Michelle, 86
dependent/independent variable, 99,
    102
Desert Storm, 58–59
designer driven dresser, 59
Dickinson, Matthew, 18
DNC speeches. *See* Democratic
    National Convention (DNC)
    speeches
Dukakis, Kitty, 15, 17

East Wing-West Wing tension, 89
economic speeches, 44
*Edith Bolling Galt Wilson: The
    Unintended President*
    (McCallops), 16
education and health care speeches,
    44
Edwards, George, 99–100, 125
Eisenhower, Mamie, 1, 14
Eksterowicz, Anthony, 18
elite interview process: interview
    participants, 48–49; methodology,
    172–173; questions asked, 49
external validity, 104, 105

favorability, 141–142
favorability ratings, 35, 36 (figure),
    123, 159 (table), 160 (table), 161
    (table)
feeling thermometer, 35, 36, 140, 171
Ferraro, Geraldine, 79

first ladies. *See* presidential spouses
First Ladies that Shaped the Image
    and the Role of the Office of the
    First Lady (1789–1817), 10
first lady activism, 10, 11, 12
first lady effect vs. vice presidential
    effect, 115–119, 157 (figure), 158
    (figure), 166 (table)
first lady speeches vs. husband's
    speeches, 109–113
first lady speeches vs. no speech, 106
    (figure), 107–109, 107 (figure)
first lady videos vs. husband's video,
    109–113, 153 (figure), 154 (figure)
first lady videos vs. no video, 107–
    109, 151 (figure), 152 (figure)
Flowers, Gennifer, 66
foreign affairs speeches, 44
foreign policy: Bush, Laura, 64–65,
    83–84, 96–97, 112, 120, 158
    (figure); Clinton, Hillary, 11;
    Obama, Michelle, 43–44, 84, 113.
    See also traveling abroad
Foster Care Independence Act, 33
4 P's of political activism, 10
front-porch campaigns, 13
F-test, 175
Furman, Bess, 15

Gallup feeling thermometers, 171
gender-based personality issues, 21
gender gap, 19
gender scholars, 20
gender stereotypes, 20, 21, 101
generalizability, 105
Gerber, Alan, 100
going personal, 82–88
going positive, 92–98
going public, 27, 107, 125
going purple, 88–92
Goldstein, Joel, 23
good will tours, 124
Gore, Al, 24 (table), 118, 157 (figure)
Graham, Lindsey, 134

Grandma's House, 58
Green, Donald, 100
Greenstein, Fred, 11
Grimes, Ann, 14–16
gubernatorial spouses, 131
Gutin, Myra, 17

Harding, Florence, 10, 13, 14
Harrison, Benjamin, 13
Harrison, Caroline, 13
Harrison, Carrie, 13
Hastedt, Glenn, 11
Head Start, 95
health care reform: ACA (*see*
    Affordable Care Act); Clinton,
    Hillary, 28–29, 33, 34, 45–46,
    53, 55, 56, 62, 94–95; Health
    Security Act, 29, 33, 55, 88;
    Obama, Michelle, 69, 70, 94,
    114, 122
Health Security Act, 29, 33, 55, 88
Healthcare.gov web site debacle
    (2013), 88
Hidden Power (Marton), 16
historical overview, 10, 13, 14
honesty deficit, 144
House candidates' spouses, 131
"How Bill and Hillary Work Together
    to Handle the Media" (Mueller),
    15
Hughes, Karen, 60
humble outsiders, 123
Hurricane Katrina, 65

impoverished populations, 85
internal validity, 104, 105
international relations, 11. *See also*
    foreign policy; traveling abroad
interview process. *See also* elite
    interview process
*Inventing a Voice: The Rhetoric of
    American First Ladies in the
    Twentieth Century* (Wertheimer),
    17

Jindal, Bobby, 177
job approval ratings, 36
Johnson, Lady Bird, 3, 14, 95
Johnson, Lyndon Baines, 95
Joining Forces, 28, 66, 69, 97, 98,
    113

Kahn, Kim, 101
Kennedy, Jacqueline, 2, 10, 14, 15, 18
Kernell, Samuel, 18, 27
King, Gary, 124
Kroft, Steve, 87

large aggregated data set, 99, 100
late-night talk shows, 149
Lauer, Matt, 66
legislative workshops, 11
lessons learned: deploy the spouse
    early, 146–147; deploy the spouse
    in regions where president not
    popular, 148; deploy the spouse
    often, 147–148; deploy the spouse
    separately, 148–149
Let Girls Learn, 28
Let's Move!, 28, 66, 69, 93, 97, 122
Limbaugh, Rush, 66

MacManus, Susan, 19
malaria initiative, 63
march of quantification, 124
Marton, Kati, 16
McCallops, James, 16
McCluskie, Sean, 11
McKinley, Ida, 13
McKinley, William, 13
mean annual feeling thermometers,
    171
Mechanical Turk, 105, 115, 124, 172,
    176
memoirs, 3
messengers-in-chief, 123
midterm elections, 29, 89, 90
Model Wives period, 10
Modern Spouses period, 10

Monica Lewinsky scandal, 66
Mothers' Health Protection Act, 33
Mueller, James, 15, 16
multivariate regression, 39, 100
"Mysterious Columba Bush, The"
   (Rosin), 137

name recognition, 37 (figure)
name recollection question, 37–38
Nashville, 73
National Book Festival, 60
negative honesty effect, 143 (figure),
   144
negative press attention, 79–80
Nixon, Pat, 32, 64
No Child Left Behind Act, 60–61, 62,
   94, 96, 122
"no filter" approach, 69
nonpolicy-oriented discussion, 6

Obama, Michelle: advocating for the
   president, 66; alternative media
   outlets, 67; Associate Dean of
   Student Services, 93; campaign
   speeches, 44; childhood obesity, 6,
   69; covert support of
   administrative policies, 69, 71;
   DNC speech (2012), 86; East
   Wing staff, 66; effect of speech/
   video, 107 (figure), 152 (figure);
   first lady speech vs. husband's
   speech, 111 (figure), 113; first lady
   speech vs. vice president, 117–118,
   158 (figure); focus on children, 94;
   foreign policy, 43–44, 84; foreign
   policy speech effect, 113; guest
   host on scripted network TV
   shows, 73; health care reform, 69,
   70, 94, 114, 122; humanizing
   president's image, 86; Let's Move!
   speeches, 94; major public
   remarks, 1, 9; media strategists,
   68; most trusted political figure
   (2013), 20; multifaceted concerns,

82; negative press attention, 80;
   normal role model, 87; Oscars
   (2013), 72; pet project and
   campaign-related remarks, 69; pet
   projects, 28; pet projects as soft
   frames for husband's domestic
   policies, 93–94; politicized pet
   project speeches, 34; public
   speeches, 24 (table); reinforcing
   Obama brand with the public, 69;
   social media presence, 68; speeches
   by type and topic, 31 (figure);
   summary of experimental findings,
   127–128; tandem policy speeches,
   34; University of Chicago
   Hospitals, 93; valence issues, 97.
   See also spouses of last three
   presidential administrations
observational studies, 101
Office of the First Lady: effect of
   Clinton's involvement in health
   care formation, 11; first lady's
   chief of staff at president's
   morning briefing, 52; fully
   professionalized office, 2, 18–19;
   integration into White House, 10,
   51–52; pet projects, 122; political
   rather than ceremonial role, 20;
   politicization, 18; positive
   reputation, 88; public relations
   role, 19; staff size, 66. *See also*
   presidential spouses
On Behalf of the President (Wright):
   author's intention, 3; book's
   contributions to the literature,
   121–124; central argument of the
   book, 5; focus, 2; methodology,
   2–3; perspective, 3; primary
   theories, 26; questions to be
   answered, 1; roadmap/preview,
   4–8; unique traits, 2–3; what the
   book is about, 4
On Deaf Ears (Edwards), 99–100, 125
overt policy cues, 35 (figure)

paired Welch two-sample t-tests, 174
Palmieri, Jennifer, 137
paradox of politicization, 18
partisan identification, 38–42
partisan politics, 149
Paul, Kelley, 147
Paul, Rand, 177
Paynter, Kristen, 18
PEPFAR (President's Emergency Plan for AIDS Relief), 63, 64
permanent campaign, 125
Perry-Giles, Shawn, 17
personal appeals (going personal), 82–88
pet projects, 27–28, 92–98, 113, 122
pet project speeches, 27–28, 34, 171
Pew feeling thermometers, 171
pillow influence, 16
pillow talk, 121
plausibility probe, 131
policy cues, 35 (figure)
policy first lady model, 11
policy speeches, 28–29
political advocacy in apolitical context, 34
political first lady, 11
political scandal, 36
political scientists, 4, 119, 121, 124
politicization of speeches, 32
politicization scholars, 18
politicized pet project speeches, 34
politicized speech, 29
pooled treatment effect, 117
positivity, 62
power analyses, 175
"Power dynamics of the couple's relationship," 77
presidential approval ratings, 172
presidential candidates pictured with spouse, 177. See also candidate spouse experiment
Presidential Companion, The (Watson), 10

presidential election (2016), 176–177. *See also* candidate spouse experiment
presidential responsiveness, 71
presidential speeches, 100
presidential spouses: approval ratings, 20; daily schedules, 25, 131; evolution of role over time, 9; formal office (*see* Office of the First Lady); humanizing president's image, 19, 86; image making tools, 14, 16–18; participation in political process, 78–79; presidential defender/image softener, 14; proximity to the president, 45–46; public appearances, 4; public counterweight, 15; public fascination, 3, 5; public sphere work as extension of private sphere priorities, 20; types of speeches, 27–29; typologies, 9; Watson's historical categorizations, 10. *See also* spouses of last three presidential administrations
President's Emergency Plan for AIDS Relief (PEPFAR), 63, 64
president's morning briefing, 52
President's Partner: The First Lady in the 20th Century, The (Gutin), 17
president's public image, 85–86
Presidents' Wives, The (Watson), 9, 29
private speeches, 25
proximity to the president, 45–46, 74–75, 83
public appearances, 26
Public Law 95-750, 52
public opinion, 99, 100, 107

Qualtrics, 124, 172, 176
Quecan, Andrew, 19

randomized block assignment, 102, 105

randomized survey experiments, 99–120, 124–125; block random assignment, 102; conclusions, 115; effect of speeches and videos on women, 113–115, 154–157; example of speech excerpt, 103, 116; experimental design, 101–105; first lady effect vs. vice presidential effect, 115–119, 157 (figure), 158 (figure), 166 (table); first lady speeches vs. husband's speeches, 109–113; first lady speeches vs. no speech, 106 (figure), 107–109, 107 (figure); first lady videos vs. husband's video, 109–113, 153 (figure), 154 (figure); first lady videos vs. no video, 107–109, 151 (figure), 152 (figure); possible adjustments to existing experimental design, 128–130; results, 105–120; speech excerpt experiment, 101–104, 164 (table); statistical concepts, 101–105, 174, 175; subconscious effects, 101; summary of experimental findings (Bush), 126–127; summary of experimental findings (Clinton), 125–126; summary of experimental findings (Obama), 127–128; validity, 104, 105; video clip experiment, 104, 105, 165 (table)

Reach Higher, 28
Reach Out and Read, 61
Ready to Read, 61
Reagan, Nancy, 57, 83
Reagan, Ronald, 100
RealClearPolitics, 175
regression analysis, 39
"Remarks by the First Lady on What Health Insurance Reform Means for Women and Families" (Obama), 70

Riverdance, 97
Roosevelt, Eleanor, 10–15, 32
Rosin, Hannah, 137
Rubio, Jeanette, 147
Rubio, Marco, 177
Running Mates (Grimes), 16

Salvation Army bell ringers, 58
sample size, 130
Santorum, Rick, 176, 177
security concerns, 124
self-deprecation, 123
Senate candidates' spouses, 131
7 AM meeting, 52
sex stereotypes, 101
Sniderman, Paul, 121
snowball sampling, 172
social desirability bias, 101
social media, 68
"Source Material" (Watson), 16
"sovereign," 42
speech excerpt experiment, 101–104, 164 (table)
speech frequencies, 122
speech topics (first lady vs. husband), 162–163 (table)
speech types, 27–29
speech type vs. speech topic, 29, 30 (figure), 31 (figure)
Spellings, Margaret, 60
Spoken From the Heart (Bush), 86
spouse mobilization. *See* lessons learned
spouses of last three presidential administrations: acting in ways they would not have otherwise, 56; adequate presidential replacements, 125; aversion to spouses as policy makers, 60; bully pulpit, 58, 73, 88, 123; Bush administration (*see* Bush, Laura); campaign trail, 71–72; changes in

public appearances, 35, 122; Clinton administration (*see* Clinton, Hillary); controversial policy questions, 88–89; effectiveness of first ladies vs. president, 83; effectiveness of spouses on campaign trail, 73; favorability ratings, 35, 36 (figure), 123; first three professional first ladies, 77; formal office (*see* Office of the First Lady); fundraising prowess, 73; goals of mobilizing spouses, 7, 50; good will tours, 124; highly likable and visible public figures, 38; hiring public relations experts, 66; humble outsiders, 123; impervious to political scandal, 36; impoverished populations, 85; laymen's opinions, 133–134; lessons learned (*see* lessons learned); messengers-in-chief, 123; name recognition, 37 (figure); Obama administration (*see* Obama, Michelle); part of U.S. celebrity cultures, 73; partisan identification, 38–42, 149; president's "number one person," 83; president's public image, 85–86; proximity to the president, 45–46, 74–75, 83; public interest, 72; reasons for increase in public appearances, 77; security concerns, 124; self-deprecation, 123; "sovereign," 42; special appeal of first ladies overseas, 84; special surrogates, 45; special treatment from media, 42–43, 123; "stay above the fray," 88; "tightrope walk," 80; tremendous communications asset, 42; women's rights campaigns, 92. *See also* presidential spouses
STATA, 175

statistical concepts: bivariate regression, 39, 40; confidence level, 50; correlation, 39; dependent/independent variable, 99; F-test, 175; multivariate regression, 39, 100; paired two-sample t-tests, 174; power analyses, 175; regression analysis, 39; sample size, 130; snowball sampling, 172; statistical sensitivity, 130–131; statistical significance, 39, 175. *See also* randomized survey experiments
statistical sensitivity, 130–131
statistical significance, 39, 175
"Stay above the fray," 88
strategic appearances hypothesis, 26, 49
subconscious effects, 101
Sulfaro, Valerie, 9, 11, 12, 20, 38–40
supply-side explanations, 5, 49
survey experiments. *See* randomized survey experiments

Taft, Helen, 10
Tag Teaming the Press (Mueller), 16
tandem policy speeches, 33–34
Tetlock, Phillip, 121
theories: personal attributes, 48; preliminary support for strategic communications theory, 26–34; primary theories advanced in book, 26; strategic appearances hypothesis, 26, 49; weaknesses, 47
"tightrope walk," 80
Top Chef, 73
trait approach to gender stereotypes, 21
Transitional Spouses period, 10
traveling abroad: Bush, Laura, 90–91; Clinton, Hillary, 91, 92. *See also* foreign policy
trial and error approach, 51

Truman, Bess, 10, 14
24-hour news cycle, 5, 72
"two for the price of one" slogan
    (1992), 75

University of Chicago Hospitals, 93

valence issues, 44, 93, 97
validity, 104, 105
"vast right-wing conspiracy," 66
vice presidents: comparable to
    presidential spouses, 23; effect of,
    vs. first lady effect, 115–119, 157
    (figure), 158 (figure), 166 (table);
    favorability ratings, 36 (figure);
    name recognition, 37 (figure);
    public speeches, 24 (table); speech
    frequency, 73
video clip experiment, 104, 105, 165
    (table)

War on Terror, 43, 122
Washington, Martha, 13
Watergate, 71
Watson, Robert, 9, 10, 14, 16, 29
Wertheimer, Molly, 17
White House Briefing Room web
    sites, 2, 23, 25, 122, 172
White House centralization, 18–19
White House Diary, A (Johnson), 3
White House staff size, 18
women, effect of speeches and videos
    on, 113–115, 154–157
women and family speeches, 28
Women's Health and Cancer Rights
    Act, 33
"Women's Rights are Human Rights"
    (Clinton), 92
women's rights campaigns, 92
Wright, Lauren. See *On Behalf of the
    President* (Wright)

About the Author

LAUREN A. WRIGHT received a PhD in Government from Georgetown University in December 2014 where she majored in American politics and political methodology. Lauren's dissertation received distinction and was nominated for the George C. Edwards III Award in presidency research. Lauren is also a board member of the White House Transition Project, a nonpartisan group of scholars, journalists, and policy experts whose combined efforts and knowledge aim to ensure a smooth presidential transition every four years.

Lauren graduated *summa cum laude*, Phi Beta Kappa, from Wake Forest University in 2010, where her research won the John Allen Easley Medal and Award for Excellence in Religion and the Elizabeth Phillips Award for the Best Essay in Women's and Gender Studies. Lauren joined the Meg Whitman for Governor campaign shortly after her college graduation, where she became one of the youngest field representatives for the California Republican Party. Her interest in politics began in college when she spent one semester in Washington interning for *Face the Nation* anchor Bob Schieffer at CBS News, and another summer interning for U.S. Senator Dianne Feinstein.

Lauren's expertise in strategic communications spans the public and private sectors. She currently serves as Director of Investor Relations for NV5 Global, Inc., a publicly traded engineering and environmental services corporation with offices nationwide (Nasdaq: NVEE). There, she is responsible for crafting and disseminating a clear and compelling investment message to the public on behalf of the company. Lauren lives in Northern California with her fiancée Jonathan, a PhD candidate in political science at Stanford University.